F.V.

WITHDRAWN

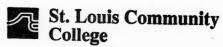

THE
TRIBAL ARTS
OF
AFRICA

THE
TRIBAL ARTS
OF
AFRICA

Jean-Baptiste Bacquart

with 865 illustrations, 195 in color

Thames and Hudson

On pages 1–7: **p. 1** A Boa figure; *wood; height: 57.1 cm (22^1/$_2$ in)*; **p. 2** A Fon figure; *wood; height: 86.5 cm (34 in)*; Prince Sandrudin Agha Khan, Geneva; **p. 6** A Dogon figure; *wood; height: 35 cm (13^3/$_4$ in)*; **p. 7 (left)** A Zulu club; *wood and glass beads; height: 70 cm (27^1/$_2$ in)*; K. Conru Collection; **p. 7 (right, above)** A Ngbaka figure; *wood and glass; height: 87 cm (34 in)*; provenance: Alduingk Collection, Amsterdam; K. Koznietsko Collection, Hamburg; P. Dartevelle, Brussels; private collection; **p. 7 (right, below)** A Kongo dog fetish figure; *wood, nail and glass; length: 68.9 cm (27 in)*; provenance: A. Brandt, New York; F. Rolin, New York; private collection

On the section openers: **p. 18** An Attye figure (detail); *wood; height: 87 cm (34^3/$_8$ in)*; **p. 19 (left)** A Bete figure; *wood and metal; height: 52 cm (20^1/$_2$ in)*; **p. 19 (right)** A Baule figure; *wood; height: 50 cm (19^5/$_8$ in)*; **p. 54 (left)** A Dogon figure; *wood; height: 29 cm (11^1/$_4$ in)*; **p. 54 (right)** A Bambara Segou-style figure; *wood; height: 57 cm (22^1/$_2$ in)*; **p. 55** A Djenne figure, 12th–15th century (detail); *terracotta; height of the animal and rider: 44 cm (17^1/$_4$ in)*; **p. 78** A Dakakari grave-marker figure (detail); *terracotta; height: 73 cm (28^5/$_8$ in)*; **p. 79 (left)** A Jukun figure; *wood; height: 83 cm (32^5/$_8$ in)*; **p. 79 (right)** A Mama figure; *wood; height: 22 cm (8^5/$_8$ in)*; **p. 114** A Yombe maternity figure (detail); *wood; height: 36 cm (14^1/$_4$ in)*; **p. 115 (left)** A Songye figure; *wood and metal; height: 68 cm (26^3/$_4$ in)*; **p. 115 (right)** A Tchokwe tobacco container; *wood and metal; height: 12 cm (4^3/$_4$ in)*; **p. 194 (left)** A Nguni figure; *wood; height: 28 cm (11 in)*; **p. 194 (right)** A Nyamezi figure; *wood and metal; height: 75 cm (29^1/$_2$ in)*; **p. 195** A Hehe figure (detail); *wood; height: 35 cm (13^3/$_4$ in)*

Maps on pages 16, 52, 76, 112, 192: Mountain High Maps® Copyright 1993 Digital Wisdom, Inc.

First published in the United States of America in 1998 by Thames and Hudson Inc., 500 Fifth Avenue, New York, New York 10110

Library of Congress Catalog Card Number 98-60234
ISBN 0-500-01870-7

Printed and bound in Singapore

Acknowledgments

This book would not have been possible without the help of Tony Babarik, who not only ensured that the English text was clear and comprehensible, but also contributed to the general concept of the book – his dedication, time and patience helped to transform a 'good idea' into a finished project.

Special gratitude and thanks must go to Colin MacKay of Sotheby's who understood that writing a book is part of an expert's job. Also at Sotheby's, I wish to extend my thanks to the photographic department who printed and reproduced so many of the illustrations that appear in the book; and, of course, to Richard Pearson, a remarkable photographer whose professional skills and personal qualities made the photographic trips an enjoyable experience.

Tim Teuten, formerly of Christie's, must also be thanked for his generous hospitality while I was in New York and for allowing me access to Christie's rich photographic library.

I wish to thank the following collectors and dealers for their support and trust throughout the production of this book. They generously allowed their objects to be photographed, provided invaluable information and more generally contributed in making the tribal art market such an enjoyable field to be involved in:

In France, M. André Fourquet, whose fabulous collection and encyclopaedic knowledge have been a continuous source of inspiration; M. Hubert Goldet for his trust, friendship, help and support in the past and during the production of this book; M. and Mme Max Itzikovitz for their warm hospitality and openness; M. and Mme Leloup for their intelligent counsel and astute opinions on the tribal art world; M. Alain de Monbrison and his assistant Florence Carrié, who supplied numerous illustrations for this book; M. Daniel Ourdet, Philippe Ratton and their assistant Charlotte Jonville for their enormous help.

In Belgium, M. Marc Blanpain, who as a pioneer in collecting African terracottas is among the foremost collectors of African art; M. Joseph Christiaens for his trust and help; M. Pierre Dartevelle, whose constant help and enormous knowledge have made the achievement of this project easier; M. Marc Félix for his advise about the concept of the book; M. David Henrion for his friendship and assistance; M. and Mme Willie Mestach for their academic and artistic views on tribal art; M. and Mme René Van Der Straete for their warm hospitality, enthusiasm and the wonderful cooking that made visits to their home so enjoyable; M. Jacques Van Overstraete, whose direct and straightforward approach was a refreshing experience.

In England, Mr Lance Entwistle and his assistant, Victoria Young, whose continuous support and impressive photographic library were of enormous help.

In America, Mr Ernst Anspach, whose historical knowledge on tribal art has been extremely helpful in producing this book; Mr and Mrs Marc Ginzberg for their warm hospitality; Mr and Mrs Daniel Malcolm, whose eclectic taste and fabulous collection is matched only by their friendliness and warmth; and to the private individuals who wish to remain anonymous, but who nevertheless perpetuate the American tradition of great collectors.

Thanks also to M. Pierre Amrouche, M. and Mme Patrick Caput, Mme Anita Chaberman, Mr Kevin Conru, Ms Jean Fritts, M. Alain Guisson, Mr Fred Jahn, M. Olivier Klejman, Mr Myron Kunin, Mr Raoul Lehuard, Mme Francine Maurer, Prof. Werner Musterberger, M. Guy Piazzini, M. and Mme Guy Porré, Mrs Franyo Schindler, Mr and Mrs Saul Stanoff, and to all the other collectors who wish to remain anonymous.

Finally, words are not sufficient to acknowledge the continuous support from my family and especially from my parents who, over the years, have been a constant source of reference for me and a limitless reservoir of understanding.

Contents

Introduction

WHILE NO ONE could write a book that embraced the entire expression of tribal Africa, this selection ranges widely and aims to create a work that is both accessible and at the same time useful to professionals. It includes objects that are representative and characteristic of traditional artistic production throughout Africa south of the Sahara. The earliest pieces date from the beginning of the first millennium and the more recent examples from the beginning of the 20th century, before the commercialization of tribal art for the tourist trade.

Defining a 'genuine' tribal art object is a complex process. Technically, the term means all objects created by African artists, but Western scholars and collectors have applied a more restrictive definition that depends on how an object was used. Thus a genuine African artefact must have been made by an African artist, and also must have been used during tribal ceremonies. This concept excludes most of the modern creations of African art, including objects manufactured for the tourist trade, and the elaborate contemporary African art from Zimbabwe and Kenya.

African tribal art is not just about an aesthetic, it is also about meaning and function. African objects were almost never created as 'art for art's sake', rather these objects always related to magical or social rites – to the supernatural world – and were rarely produced by a single individual. Before the making of many artefacts, there was a long, controlled process including close collaboration between the 'commissioner', the village diviner and the sculptor.

There are many reasons why African art is collected in the West. For some collectors, African art serves as a reference point for the cubist and abstract art movements, in as much as it liberated European artists from the constraints of representational traditions. For others, collecting African art is about preserving a dynamic and rich cultural heritage. Yet, for all of them, African art demands a dialogue and a response

A Kongo figure;
wood; height: 26 cm (10¹/4 in)

A Dogon figure;
*wood and metal; height:
54.5 cm (21³/8 in)*

to the universal artistic statements inherent in these powerful objects. Once removed from their African context, these artefacts are often fragments, literally and metaphorically. Most have lost their original patinas and some of their paraphernalia including applied jewelry, cloth and magical substances. Such adornments, meaningless to Western eyes, were of prime importance to African tribespeople and were regularly considered more important than the statues or masks themselves. And in a metaphorical sense, the objects have a 'fragmentary nature', since they are no longer used in the West – what remain are lifeless shells, retained because they are 'beautiful' or are of ethnographic interest.

Recently, the tribal notion of beauty has been scrutinized by scholars and not surprisingly shown to differ from a Western concept, which is based only on its aesthetic appeal. The African idea of a beautiful object – a statue or mask – is that it should not only correspond to tribal artistic rules and concepts, but that it should also have the ability to cure, to place curses, to instruct, and indeed to protect individuals and communities.

The first contact between Europe and Africa can be traced to Roman times. Commercial links generated by an interest in exotic animals, ivory and slaves, and trade with black Africa via Egypt and the Upper Nile River made Africa an exciting continent with amazing prizes. The first mention of an African object collected in the Western world dates from the 1480s when the Duke of Burgundy, Charles the Reckless, bought an 'Ydoilles' – an idol – from a Portuguese nobleman. Portuguese sailors had established contact with the Kongo empire, in what is now northern Angola, around this time. They not only brought back figures and other 'curios' to Europe, but also encouraged the production of the so-called 'Afro-Portuguese' ivories, which merged an African material with a European iconography. For centuries, however, contact was sparse and intermittent, mostly related to the slave trade in West Africa. Curiously, the Age of Enlightenment at the end of the 18th century, which fostered the development of new interest in Polynesian societies, seems to have ignored African civilizations. Thus very few objects were recorded in the West before the great colonial period of the second half of the 19th century.

A Kwere throne;
wood; height: 139 cm (54⅝ in);
Bareiss Family Collection

A Tchokwe mask;
wood and vegetal fibres;
height: 22 cm (8⅝ in)

In France, the first efforts to assemble dispersed ethnographic collections led to the creation in Paris of the Musée Ethnographique des Missions Scientifiques in 1878. Following the establishment of this museum, the 1878 World's Fair and French colonial involvement in Africa, another museum, the Musée d'Ethnographie, was inaugurated in 1882 within the Trocadéro building. The Musée des Arts Africains et Océaniens was established in the second half of the 20th century in the Porte Dorée and it is likely that its collections will be displayed with those of the Musée de l'Homme (formerly known as the Trocadéro Museum) in what will be called the Musée des Arts Premiers.

In Germany, mid-19th-century expeditions to Africa brought back a considerable amount of tribal objects, which were displayed in Berlin's Museum für Völkerkunde as early as 1886. Great curators, such as Von Luschan, added to the quality and the number of their collections through the acquisition of Benin works of art.

The British collected widely as a by-product of their imperial expansionism. Several African objects were recorded among Sir Hans Sloane's art collections, which ultimately prompted the creation of the British Museum in 1753. During the 19th century black African art objects entered the museum's collections through English expeditions and via British colonial administrators to Africa, among them T. E. Bowdich in 1819, the Niger Expedition of 1843, Sir Bartle Frere in South Africa during the late 1870s and Sir John Kirk in East Africa a decade later. With the arrival of Benin loot in 1897, following the British conquest of Benin, and through continuous expeditions and acquisitions, the British Museum's collections expanded to such an extent that in 1970 the Museum of Mankind was separately established to house them. However, in 1997 the museum closed and its collections were moved back to the British Museum.

In America, the creation of the first private and public collections of African art, such as the Barnes Foundation Collection, dates from the first half of the 20th century, and was generated by an interest in early 20th-century European art movements. Thereafter Western interest as a whole developed rapidly, culminating between the World Wars in the first major international exhibitions to draw popular attention to the

A Yoruba Gelede mask;
wood; height: 23 cm (9 in)

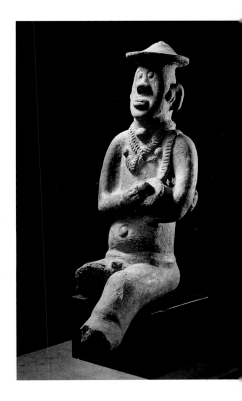

A Bankoni drum player;
terracotta; height: 53 cm (21 in)

artistic qualities of black African art, held in New York, Antwerp and Paris. At the same time, owning an African object began to become fashionable, thus removing the African achievement from the exclusive preserve of artists and siting it in the somewhat wider arena of the social and cultural elite.

The artistic value of tribal works of art was highlighted in Paris by such artists as Braque, Derain, Picasso, Matisse and Vlaminck in the early 20th century. In 1911, Paul Guillaume opened the first gallery in Paris concentrating on black African art. So significant was his authority that he influenced the purchasing patterns of new collectors, in particular Georges de Miré. Even today, the analysis that Guillaume applied to black African art is still respected. He considered Fang sculptures to be the epitome of such art and insisted upon the importance of patina and of the relationship between the statue or mask and its base. To this end, he employed a Japanese stand maker called Inagaki, who stamped his seal beneath his veneered wood bases. By the end of the First World War, during which there had been many acts of bravery by black African troops, the French were beginning to move from a position of prejudice to one of curiosity about the so-called 'primitive cultures'.

Prior to the 1980s, exhibitions concentrating on a single category of objects or a single tribe were rare. They tended instead to include a variety of objects from different areas of Africa. Eventually, private institutions, such as the Dapper Museum in Paris, began to exhibit objects dedicated to a single tribe – the Fang or the Dogon – or theme, such as body ornament. This trend is currently being reinforced through the publication of books focused on single tribes. The present book, however, deliberately sets out to provide the reader with an overview of the most artistically significant tribes living in black Africa.

Since the birth of a commercial black African art market in the 1920s, objects of good quality have become rarer. The original sources of supply were white colonials returning from Africa. Indeed, as early as 1912 Paul Guillaume advertised for objects and masks in newspapers read by colonials. Then, for two decades between the mid-1950s and the mid-1970s, when it became apparent that these original sources were

A Luba neckrest;
*wood and glass beads;
height: 14.1 cm (5¹/₂ in)*

nearing exhaustion, a new generation of suppliers travelled to Africa and appropriated statues and masks. By the early 1980s, with the toughening of export laws and the depletion of artefacts from certain tribal areas, the market turned towards new countries and new forms of collectable objects. Zambia, Tanzania and all of East Africa became major suppliers to the world's stage. Terracottas from the Niger River inland delta or from the Jos plateau in Nigeria are currently further fuelling the Western market for black African art.

The pieces referred to above have often been illegally exported and thus raise difficult questions about the protection of the cultural heritage of the countries in question. For example, controversy surrounds certain funerary figures from Madagascar and a number of terracotta statues originating from West Africa. With looting and clandestine excavations, much scientific information about these objects has been lost. The international community has rightly condemned these practices. Nevertheless, it may be worth considering that, with their arrival on the Western market, these archaeological pieces draw the attention of Westerners still more to the antiquity and sublime beauty of black African art traditions.

This book has been created with the aim of helping professional and amateur collectors alike to find visual and textual references to tribal objects they have seen or collected. Its format is based on photographs supported by a text whose purpose is to set each object in a social, artistic and sometimes religious context. The first part of each section provides the reader with important information concerning the artistic output of each major tribe of black Africa. The second part engages the reader in a visual dialogue: it includes illustrations of objects – either previously unpublished or famous – which all demonstrate the ability of black African carvers to resolve artistic challenges.

Forty-nine sections correspond to specific cultural areas. Each one studies the most important tribe within an area, including a survey of its political and social structures as well as its artistic production. In most instances this includes masks, statues and everyday objects such as textiles, furniture and jewelry. Where relevant, a short description of artistically related tribes follows. Each section ends with a bibliography providing the reader with the possibility of further deepening his knowledge of each tribe.

A Fang figure;
wood and metal;
height: 40 cm (15³/₄ in)

A Bamileke beaded throne;
wood, vegetal fibres and glass beads;
height: 160 cm (63 in);
private collection

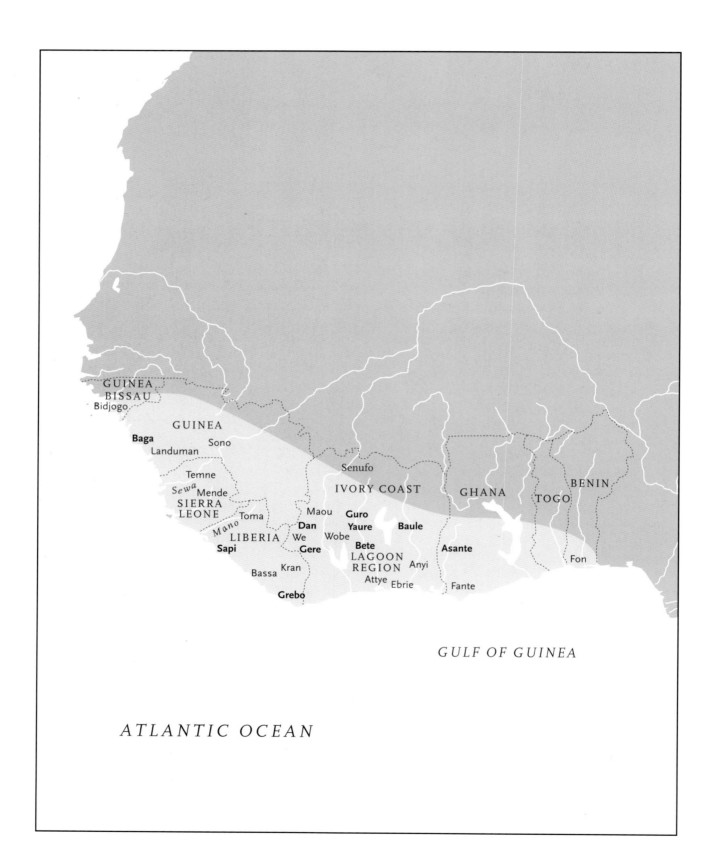

GUINEA
BISSAU
Bidjogo

GUINEA

Baga
Landuman   Sono

Temne
Sewa Mende   Senufo

SIERRA   IVORY COAST   GHANA   BENIN
LEONE   TOGO
       Toma   Maou   **Guro**
Mano   **Dan**   **Yaure**   **Baule**
     LIBERIA   We Wobe
Sapi   **Gere**   **Bete**   **Asante**
                           LAGOON   Anyi
        Kran   REGION
Bassa   Attye Ebrie   Fante   Fon

       Grebo

GULF OF GUINEA

ATLANTIC OCEAN

I

THE COAST OF WEST AFRICA

BAGA
SAPI-GREBO
THE LAGOON REGIONS
ASANTE
DAN
GURO-YAURE
BETE-GERE
BAULE

Baga

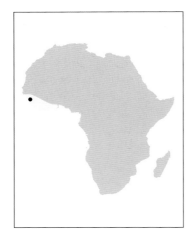

The Baga people, 45,000 in total, live along the coast of Guinea Bissau, in villages divided into between two and four *quartiers*, which are in turn divided into five or six clans. Traditionally, each village was headed by the eldest member of each clan, who met secretly, but today this system has been replaced by an elected mayor. Spiritually, they believe in a single god, known as Kanu, who is assisted by *Somtup*, a male spirit, and by *A-Bol*, a female spirit. Below them, the spirit *A-Mantsho-nga-Tshol*, who is often represented as a snake, serves as the patron of the two lowest grades of the To-lom society which overseas the different initiation ceremonies.

1

Baga figures first appeared in the West in the 1950s after the conversion to Islam and the abandonment of traditional rites and beliefs. These circumstances meant that Western dealers were able to export Baga masks and headdresses. Today, Baga people are attempting to revive their culture with the help of their elders – they are re-creating the ceremonies and festivities that once gave their lives rhythm.

MASKS

The most famous Baga mask is known as the *Nimba* (*d'mba* in the Baga language). It is a shoulder mask which stands on four legs, has a large pair of breasts, a typical enlarged head with semi-circular ears, a pointed chin and nose and is worn by dancers at births, marriages, harvest festivals and other joyful ceremonies. Two styles of *Nimba* mask have been identified: the first, better known in the West, has a concave face **[A]**, while the second has a convex face (3).

North and south of the territory occupied by the Sitemu and Pukur people, the *Ziringen-Wonde* headdress (5) was worn by dancers during ceremonies marking the end of a girl's initiation period, harvest festivals and wakes for the dead. It symbolizes a young bride and is characterized by a front panel supported by two legs set under an annulated neck and a diminutive head. Like the *Nimba* mask, the large pair of breasts on the *Ziringen-Wonde* headdress serve as an allegory for multiple births and fecundity.

Baga snake headdresses (1), representing the spirit *A-Mantsho-nga-Tshol*, can be up to 260 cm high and typically display undulation, polychrome decoration and sometimes have eyes inset with glass. They were held on the shoulders of a dancer with the help of a light framework and appeared in ceremonies in which clans of a *quartier* took part.

Other smaller headdresses, representing the medicine spirit *A-Tshol*, known as *Etiol* in the West (4), were worn by dancers either during ceremonies celebrating the end of an adult initiation or the beginning of the cultivation period. These headdresses are characterized by a pierced conical base issuing an elongated neck, which supports a horizontal head with a pointed chin.

Headdresses representing chimpanzees and bird spirits (12) symbolize the inherent qualities of the animals they represent.

The Baga still use the *Banda* headdress, which is large and an amalgamation of zoomorphic and anthropomorphic features (7). It has an elongated human face with the jaws of a crocodile, the horns of an antelope, the body of a serpent and the tail of a chameleon. It measures between 120 and 200 cm and is worn by dancers only for entertainment, but, traditionally, it was employed during apotropaic rites and the ending of male initiation ceremonies.

The headdress known as *Tonkongba* (13) is erroneously attributed to the Landuman people, a small group neighbouring the Baga people. It is in fact found among all northern Baga people and is usually kept in front of a clan's shrine. It is sometimes worn by dancers during ceremonies involving

2

1   A Baga snake headdress; *wood and pigments; height: 123 cm (48¹/₂ in)*

2   Two Bidjogo figures; *wood; height of the taller: 43.2 cm (17 in)*

3   A Baga *Nimba* shoulder mask; *wood; height: 130 cm (51 in)*

4   An *Etiol* headdress; *wood; height: 35 cm (13⁵/₈ in)*

5   A *Ziringen-Wonde* headdress; *wood and copper nails; height: 74 cm (29¹/₈ in)*

6   A Baga drum; *wood; height: 92.3 cm (36³/₈ in)*

7   An elongated Baga headdress; *wood and pigments; length: 142 cm (56 in)*

8   A Menda mask; *wood; height: 49.5 cm (19¹/₂ in)*

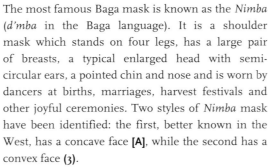

3

4

5

6

7   8   9   10

sacrifices – for instance, funerals. *Tonkongba* is alleged to be omniscient, thus he has the power to know and promulgate both good and bad news. Western scholars describe this mask as a stylized dolphin, based on its triangular snout, globular head with central crest and pair of horns, which are thought to symbolize the tail of the dolphin.

A rare type of mask thought to be related to *Menda* female society ceremonies displays an elongated face with a pointed chin, a linear nose and an arched domed forehead (8).

STATUES

So far, two types of Baga figure have been identified. The first, representing the *A-Tshol* spirit (11), is found primarily among northern Baga people and is kept on the clan's altar, guarded by the eldest man in the family. It has a conical base surmounted by a large head with a pointed beak-like chin. It is similar to the homonymous headdress described above, but the stylization is more exaggerated. The second type of figure [B] represents either a man or a woman with a stylized head similar to the one seen in *Nimba* shoulder masks [A]. These statues are thought to be the precursors of such masks, but unfortunately their function remains obscure.

EVERYDAY OBJECTS

Rare caryatid drums (6) were used to beat out the rhythm during initiation ceremonies. According to the gender of the caryatid figure, they were played either by female initiates at the end of their ceremonies, or by male initiates during their rites.

Caryatid stools were carved as prestige objects and were used by the elders during their secret meetings. Combs, which were also considered to be prestige objects, were often decorated with masks or decorative motifs.

RELATED TRIBES

Off the shore of Guinea Bissau lie the thirty islands that comprise the **Bidjogo** archipelago. Its population

lives primarily from fishing and rice farming. Although there is evidence that the Bidjogo archipelago was inhabited as far back as the mid-15th century, little is known about the people's customs and ceremonies.

Bidjogo masks are worn during initiation ceremonies related to an age-classing society, either on top of the head or in front of it. They symbolize indigenous animals such as cows, sharks [C] and sword fish (9) and the dancing movements of the wearer reflect the nature of the animal they represent.

Although Bidjogo figures, also called *Iran*, can be either realistic or abstract (2), they all have a head with a pointed chin, a flattened face with rounded eyes and semi-circular ears. These *Iran* figures are believed to be possessed by divinities and have many functions – they serve as the focus of divination ceremonies, as protectors of households against curses and as healers. Kept in small sanctuaries or in special places in houses, these figures are offered sacrifices and libations which create a thick patina on the surface.

At the beginning of the 1960s, a group of bronze staffs (10), called **Sono**, were discovered by Western scholars in Guinea Bissau. These staffs are thought to have been produced by local people colonized by Malian conquerors between the 13th and the 15th century.

BIBLIOGRAPHY
BASSANI, EZIO, 'Sono from Guinea Bissau', *African Art*, XII, 4, pp. 44–47, 1979
GALLOIS-DUQUETTE, D., *Dynamique de l'Art Bidjogo*, Lisbon, 1983
GORDTS, ANDRÉ, 'La Statuaire traditionelle Bidjogo', *Arts d'Afrique Noire*, XVIII, summer 1976, pp. 6–21
LAMP, FREDERIK, *Art of the Baga*, Exh. Cat., The Museum for African Art, New York, 1996
TEIXERA DA MOTA, A., 'Bronzes Antigos das Guine', *Actas do Congresso Internacional de Etnografia* (Lisbon, 1965), vol. 4, pp. 1–6, Santo Tirso Municipal Council, 10–18 July 1963
VAN VEERTRUYEN, G., 'Le Style Nimba', *Arts d'Afrique Noire*, 1968

9 A Bidjogo sword-fish mask; *wood, pigments and vegetal fibres; length: 66 cm (26 in); private collection*

10 A Sono staff; *bronze; height: 20 cm (8 in)*

11 An Etiol figure; *wood and copper nails; height: 81 cm (32 in)*

12 A Baga bird headdress; *wood and pigments; length: 45 cm (17 3/4 in)*

13 A 'Landuman' *Tonkongba* mask; *wood; length: 90.2 cm (35 1/2 in)*

11

12

13

[A] Left: a **Baga** *Nimba* **mask**
wood and copper nails;
height: 135 cm (53¹/₈ in)

Shoulder masks like this one were
used during joyful ceremonies such
as weddings and harvest festivals.
The wearer of the mask had a raffia
costume and performed dances while
surrounded by villagers.

[B] Below: a **Baga figure**
wood and beads; height: 86 cm (34 in);
provenance: Charles Ratton, Paris;
private collection

This unique Baga figure embodies
all the characteristics of Baga art with
its elegance and stylization. This type
of figure may have been a prototype
for the *Nimba* masks which display
similar cephalomorphic features.

[C] Right: a **Bidjogo Shark headdress**
wood, pigment and vegetal fibres; length
34 cm (13³/₈ in); private collection

Worn during age-classing ceremonies
that structured Bidjogo life, this
extraordinary headdress, with its
stylized shark head, reflects the
strong influence of the ocean on
Bidjogo beliefs.

Sapi-Grebo

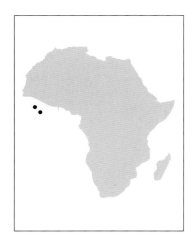

The various peoples of Sierra Leone predominantly belong to the Mende and Kissi tribes who make their living from rice farming. They are led by chiefs whose power is counterbalanced by the powerful *Poro* male society; the female society is called *Sande*.

1

The Mende and Kissi people revere stone anthropomorphic carvings which are found in fields and rivers in an area centred around the Sewa and Mano rivers. The Kissi people call them *Pombo* (pl. *Pomtam*), which means 'the deceased', while the Mende refer to the carvings as *Nomoli* (pl. *Nomolisia*). These carvings are extremely old and it was not until 1959 that Western scholars associated them with the so-called **Afro-Portuguese** ivory objects. The latter – made between 1490 and 1530 and found in all the European royal courts – display a mixture of European themes in an African style. Oliphants, salt cellars **[A]**, spoons and forks were designed on paper by Europeans and were executed in ivory by mainly Sapi artists.

The **Sapi** kingdom, which included a number of tribes such as the Temne and the Sherbro, encompassed present-day Guinea and Liberia, but collapsed in the 16th century under pressure from the Manes people. Today, these Sapi stone carvings have different associations for the Kissi and the Mende peoples. The Kissi wrap them in cotton cloth, and place them either on small altars or in a deep bowl with other amulets and worship them. According to Kissi belief, they are thought to act as intermediaries with their ancestors. The Mende generally honour their figures by placing them on altars set under small huts where libations are poured over them to procure a good crop.

These Sapi stone figures all appear to date from between the 13th and 18th centuries (except some rougher carvings made during the 19th–20th centuries) and measure from 8 to 40 cm, but there are several types and styles. The first type, identified by the Kissi people as *Pombo* **(4)**, comprises stone figures with an elongated head, a rectangular mouth showing filed teeth and, generally, a ridged coiffure. A second type, which the Mende people called *Nomoli* **(5)**, includes statues with an enlarged head, globular eyes and a typical enlarged, flared nose. A third type, called *Mahen Yafe* **(3)** meaning 'spirits of the chief', have large heads adorned with jewelry, and appear to represent the heads of chiefs. Unfortunately, no information exists detailing the function of these statues.

Today, the 1,000,000 **Temne** people live in small chiefdoms within Sierra Leone. Ruled by a central chief, they are socially regulated by secret societies such as the male *Poro* society and the female *Bondo* association. During initiation rites related to the

1 A Bassa dog figure;
  wood; length: 31.7 cm (12¹/₂ in)

2 A Mende figure;
  wood; height: 60 cm (23¹/₂ in);
  Dr Michel Gaud, St Tropez

3 A *Mahen Yafe* head;
  stone; height: 25.4 cm (10 in)

4 A *Pombo* figure;
  stone; height: 16.2 cm (6¹/₂ in)

5 A *Nomoli* figure;
  stone; height: 31.1 cm (12¹/₄ in)

2

3   4   5

6   7   8   9

latter, young girls were led by the head of the association, called the *Soko*, to a sacred grove by a river. At the head of the procession, the *Soko* may carry a female figure which is a representation of an ideal woman **(10)**.

Bassa territory lies in the middle of present-day Liberia. Their economy is based on rice which they cultivate around small villages which have a population of around two hundred. Bassa artistic tradition has been influenced by their north-eastern neighbours, the Dan, who live on the Ivory Coast. Bassa carvers are famed for their *Gela* masks worn during the *No* men's society ceremonies when the wearer of the mask moves with feminine and elegant grace. This mask displays a characteristic two-planed face with a protruding mouth inset with wooden teeth and semi-closed eyes **(7)**. They are worn by dancers during entertainment ceremonies related to visits of foreign dignitaries and at the end of a boy's initiation rite. Rare figures of dogs **(1)** carved with a human face on the side, as well as stools **[B]**, are known to exist, although the purpose of the dog statue remains unknown.

The **Toma** people of Guinea (known as Loma in Liberia) number 200,000 and live in the high-altitude rain forest lying across the Guinea–Liberia border. Artistically, their reputation rests on their *Landai* mask which has an articulated crocodile jaw and a flattened, stylized human face **(6)**. This mask symbolically devours *Poro* society candidates at the end of their initiation period, after which they are revived as full members of this sodality. Some rare figures exist which are kept within each household.

The **Mende** settled in Sierra Leone during the 16th century, having migrated from the north. Today, the 2,000,000 Mende live mostly from rice and cocoa farming and are organized into different chiefdoms. Social order and structure are regulated through the *Poro* male and the *Sande* female societies. During ceremonies associated with the latter, women wear *Bundu* masks **(9)** which embody idealized female beauty and represent an ancestor of the society.

Other Mende societies are responsible for protecting their members from illness or curing them. Female figures **(2)** are carved and revered for their healing properties and also serve as emblems for the society when they are formally displayed during processions. Stylistically, they can be identified by their enlarged breasts, their hands resting on their abdomen and their typical head with an exaggerated coiffure.

Unlike the other populations living in Liberia, the **Grebo** people are not structured by the *Poro* society. They are ruled by a chief known as *Bodio* who lives in near total isolation. The characteristic feature of Grebo masks is an elongated nose set between tubular eyes **[C, 8]**. These masks were recently attributed to a neighbouring tribe, the Kru, who live on the Ivory Coast. Since they have one or several pair of eyes, it is thought they may represent seers.

BIBLIOGRAPHY

BASSANI, E., and WILLIAM FAGG, *Africa and the Renaissance*, New York, 1988

FAGG, WILLIAM, *Afro-Portuguese Ivories*, London, 1959

LAMP, F., 'House of Stones: Memorial Art of Fifteenth Century Sierra Leone', *Art Bulletin*, 65, 1983, pp. 219–37

MENEGHINI, M., 'The Grebo Mask', *African Art*, VIII, 1, 1974

PHILLIPS, R., 'Masking in Mende Sande Society Initiation Rituals', *Africa* (London), 48 (3), 1978, pp. 265–78

TAGLIAFERRI, A., and ARNO HAMMACHER, *Fabulous Ancestors, Stone Carvings from Sierra Leone and Guinea*, New York, 1974

VAN DAMNE, A., *De Maskersculptuur binnen het Poro-genootschap van de Loma* (Working Paper), Ghent, 1987

6   A Toma mask;
    wood; height: 88 cm (34 1/2 in)

7   A Bassa mask;
    wood; height: 27 cm (10 1/2 in)

8   A Grebo mask;
    wood; height: 55 cm (21 3/4 in)

9   A Mende *Bundu* mask;
    wood; height: 37 cm (14 1/2 in);
    Archives Monbrison, Paris

10   A Temne figure;
    wood; height: 61 cm (24 in)

10

[A] Left: an Afro-Portuguese salt cellar (c. 16th century)
ivory; height: 19.5 cm (7³/₄ in)

It is likely that this Afro-Portuguese salt cellar was made by Sapi ivory craftsmen for export to the royal courts of Europe. The depiction of European figures is not surprising since it was designed in Europe.

[B] Above: a Bassa stool
wood; height: 41 cm (16¹/₄ in)

Four male and female figures with typical Bassa features appear on this important stool. These figures may represent Bassa ancestors and confer to the owner of the stool respectability and prestige.

[C] Right: a Grebo mask
wood; height: 53 cm (21 in);
private collection

Grebo masks of this type are characterized by highly stylized features which have appealed to Western artists since the early 20th century. Such masks usually display several pairs of eyes, which are thought to represent ancestors.

The Lagoon Regions

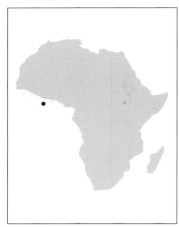

2

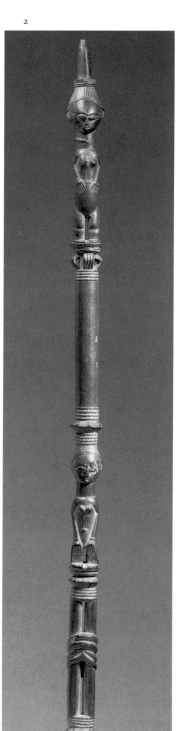

1

The eastern coast of the Ivory Coast comprises an area of lagoons, where the population is divided into twelve different language groups. The cultural and stylistic unity of these people justifies grouping them together for the purposes of this chapter. Before colonization, each village was autonomous and, when threatened, they united to form a 'confederation'. Unusually, these people are not governed by chiefs, although a man's social position is determined by his age.

The sculptural art of this area can be identified by common characteristics. Carvings feature an elaborate coiffure divided into raised masses and small button-like scarifications on the face [A], while the influence of their neighbours, the Akan to the east and the Baule to the north, is also apparent.

The two principal groups of the Lagoon area are the **Ebrie** and the **Attye** (also called Akye). The **Anyi** people live to the north-east of this area and evolved an artistic tradition reflecting the influence of both the Lagoon and the Baule people.

MASKS

Masks from the Lagoon area are extremely rare, but usually have a rough-looking appearance (5). Their function is unknown.

STATUETTES

The Lagoon people produced a corpus of figures, varying from 25 to 70 cm in height, which were usually full-frontal, standing female figures with muscular legs and arms. Their faces have an incised mouth, a T-shaped nose, enlarged globular eyes (11), button-like scarifications (8) and an elaborate coiffure divided into raised masses. They are characterized by a rich patina and are sometimes wearing miniature gold necklaces [C].

The western Lagoon people (Ahizi, Alladian, Adiukru) carved figures in a slightly different style, with asymmetrical poses, flat breasts and a thin aquiline nose; while the statues made by the eastern Lagoon tribes (Abure, Gwa, Attye) have a central incised scarification on their body, reminiscent of their eastern neighbours, the Anyi. Anyi figures have rounded features and do not show the inset pegs typical of the Lagoon people (9, 10).

Used by traditional healers, the role of these figures was to convey messages to spirits living in the other world. Occasionally, they were given as prizes to outstanding dancers.

EVERYDAY OBJECTS

The stools carved by the Lagoon people visibly show that they have been influenced by their Akan neighbours. They were carved with a single foot in the shape of an animal (4), whereas the Akan model has a central geometric foot surrounded by four columnar ones. Moreover, they produced elongated drums (170 cm long) which were beaten during the age-classing society ceremonies.

Using the 'lost-wax' technique, the Lagoon people created elaborate gold jewelry, often in the shape of a stylized ram's head (3) or a human face. The surface was covered with minute linear geometric decorations. Traditionally, they were hair ornaments, but today they function more as necklaces.

The Attye people carved ivory combs (6) and wooden canes (2) that suggest a European influence.

BIBLIOGRAPHY
Art of the Côte d'Ivoire, Musée Barbier-Mueller, Geneva, 1993
VISONA, M., *Art and Authority among the Ayke of the Ivory Coast*, Santa Barbara, 1983

3

4

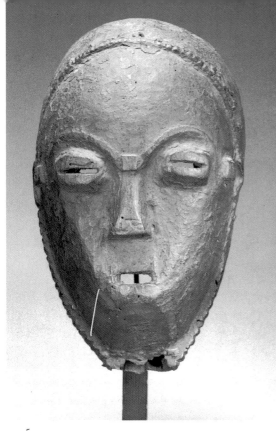

5

6

7

1   A Fon *Bocio*; wood and magical
    substances; height: 53 cm (21 in)

2   An Attye cane;
    wood; height: 96 cm (37³/₄ in)

3   Attye jewelry;
    gold; height: 8.9 cm (3¹/₂ in)

4   A Lagoon area stool;
    wood; height: 43 cm (17 in)

5   A Lagoon area mask;
    wood; height: 39 cm (15¹/₄ in)

6   An Attye comb;
    ivory; height: 10 cm (4 in)

7   A Fon royal sceptre;
    wood and iron; height:
    39 cm (15¹/₄ in)

8   A Lagoon area figure;
    wood; height: 78 cm (30³/₄ in)

9   An Anyi figure;
    wood and beads; height:
    37 cm (14¹/₂ in)

10 An Anyi figure;
    wood; height: 38 cm (15 in);
    private collection

11 A Lagoon area figure;
    wood; height: 17 cm (6⁵/₈ in)

FON

The Fon people live in the Dahomey kingdom, which is part of the Republic of Benin. Oral tradition suggests the Dahomey kingdom was created by a Yoruba princess some time before the 17th century. During the 18th century, its territories expanded and they took part in the slave trade with the French colonials.

Two categories of Fon objects can be distinguished. The first includes royal paraphernalia such as king figures, commemorative iron staffs, called *Asen*, small metal emblematic figures and sceptres decorated with a zoomorphic blade (7). The second category of objects is called *Bocio* **[B]** and relates to the *Vodun* or magical ceremonies undertaken to contact the spirit world and trap harmful forces. The word *Vodun* is derived from the Yoruba language and also refers to the Fon gods. The *Bocio* are wooden figures made by blacksmiths under the order of a *Fa* diviner. They are usually set on a peg and covered with magical substances to the extent that the figure may be hidden. These substances are made of blood, palm oil, beer and animal parts **(1)** and are believed to give power to the *Bocio*.

BIBLIOGRAPHY

ADANDE, C., 'Le Bochio: une sculpture de rien qui cache tout', *Mélanges Jean Pliya*, Cotonou, 1994
BLIER, P. S., *Vodun: Art, Psychology and Power*, Chicago, 1995
MERLO, C., *Un Chef-d'oeuvre d'art nègre: le buste de la prêtresse*, Auvers-sur-Oise, 1966

8

9

10

11

[A] Left: **an Attye figure**
wood; height: 87 cm (34³/₈ in)

This tall Attye figure may have been used as a
post. It is refined and elegant like all the art made
by the Lagoon people. The small face and neck
pegs are typical of the artistic output from this
region of the Ivory Coast.

[B] Above: **a Fon *Bocio* figure**
wood, metal and magical substances;
height: 35cm (13⁵/₈ in); private collection

Unusually refined, this *Bocio* figure conveys a
serenity rarely found in this type of Fon figure.
It was made collectively by a carver, a blacksmith
and a magician.

[C] Right: **an Anyi figure**
wood, beads and gold; height: 35 cm (14 in);
provenance: Vlaminck Collection, Paris; Dr Chauvet
Collection, Paris; private collection

Glass and gold beads, such as those worn by this
exquisite figure, are usually associated with the
Baule people, but this figure's facial features and
elaborate coiffure suggest it was made by the
Anyi. It was probably used to convey messages
to the spirits who, according to Anyi beliefs, rule
the world.

COLLECTION D.ᵉ STEPHEN CHAUVET

Asante

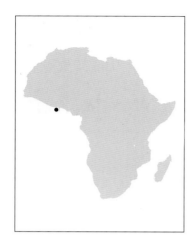

When they arrived on the coast of Ghana in 1471, Portuguese sailors were astonished by the highly structured kingdoms they encountered. This initial contact, along with the area's reputation for being wealthy, encouraged Westerners to settle in the region and to trade bronze and European-manufactured objects for Ghanaian gold and slaves. These first Europeans only met a fraction of the Ghanaian population who occupy a large territory that can be separated into three distinct areas for the purpose of this chapter.

The first area, which lies along the coast of the Gulf of Guinea, is a flat plain covered with shrubs occasionally interrupted by lagoons. It is divided into numerous kingdoms of which the most well known are the Fante and the Ewe. The second area includes the central part of the country. It is a forest area where the most renowned tribe is undoubtedly the Asante (also known as Ashanti). The Asante tribe, as well as other peoples living in central and south Ghana, speak the Twi language and collectively form the Akan people. The third area, in northern Ghana, is covered by savannah and is the habitat of Gur-speaking people whose traditions and religions are still poorly understood.

1

1 A group of gold-weights;
   brass; height of the tallest: 8 cm (3 in)

2 Two Fante *Akuaba* doll;
   *wood; height of the tallest: 33.7 cm
   (13¹/4 in)*

3 A Bono *Akuaba* doll;
   *wood; height: 26.5 cm (10¹/2 in);
   E. Anspach Collection; New York*

4 An Asante *Akuaba* doll;
   wood; height: 35.5 cm (14 in)

2

Akan artistic production focuses primarily on decorative art objects. These fall into several categories – statues, furniture and jewelry. Statues and stools were occasionally placed in royal and commoner shrines – a room where magical materials such as brass vessels and amulets were kept.

The artistic production of the entire Ghanaian tribal population is strongly influenced by the aesthetic traditions of the Asante tribe. In fact, it is almost impossible to attribute a specific type of sculpture to a specific tribe, given that Asante carvers and artisans travelled across Ghana and spread the Asante aesthetic tradition countrywide.

MASKS
Only one type of headdress has been found in Ghana. It comes from the north and is a vegetal cap surmounted by two horns.

STATUES
Asante carvers are famed for their female dolls, known as *Akuaba*, which measure between 20 and 40 cm in height and display a stylized elongated body and an enlarged circular head **(4)**. These dolls, consecrated by priests, are thought to have the power to make barren women conceive and are carried around and treated like a real child by Asante women. After use, they are placed in a domestic shrine.

Fante and Bono people, who live respectively to the south and the north of the Asante, also employ *Akuaba* dolls, but they are carved in a different style. The heads of Fante dolls are rectangular **(2)** whereas Bono *Akuaba* have a triangular profile **(3)**.

The Asante also carve maternity figures called *Esi Mansa*. They are kept in royal or commoner shrines where they emphasize the importance of the family and lineage **[B]**.

From the 16th to the 18th centuries, southern Akan people incorporated terracotta heads – and more

3   4   5   6   7

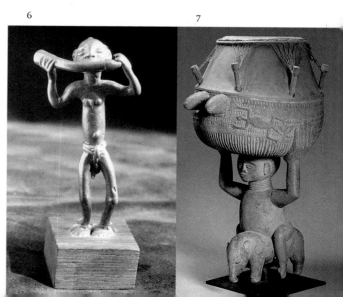

8   9   10   11   12

rarely, figures – into the funeral ceremonies of their chiefs. They were paraded through the village and then either left on the grave or set on a shrine where libations were offered to them.

Different styles of head can be distinguished. The first major style, related to the Fante and the Fomena-Adanse people, shows a rounded head **[C]**. A second important style, found among the Kwahu people, has a flattened face (**5**) which suggests a connection with *Akuaba* dolls.

Large elaborate drums (**7**) were played during Fante festivities. The lead drum, sometimes called *Queen Mother*, is characterized by its legs and breasts and is covered by motifs recounting local proverbs.

EVERYDAY OBJECTS

The Asante are famous for their ceremonial stools (**8**) carved with an arched seat set over a foot, referring to a proverb or a symbol of wisdom. They are usually made for a chief when he takes office and are adorned with beads or copper nails and sheets. In rare cases, when the chief is sufficiently important, the stool is placed in a special room following his death to commemorate his memory.

Asante chairs (**9**) are based on 17th-century European models and, unlike stools, do not have any spiritual function. They are used as prestige objects by important chiefs during festivities or significant gatherings.

The extent of the gold trade among the Akan people encouraged the use of brass gold-weights which are cast using the 'lost-wax' process and have geometric or figurative shapes. Western scholars have identified two major periods of gold-weight production.

The first period dates from 1400 to 1720 and is thought to have been the result of influence of traders from the Mali empire. These weights are thick and usually geometrically shaped. Figurative weights are rare. They are large in size (7–10 cm) and usually lack detail (**6**).

Weights produced during the second period date from 1720 to 1930. They are either geometric or figurative and show a greater variety of shape and detail. For example, animals, proverbs or, more simply, people doing everyday activities have been represented (**1**).

The elaborate coiffures of Akan women led to the production of wooden combs which were often given as presents from fathers or husbands (**11**). They are frequently decorated with a scene depicting the occasion when the gift was presented.

Two major types of brass vessel are used by the Akan. Called *Forowa* and *Kuduo*, they were used respectively for storing vegetable fat, or precious possessions or as receptacles for religious ceremonies (**12**).

The Akan prize gold jewelry (**10**) and have fashioned rings, necklaces and bracelets in geometric or animal shapes which are worn during festivities. Zoomorphic and cephalomorphic amulets **[A]** were usually worn by chiefs at important meetings.

The Akan people are famous for their textiles, which are worn during important festivities. They are narrow strips of fabric, which have orange, red and blue threads sewn together. While the Asante chiefs wore textiles decorated with abstract patterns which were often made from silk, the Ewe people, their eastern neighbours, tended to weave figurative motifs and symbols into their fabric designs that were later sold at market.

Among the Fante people, warrior 'companies', known as *Asafo*, defended villages from invaders. Today, they have a more social and fraternal function and are headed by a chief known as *Omanhene*, who initiates inter-company competitions. Each *Asafo* rallies around a shrine, called *Posuban*, and is associated with certain colours and a specific flag. These appliqué flags display scenes and symbols that relate to proverbs (**13**).

RELATED TRIBES

The **Moba** people reside in the north-east corner of Ghana and in Togo and are known primarily for their highly abstract sculptures called *Tchitchiri* (**14**). These represent ancestors or house spirits and are often covered with a thick encrusted patina.

5 A Kwahu-style head;
terracotta; height: 37.8 cm (14⁷/₈ in)

6 A figurative gold-weight;
brass; height: 9 cm (3⁵/₈ in); E. Anspach Collection, New York

7 A Fante drum;
wood; height: 75 cm (29¹/₂ in)

8 A stool;
wood; height: 39 cm (15¹/₂ in)

9 A chair; *wood covered by copper sheet; height: 92 cm (36 in)*

10 A piece of gold jewelry;
diameter: 15.2 cm (6 in)

11 A comb; *wood; height: 26 cm (10 in); private collection*

12 A *Kuduo* vessel;
brass; height: 14 cm (5¹/₂ in)

13 An Asafo flag;
cotton; length: 129 cm (51 in)

14 A Moba figure;
wood; height: 140 cm (55 in); Archives Monbrison, Paris

13

14

BIBLIOGRAPHY

COLE, HERBERT, and DORAN ROSS, *The Arts of Ghana*, University of California, Los Angeles, 1977
GARRARD, TIMOTHY F., 'Studies in Akan Goldweights', *Transactions of the Historical Society of Ghana*, 13:1; 13:2; 14:1; 14:2; 1972–73 (vol. 4)
ASANTE: AMROUCHE, PIERRE, and AMADOU THIAM, *Art Moba du Togo*, Galerie Amrouche, Paris, 1991
DE GRUNNE, BERNARD, *Terres cuites anciennes de l'Ouest Africain*, Louvain-la-Neuve, 1980

[A] Left: **an Asante bowman figure**

brass; height: 7 cm (2³/₄ in); private collection

This remarkable brass figure may have been used either as a pendant or as a gold weight. Its bun-like coiffure is also found on terracotta heads (*see* C) and suggests early dating.

[B] Below: **an Asante maternity figure**

wood; height: 56.6 cm (22¹/₄ in)

Maternity figures are commonly found within West Africa. This one is rare because it is so magisterial – the chair on which the figure is seated is a throne used by chiefs of the region. Its design is derived from a 17th-century European model.

[C] Above: **a Fante-style (Fomena-Adanse substyle) Asante head**

terracotta; height: 28 cm (11 in)

Probably dating from between the 16th and the 18th centuries, this Asante head has an elaborate coiffure and scarification typical of the nobility of the region. It was used either as a grave marker or to receive offerings.

Dan

Dan people, who are also known by the name Yacuba, live in the western part of the Ivory Coast and into Liberia where the land is forested in the south and bordered by a savannah in the north. The 350,000 Dan people make their living from farming cocoa, rice and manioc. Before unifying secret societies were set up at the turn of the century, each Dan village was an autonomous socio-political unit governed by a chief elected on the base of his wealth and social position. Today, the leopard society acts as a major regulator of Dan life and initiates young men during their isolated periods of three to four months in the forest. Dan people have achieved notoriety in the area for their entertainment festivals which were historically village ceremonies, but are today performed largely for tourists. During these festivals, masked performers dance on stilts.

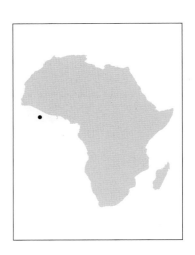

1

2

1 A figure;
   brass; height: 17.8 cm (7 in)

2 A *Tankagle* mask;
   wood and pigments;
   height: 27.9 cm (11 in)

3 A *Bagle* mask;
   wood; height: 27 cm (10³/₄ in)

MASKS

Dan masks are characterized by a concave face, a pointed chin, a protruding mouth, an upturned nose, a high-domed forehead and are often covered in a rich brown patina. Similar masks are found throughout the country, but regional stylistic variations occur. For example, northern face masks tend to have very fine features, a high-domed smooth forehead, eyes set in the middle of the face and a very smooth brown patina obtained by immersing the mask in a pool of mud. Southern masks, on the other hand, have protruding features and a rougher patina obtained by applying vegetal pigments.

There are a variety of Dan face masks, each of which has a different function.
• The *Deangle* mask (4) has a ridge in the middle of the forehead and slit eyes, which are occasionally covered with white kaolin. It is worn by the

intermediary who acts between the village and the forest initiation camp.
• The *Tankagle* mask (2) is worn during entertainment celebrations and has similar features to the *Deangle* mask, but is larger and more detailed.
• The *Gunyeya* mask (10), also called a racing mask, has a pointed face and typical large circular eyes. Its wearer is pursued by an unmasked runner and, if caught, the unmasked runner wears the mask and is, in turn, pursued. Historically, these races trained men to fight and the winner gained social recognition. Nowadays, the races are more like a game.
• The *Zakpai* mask (6) has similar features to the *Gunyeya*, but has a red cloth over its eyes. It acts against bush fires during the dry season.
• The *Bagle* mask (3) has an oval, concave face, a low forehead and typical tubular eyes. It is worn to entertain while the wearer dances, beats the musicians with a curved stick and throws objects he finds in their way.

3   4   5   6   7

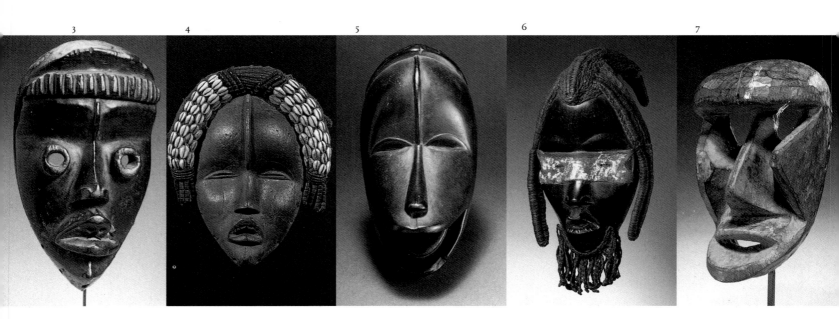

8   9   10   11   12

• The *Bugle* mask (8) is characterized by an exaggerated mouth, a dark, thick patina, a row of stylized horns on the forehead and, when preserved, a high feathered coiffure. Its wearer dances and makes trouble in order to provoke a reaction from the people watching. It was worn in pre-war ceremonies.

• The *Kaogle* mask (7) has triangular cheek-bones and eyes and its wearer is meant to stimulate a festive mood among the audience by throwing sticks at them.

• The *Dugle* mask (5), or 'the cow', has a high forehead and a huge mouth resembling a beak and is worn for entertainment purposes.

• The *Gagon* mask (9) has the same function as the *Dugle* and is predominantly found in the northern Dan territory. It has a high-domed forehead, slit eyes, a long, beak-like nose with black monkey fur attached underneath, and a long, mobile jaw.

• The *Glewa* mask is worn for peace-making purposes. It is a large mask, either in the shape of a stylized elephant with tubular eyes and a domed forehead with a medium ridge, or in the form of a human face with exaggerated features.

• The *Go Ge* mask [C] belongs to the *Go* secret society and is worn to announce the death of important chiefs. Its features vary from one village to another, but the masks are usually large, and have an elaborated plaited coiffure.

The Dan people also carried small masks (less than 20 cm high) which are sometimes called 'passport' masks (12). They were sewn onto a piece of cloth and kept in a leather pouch and possibly worn in the small of the back. They are miniature copies of a family mask and sometimes received libations. These apotropaic masks also act as witnesses during initiation ceremonies.

STATUES

Dan figures [B], which were commissioned by powerful chiefs as three-dimensional portraits of their favourite spouse, are relatively rare. They measure about 60 cm in height and function as maternity figures with babies on their backs. These statues are kept hidden inside houses and are only revealed during important occasions such as visits by foreign dignitaries.

Since the turn of the century, Dan blacksmiths have cast brass figures (1) which serve as prestige objects. They usually represent soldiers or people engaging in daily activities.

EVERYDAY OBJECTS

Wooden carved ladles are given to the most generous and hospitable women in each village. They have an elongated scoop and their handle is carved either in the shape of a pair of legs [A], or a face or an animal head.

Dan jewelry, such as brass necklaces with ornamental leopards' teeth (13), and armlets and bracelets with spherical bells, is cast by village smiths.

RELATED TRIBES

The **Dan Maou** people occupy the north-west part of the Dan territory. They carve large face masks with chins issuing a long beak which are covered in a thick encrusted patina (11). This type of mask is feared by the population as it has a judiciary function and is worn to denounce spell-casters. Dan Maou masks can also be recognized by the triple incised grooves on their edges.

Dan Kran people inhabit the southern part of the Dan territory and have powerful carved masks with geometric triangular features (7).

BIBLIOGRAPHY
Art of the Côte d'Ivoire, Musée Barbier-Mueller, Geneva, 1993
FISCHER, E., 'Dan Forest Spirits: Masks in Dan Villages', *African Arts*, II, no. 2 (1978), pp. 16–23, 94
FISCHER, E., and H. HIMMERHEBER, *The Arts of Dan in West Africa*, Rietberg Museum, Zurich, 1984
VERGER-FÈVRE, M., *Masques Faciaux de l'ouest de la côte d'Ivoire dans les collections publiques françaises*, Mémoire de l'école du Louvre, 2 vols, 1980

4   A *Deangle* mask;
    wood, cowrie shells and beads;
    height: 30 cm (11³/₄ in);
    Archives Monbrison, Paris

5   A *Dugle* mask;
    wood; height: 25.5 cm (10 in);
    R. Mendes France Collection, Paris

6   A *Zakpai* mask;
    wood; height: 28 cm (11 in)

7   A Dan Kran *Kaogle* mask;
    wood; height: 24.1 cm (9¹/₂ in)

8   A *Bugle* mask;
    wood; height: 26.7 cm (10¹/₂ in)

9   A *Gagon* mask;
    wood, metal and hair;
    height: 33 cm (13 in)

10 A *Gunyeya* mask;
    wood and vegetal fibres;
    height: 22 cm (8³/₄ in)

11 A Dan Maou mask;
    wood and horn; height:
    74 cm (29 in)

12 A 'passport' mask;
    wood; height: 18 cm (3 in);
    Archives Monbrison, Paris

13 A necklace;
    brass; diameter: 33 cm (13 in);
    private collection

13

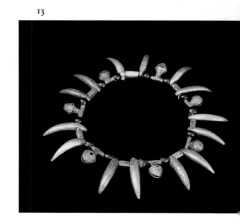

[A] Left: a Dan spoon
wood; height: 69 cm (27 in);
private collection

Large anthropomorphic spoons were coveted
prizes given to the most hospitable village women.
The refined treatment of the legs juxtaposed with
the roughness of the scoop symbolizes the freedom
of expression of African carvers.

[B] Left: **a Dan figure**
wood; height: 51.3 cm (20¹/₄ in)

This Dan female figure with applied
hair is a representation of a favourite
spouse and was only displayed
on important occasions. The shiny
patina attests to the attention and
pride accorded to this figure by
the Dan woman who was entrusted
with its care.

[C] Right: **a Dan *Go Ge* mask**
*wood; height: 26 cm (10¹/₂ in);
private collection*

A superb example of a *Go Ge* mask,
it is set under an elaborate coiffure
with inset talismans. It was only
worn during the funeral ceremonies
of important chiefs and epitomizes
the elegance of Dan masks.

Guro-Yaure

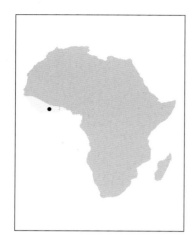

GURO

Between the Baule and the Yaure to the west, the Malinke to the north and the Bete and We to the south, the Guro people live surrounded by savannah and forest. They migrated from the north during the 16th century and number about 200,000. Originally they were called Kweni, but they were violently colonized between 1906 and 1912 and were given the Baule name Guro by the invading French colonials. Guro villages have rounded houses in the northern area and rectangular houses in the southern region. Village life is regulated by a council of elders, representing each main family, and by secret societies. The Guro farm predominantly cotton, rice, coffee and cocoa – the men clear the fields and the women plant.

Guro art is characteristically elegant. Their artistic output is dominated by masks carved with elongated faces, concave profiles and slanted eyes.

MASKS

Three different regional styles of mask can be distinguished:

In the western Guro area, face masks are carved with extremely pointed chins, protruding mouths, long linear noses, bulging slanted eyes and a high-domed forehead which is sometimes adorned with scarifications (2). These masks have apotropaic functions and are worn by an adjudicator when guilty individuals are punished.

The southern style is influenced by the neighbouring Bete tribe. Their masks can be distinguished by their human physiognomy, raised scarification in the middle of the high forehead, a triangular nose and pierced eyes surrounded by incised scarifications [D]. Another type of mask found in this region has a domed forehead, an upturned nose, slanted eyes and a pointed chin (1). *Dye* masks, either in the shape of a man's face or an antelope or elephant's head, tend to be worn at the funerals of important chiefs and can be viewed only by men.

In the northern area, four major types of ceremonial mask are carved:

The *Gye* helmet mask represents a stylized antelope and is worn during memorial festivals (3). Three

other masks appear at the same time during entertainment ceremonies and are owned by an appointed family. The *Zamble* face mask (4) represents yet another stylized antelope [C]; the *Gu* face mask resembles an elegant woman's face with forehead scarifications and an elaborate coiffure incorporating some amulet symbols; and the *Zauli* face mask takes the form of a stylized antelope head with tubular eyes, a pair of horns and a beak-like square mouth.

STATUETTES

Guro artists carved figures, varying in height from 20 to 80 cm, which appear either during entertainment festivals on the head of a dancer, or are kept in houses and employed as divination figures. These standing statues are carved with their hands on their hips and have a columnar neck supporting a head with similar features to the face masks (6, 7, 8).

EVERYDAY OBJECTS

Guro carvers produced elegant heddle pulleys [B, 9, 10] and spoons decorated with human or animal faces.

BIBLIOGRAPHY

Art of the Côte d'Ivoire, Musée Barbier-Mueller, Geneva, 1993
FISCHER, E., and L. HOMBERGER, *Art of the Guro*, Rietberg Museum, Zurich, 1985
SIROTO, L., 'A Note on Guro Sculpture', *Man*, 53, 1953, pp. 17–18

1 A southern (?) Guro mask;
   wood; height: 52 cm (20¹/₂ in)

2 A western Guro mask;
   wood; height: 63.5 cm (25 in)

3 A northern Guro *Gye* mask;
   wood; length: 50.8 cm (20 in)

4 A northern Guro *Zamble* mask;
   *wood; height: 27.3 cm (10⁷/₈ in);
   private collection*

5 A Yaure mask;
   wood; height: 42 cm (16¹/₂ in)

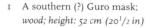

1

2

3

4

5

6   7   8   9

YAURE

The Yaure people, 20,000 in total, settled in the territory between the Baule to the west, the Guro to the east and Lake Kossou to the north. They are divided into three main groups living in approximately twenty villages scattered over a rich savannah where baboons, bush-cows, deer and elephants are hunted. A chief, assisted by a council of elders, leads each village. Their language, culture, religion and art are influenced by their powerful neighbours, the Baule and the Guro. Nevertheless, they possess a strong sense of identity and have evolved a characteristic and refined art.

The Yaure adorn a variety of everyday objects with figurative representations, but it is their masks that reveal their artistic abilities.

MASKS

Yaure masks symbolize the 'yu' or spirit power. They have an elongated face with a protruding mouth and pierced semi-circular eyes set under a high forehead. An elaborate plaited coiffure parted on each side, with horns or birds at the end, completes the image, while the outline of the mask is characteristically surrounded by a serrated edge (5).

Yaure masks are worn predominantly on two occasions: the *Je* celebration and the *Lo* ceremony. The first purifies the village after a death and helps the deceased's soul on its way to its final resting place. Painted masks are mainly worn by dancers during this ceremony, while for the *Lo* ceremony, masks covered with black pigments appear [A]. The function of each type of mask is not rigidly fixed, which leads to their appearance during either ceremony.

STATUETTES

Small Yaure statuettes are carved to protect and help in difficult situations. They amalgamate the Baule concept of 'spouse from the other world' (*Blo Blo Bian*) with a bush spirit (*Asie Usu*). They are usually about 30 cm high and have the same characteristics as their Baule equivalent – realistic features with the emphasis placed on the head.

EVERYDAY OBJECTS

The Yaure use drums to announce the death of a chief. They also make fly-whisks, monoxylous seats with a circular concave base, seats supported by bent square legs and ivory bracelets with a protruding ridge.

BIBLIOGRAPHY

Art of the Côte d'Ivoire, Musée Barbier-Mueller, Geneva, 1993

6   A Guro figure;
    wood; height: 69 cm (27^1/8 in)

7   A Guro figure;
    wood; height: 40 cm (15^5/8 in)

8   A southern Guro figure;
    wood; height: 84 cm (33 in);
    private collection

9   A Guro pulley;
    wood; height: 18.2 cm (7^1/8 in)

10 A Bete-Guro pulley;
    wood; height: 25.5 cm (10 in)

10

[A] Left: **a Yaure mask**
wood; height: 43 cm (17 in); provenance:
O. Lecorneur, Paris

The coiffure with two recesses under
a comb-like structure and the serrated
edges makes this mask archetypal.
The meaning of the comb-like
structure is unknown, but it
is sometimes also found on
Bambara masks.

[B] Below: **a Guro pulley**
wood; height: 26 cm (10³/8 in);
provenance: C. Ratton, Paris;
G. Rodier, Paris; M. Pinto, Paris;
private collection

The enlarged head set on top of this
heddle pulley displays features typical
of southern Guro art. The hole on top
of the head allowed the pulley to be
attached to a loom.

[C] Above: **a northern Guro mask**
wood; height: 28 cm (11 in);
private collection

This elongated mask's stylized
features and face scarifications are
typical of northern Guro carvings.
The backward-swept horns may refer
to an antelope.

[D] Right: **a southern Bete-Guro mask**
wood; height: 27 cm (10⅝ in);
private collection

The applied hair and carved teeth on
this mask convey a fierce expression.
Its function was apotropaic and
judicial. The high-domed forehead
with a vertical ridge is typical of the
southern Guro artistic output which
was influenced by Bete art.

Bete-Gere

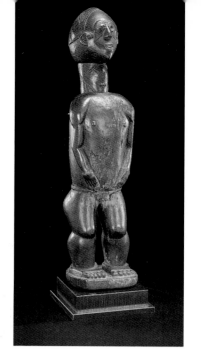

BETE

The Ivory Coast is home to the Bete – they live between the Akan tribe to the east and the Guro tribe to the north. They number 350,000 and live in villages, with the eldest man of the main family at the head. Historically, they were hunters, but nowadays they also farm. Religion, omnipresent in Bete life, aims to maintain a harmonious relationship between nature and the ancestors who are responsible for the welfare of the tribe. Elaborate masquerades and ceremonies are performed by the men of the tribe who belong to dance societies.

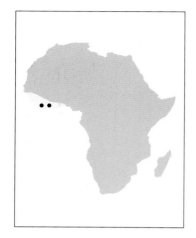

1

2

3

The Bete have carved some elegant statues, stylistically influenced by their neighbours the Guro, as well as powerful masks which are informed by the tradition of their western neighbours, the We.

MASKS

Bete carvers are renowned for one particular type of face mask which has exaggerated features (2, 3) – a large protruding mouth, an elongated nose, with nostrils sometimes extending to each side of the face, and globular eyes set beneath a high-domed forehead carved with a medium ridge. Historically, this type of mask was worn to prepare men for war; nowadays, it is worn for a variety of ceremonies, including entertainment dances.

STATUES

Bete statues [C, 1] are rare. They are between 30 and 70 cm high and were usually carved as standing figures displaying set-apart legs, an elongated torso with square shoulders, an elongated columnar neck supporting an oblong head with a pointed chin, an incised mouth and a high-domed, smooth forehead under a helmet-like coiffure. Traditionally, following the death of a dignitary, a piece of bamboo the size of the body was cut and was wrapped in cloth. This stick

was believed to keep the deceased's vital fluids among the living. Later on, the Bete replaced these abstract sticks with figures, which may fulfil the same function. Other smaller statuettes may have been carved to represent spouses from the other world, a tradition inspired by the Baule.

EVERYDAY OBJECTS

Figurative objects used in everyday activities are extremely rare among the Bete people. A few heddle pulleys do, however, exist and are decorated with faces [B].

RELATED TRIBES

The Nyabwa people, who live north of the Bete, use a type of mask related to the Bete war mask in certain ceremonies. Its features, however, are less exaggerated than its model.

A typical mask carved by people living between the Bete and the Guro has features associated with both tribes. It is referred to in the Guro-Yaure chapter (pp. 40–43).

BIBLIOGRAPHY

Art of the Côte d'Ivoire, Musée Barbier-Mueller, Geneva, 1993

4

5

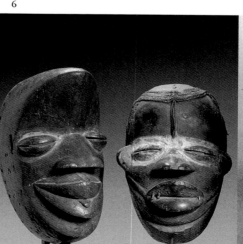
6

7

WE (GERE-WOBE)

The We, whose name means 'men who easily forgive', live in the forests on the western frontier of the Ivory Coast. They are in fact two separate tribes – the Gere (also known as Ngere) and the Wobe – although they share numerous customs and beliefs. Confederations govern the tribes – the largest is the warrior confederation which is led by a military chief, who also acts as a civil authority. The family unit plays an important role in We social life. Each is led by a patriarch, revered for his wisdom and wealth, who supervises the clan's life – he organizes weddings, settles conflicts and influences religious life.

We carvers seem to have focused their skills on carving powerful face masks to which paraphernalia such as cowrie shells, bells, nails and feathers were attached. These applied pieces were thought to reinforce the power of the mask.

MASKS

Gere masks [A, 4, 5] are characterized by a triangular face with an open mouth, an enlarged triangular nose and tubular eyes, a domed forehead and in some cases protruding ears and horns. They are worn by dancers during funerals and also act as 'detective' masks – singling out a guilty person.

Wobe masks (6, 7) have protruding globular eyes and enlarged lips. The horns found on Gere masks are usually absent from Wobe ones.

STATUES

We statues are rare. The ones that do exist display Dan-like features and are identifiable through the series of scarifications that appear on the abdomen and face – such as a curved line running from the nostrils to the temple or a central ridge on the forehead (9, 10).

EVERYDAY OBJECTS

We people used small chairs (8) with a square seat resting on four very low (8 cm high) legs. At times, they incorporated a thin curved backrest which may have been inspired by European prototypes. During circumcision ceremonies in particular, stools resting on four curved feet were used.

We blacksmiths produced jewelry that was very similar to that of the Dan – for instance, open bracelets (11) and anklets decorated with spherical bells and covered with spiralling motifs (12).

BIBLIOGRAPHY

Art of the Côte d'Ivoire, Musée Barbier-Mueller, Geneva, 1993
HIMMELHEBER, H., 'Die Masken der Guere in Rahmen der Kunst des oberen Cavally-Gebietes', *Zeitschrift für Ethnologie*, vol. 88, 1963, no. 2, pp. 216–33
HIMMELHEBER, H., 'Masken der Guere II', *Zeitschrift für Ethnologie*, vol. 91, 1966, no. 1, pp. 100–08

8

9

10

11

12

1   A Bete figure;
    wood and metal;
    height: 52 cm (20^1/$_2$ in)

2   A Bete mask;
    wood and copper nails;
    height: 29 cm (11^1/$_2$ in)

3   A Bete mask;
    wood and metal nails;
    height: 27.9 cm (11 in)

4   A Gere mask;
    wood and copper nails;
    height: 50 cm (19^3/$_4$ in)

5   A Gere mask;
    wood, fur and vegetal fibres;
    height: 40 cm (15^3/$_4$ in)

6   Two Wobe masks;
    wood; height of the taller:
    30 cm (11^3/$_4$ in)

7   A Wobe mask;
    wood, hair and copper;
    height: 30 cm (11^3/$_4$ in)

8   A We chair;
    wood; height: 47 cm (18^1/$_2$ in)

9   A We figure;
    wood; height: 57 cm (22^1/$_2$ in)

10 A We figure;
    brass; height: 20 cm (8 in)

11 A Wobe bracelet;
    brass; diameter: 15 cm (6 in);
    private collection

12 A Gere anklet;
    brass; diameter: 27 cm (10^5/$_8$ in);
    private collection

[A] Above: **a Gere mask**

wood, vegetal fibres and cowrie shells; height: 32 cm (12¹/₂ in)

This extraordinary-looking monoxylous mask has typical tubular eyes hidden
by exaggerated horns. The mask was able to single out a guilty person and its
power was reinforced by added paraphernalia such as cowrie shells and magical
substances set into its forehead.

[B] Above: **a Bete heddle pulley**
wood; height: 29.5 cm (11¹/₂ in); private collection

Continual handling and usage by Bete textile
weavers gave this abstract heddle pulley its rich
patina. Neck scarifications such as these were
also found on Bete figures.

[C] Right: **a Bete figure**
*wood and metal; height: 61 cm (24 in);
private collection*

During the funeral ceremonies of important
chiefs this archaic-looking figure, which represents
a dead chief, was paraded by the Bete people.
The typical abdomen and neck scarifications would
have identified the particular chief it symbolized.

Baule

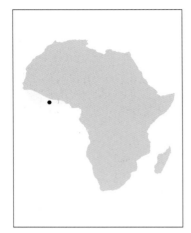

The Baule represent one of the most important tribes of the Ivory Coast. Their name is testimony to their birth – according to legend, Queen Aba Pokou led her people on an exodus towards the gold-mining areas during the 18th century and had to cross a river where she was obliged to sacrifice her son to the river god, thus giving her people the name *Bauli*, 'the son is dead'. During the 19th century, the queendom disintegrated due to internal conflicts and by the beginning of the 20th century, when the French colonials arrived, they found only a network of villages, headed by councils of venerated men.

1

2

Baule artists produced numerous works of art and Baule carvers are still very active today. With their great sense of stylization and attention to detail, they have produced some of the most elegant objects of all African art.

MASKS

The Baule people use three major type of masks: the first is a helmet mask in the shape of a buffalo head, *Bonu Amwin*; the second represents a human face with rounded, fairly realistic features; and the third type includes masks related to the *Goli* festival.

The *Bonu Amwin* helmet mask (3) represents a buffalo's head with a pair of crescent-like flat horns, a T-shaped nose and a large rectangular mouth with exposed teeth – its stylized features inspired Picasso's costume designs. It is sometimes painted with black, white and red pigments. The mask was originally worn only by warring men. Nowadays, it is mostly used to protect villages.

The second type of mask [B, 9] is characterized by a rounded face with realistic features, pointed chin, T-shaped nose, semi-circular eyes, raised scarification – typical of the Baule tribe – and an elaborate coiffure. They do not appear to have any sacred function and are worn only during festivities related to visits by important dignitaries. This type of mask sometimes has two faces, side by side (10), symbolizing twins, which for Africans is a good omen.

The *Goli* festivities date back to around 1900 and are held to celebrate new crops, the visits of dignitaries or periods of mourning. Three types of masks are used during these festivals: the first is of discoid shape and represents a highly stylized face beneath a pair of horns (8); the second is a helmet mask representing a buffalo head beneath antelope horns (2); and the third is used for closing the festivities, and has an elongated human face appearing under a pair of backward-swept horns.

STATUES

Baule statuettes vary from 10 to 60 cm in height. They are usually standing on a base with legs slightly bent, with their hands resting on their abdomen in a gesture of peace, and their elongated necks supporting a face with typically raised scarification and bulging eyes. The coiffure is always very detailed and is usually divided into plaits. They are sometimes covered with gold leaf or may represent colonials.

Statuettes were mostly used for two purposes: the first was to incarnate a spirit of the bush, *Asie Usu*; the second was to represent a spouse from the other world, *Blolo Bla* or *Blolo Bian*.

The *Asie Usu* spirits [C] live in the countryside. They are mischievous, but, if properly honoured, will grant fruitful harvests and hunts. They sometimes express desire, through the village diviner, to be associated with a specific person. A statuette is then

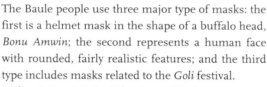

3

4

5

sculpted and worshipped in the house of the designated individual, and is often given a libation of chicken blood and egg, giving it an encrusted patina [C].

The *Blolo Bla* or *Blolo Bian* (5) represents a spouse from the spirit world. Baule people believe that every person has such a spouse. It manifests itself through a series of dreams, usually of a sexual nature, and is believed to be responsible for practical and spiritual problems that arise in the life of that individual. Once carved under the direction of the village diviner, the statuette is kept in the person's room and is offered food. Moreover, it is rubbed on the owner's skin, often giving it a shiny patina.

Figures of monkeys holding a cup were also carved by the Baule. They are usually about 80 cm high and are covered with a thick encrusted patina. They were thought to be associated with a blacksmith cult. Periodically, a senior blacksmith would sacrifice a dog or another animal to the statue and pour its blood over it.

EVERYDAY OBJECTS

The Baule are noted for decorating their everyday objects. Carved doors (1) were once quite common, but nowadays they seem to have disappeared from Baule houses. Drum tappers (6), canes (11), heddle pulleys (7) and ointment boxes are sometimes exquisitely carved with human or animal figures. They sometimes wore gold [A] and bronze pendants.

Since the end of last century, anecdotal figures depicting Baule people as colonials wearing European cloth have been carved for the tourists (4).

BIBLIOGRAPHY

Art of the Côte d'Ivoire, Museum Barbier Mueller, Geneva, 1993
BOYER, A. M., 'Miroirs de l'invisible: La statuaire Baoule', *Art d'Afrique Noire*, no. 44–45, 1982–83
RAVENHILL, P., *Baule Statuary Art: Meaning and Modernization*, Philadelphia, 1980
RAVENHILL, P., *Dreams and Reveries, Images of Otherworld Mates amongst the Baule*, West Africa, 1996
VOGEL, SUSAN, 'Baule Art as the Expression of a World View', *The Art Journal* (Institute of Fine Arts, New York), vol. 33, 1977

8

9

10

11

6

7

1 A carved door;
   *wood; height: 100 cm (39 3/8 in);
   private collection*

2 A buffalo mask;
   wood; height: 89 cm (35 in)

3 A *Bonu Amwin* helmet mask;
   wood; height: 64.8 cm (25 1/2 in)

4 A figure of a colonial;
   wood; height: 37 cm (14 1/2 in)

5 A *Blolo Bian* figure;
   wood; height: 31.8 cm (12 1/2 in)

6 A drum tapper;
   *wood and copper nails;
   height: 26.7 cm (10 1/2 in)*

7 A heddle pulley;
   *wood; height: 21 cm (8 3/8 in);
   private collection*

8 A *Bonu Amwin* abstract mask;
   wood; height: 71 cm (28 in)

9 A face mask;
   wood; height: 25.4 cm (10 in)

10 A double mask;
   wood; height: 28 cm (11 in)

11 A cane;
   wood; height: 87 cm (34 1/4 in)

[A] Above: **a gold pendant**
length: 6.8 cm (2³/4 in); provenance: Prince Sandrudin Agha Khan, Geneva

A Baule nobleperson would have worn this pendant. It displays a face with scarifications typical of Baule artistic traditions.

[B] Left: **a face mask**
wood; height: 46 cm (18 in); location: private collection

Worn during festivities related to dignitaries' visits to the village, this magnificent Baule mask epitomizes Baule art with its typical coiffure, scarifications and beard.

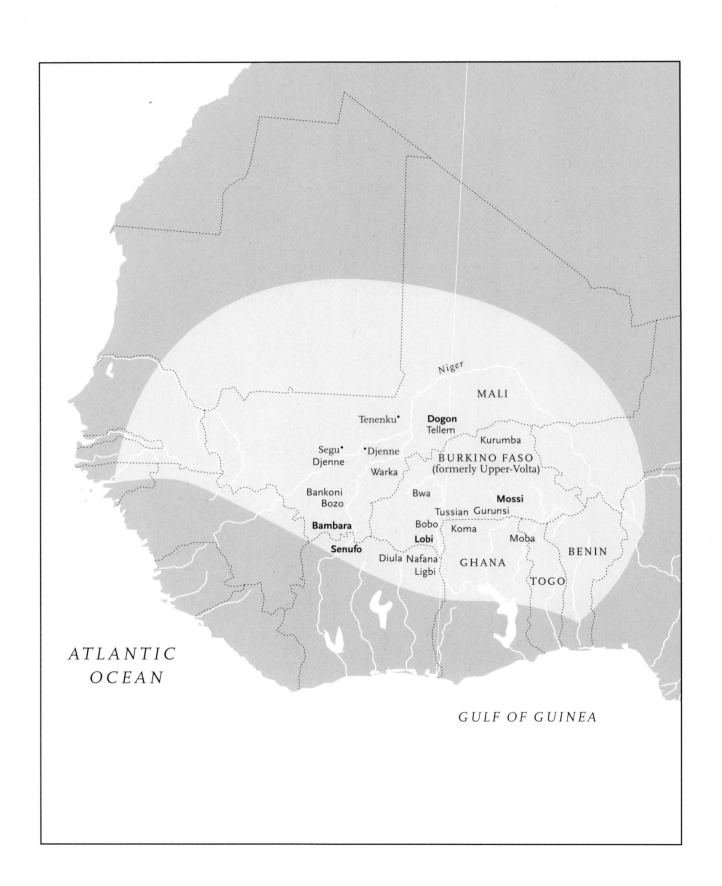

Niger

MALI

Tenenku• **Dogon**
Tellem

Kurumba

Segu• •Djenne
Djenne

BURKINO FASO
(formerly Upper-Volta)

Warka

Bankoni
Bozo

Bwa

Mossi

Tussian Gurunsi

Bambara

Bobo

Koma

Lobi

Moba

BENIN

Senufo

Diula Nafana
Ligbi

GHANA

TOGO

*ATLANTIC
OCEAN*

GULF OF GUINEA

II

INLAND
WEST AFRICA

DJENNE
DOGON
BAMBARA
LOBI-MOSSI
SENUFO

Djenne

I

Recently, a large number of looted terracotta figures attributed to the Mali empire appeared on the Western market. In the process of looting archaeological sites, relevant historical information regarding an object's function and provenance is often destroyed, but hopefully further field research in this region will clarify what is arguably one of the great African archaeological discoveries of the 20th century.

Both official excavations and the looting of archaeological sites along the Niger River have recently brought to light the existence of other cultures – identified as the Inland Niger Delta, the Tenenku, the Bura and the Koma cultures – which date from the same period. Knowledge of these cultures is based exclusively on their artistic production since neither historical, social nor political information is known to exist.

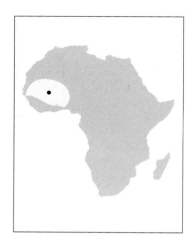

2

3

Significant numbers of terracotta figures, bronze jewelry and a few rare bronze figures appeared in France and Belgium during the 1970s – it is suspected that all of them were looted from archaeological sites.

Two major styles of terracotta statue have been attributed to the Mali empire – the first is the so-called **Djenne** style. Its name is derived from the archaeological site of Djenne-Djenno and it includes figures dating from the 12th to the 15th century which all have naturalistic rounded features and facial scarifications **[A]**. The second style, known as the **Bankoni** style, is centred around the modern town of Bamako and is characterized predominantly by figures with elongated features dating again from the 12th to the 15th century **[C]**.

Recently, a number of Mali empire satellite cultures were identified among the archaeological sites scattered along the northern part of the Niger River. One such satellite culture, referred to as the **Inland Niger Delta**, dates from the 12th to the 15th century. Their figures **(10)** display rounded features similar to the Djenne style, but lack the face scarifications and bulbous eyes typically found.

A group of ten figures, all seated in the same position **(1)**, with legs turned sideways, were discovered in the north of this region and were probably made in the same workshop. Dating from between the 11th and 14th century, they are thought to have been made for a shrine or a meeting room.

A second satellite culture, dating from the 13th to the 16th century, emerged near the site of **Tenenku** and is associated with the production of terracotta dogs and human figures with typical elongated animal-like faces **(11)**.

The corpus of figures in the Mali empire cultural area is enormous. The **Djenne** and **Bankoni** statues share similar themes – kneeling and seated figures, equestrian figures displaying large arrays of weapons, standing figures engaged in everyday activities and maternity figures. However, some themes are exclusive to the Djenne style – for instance, figures covered with pustules, thought to symbolize ill health **(5)**. Bankoni-style figures are more anecdotal and often represent people engaged in everyday activities – carrying pots **(6)** or playing drums (**see p. 13**).

The function of these terracotta figures is unclear. Some are covered with a red slip – a colour associated with death (traditionally, a corpse was covered with red pigment before burial) – while others are polychrome and show traces of wear suggesting repeated ceremonial usage. One statue was found in the wall

4

5

6

7

8

9

of a house, implying a foundation rite function. Human sacrifices undertaken during foundation ceremonies are mentioned in the oral history of the Djenne people, and it is thought that in some instances terracotta figures may have been substituted for humans in these ceremonies. Rare terracotta plaques, probably made as wall decorations, are also known to exist (4).

Wooden figures associated with the Mali empire are extremely rare and have been grouped under the name **Djennenke [B]**. They were found in caves on the eastern side of the Dogon plateau and are thought to be the products of Mali empire migrants who fled when the Songay king, Soni Ali, invaded in 1468. Their height varies from 30 to 200 cm and they are often covered with a black or a thick encrusted patina. Male, female and hermaphrodite figures were frequently carved in hieratic postures. The attention to detail on, for instance, their jewelry and loincloths is a feature shared with Djenne terracotta statues. Little is known about their function.

EVERYDAY OBJECTS

Large urns found in the Djenne area characteristically have incised, subtle geometric motifs (9). They are usually covered with a red slip which suggests a funereal purpose. Small utilitarian cups, neckrests and goblets are also known to exist. Globular vessels with long necks culminating in an animal head were excavated from the Bankoni area (8). Their precise use is unknown, but they are thought to have been associated with burial rites. Rare figurative bronze pendants were also found in the Djenne area. They have similar features to the terracotta figures.

The production of terracotta figures was not exclusive to the Mali empire. Recent excavations along the Niger River have revealed a wealth of statues which testify to the numerous cultures that flourished in this area.

The **Bura** style, characterized by figures with flattened heads and typical scarifications, is linked to the homonymous site near Nyamey. It first came to light during official excavations that revealed a necropolis dating from between the 14th and 16th century.

Corpses were buried in tall terracotta conical urns that were sometimes surmounted by a figure. These figures display considerable stylistic variations, but generally they have a flattened face, stylized features and overall typical incised body scarifications. Rare fragmentary equestrian figures **[D]**, relating to the Djenne iconography and highly stylized stone figures (2) have been found.

The archaeological site of **Koma** in northern Ghana was discovered in 1985. The Komaland culture centres around this site, where archaeologists and looters found numerous circular tumuli dating from around the 16th century. Within each tumulus, metal objects (3), terracotta vessels and figures, as well as human bones, were found.

The zoomorphic and anthropomorphic terracotta figures, ranging in height from 5 to 40 cm, show a highly original style with deformed features and large open mouths (7). It is thought that Janus figures, as well as turtles, crocodiles and other animals, may have been totemic emblems.

BIBLIOGRAPHY
ANQUANDAH, J., 'L'Art du Komaland', *Arts d'Afrique Noire*, 62, 1987
CUOQ, J. M., and R. MAUNY, *Receuil des sources arabes concernant l'Afrique Occidentale du VIII au XVIème siècle*, Paris, 1975
Dalla Terra all'arte, terrecotte Africane da collezioni cosmache, Exh. Cat., Como, Dec. 1991–March 1992
DE GRUNNE, BERNARD, *Terres cuites anciennes de l'ouest Africain*, Louvain-la-Neuve, 1980
DETAVERNIER, H., 'Terres cuites Koma du nord Ghana', *Arts d'Afrique Noire*, 74, 1990
ERNARDI, B., and B. DE GRUNNE, *Terra d'Africa, Terra d'Archeologia*, Florence, 1990
LELOUP, HÉLÈNE, *Statuaire Dogon*, Strasbourg, 1994
Vallées du Niger, Exh. Cat., Musée National des Arts d'Afrique et d'Océanie, Paris, Oct. 1993–Jan. 1994

1 An Inland Niger Delta figure; *terracotta; height: 51 cm (20 in)*

2 A Bura stylized figure; *stone; height: 36 cm (14 in)*

3 A Koma pendant; *bronze; height: 9 cm (3 1/2 in)*

4 A Djenne plaque; *terracotta; height: 37.5 cm (14 3/4 in)*

5 A Djenne figure covered with pustules; *terracotta; height: 18 cm (7 in)*

6 Two Bankoni figures; *terracotta; height of the taller: 57 cm (22 1/2 in)*

7 A Koma figure; *terracotta; height: 31 cm (12 in)*

8 A Bankoni ritual vessel; *terracotta; height: 45.7 cm (18 in)*

9 A Djenne urn; *terracotta; height: 77.5 cm (30 1/4 in)*

10 An Inland Niger Delta zoomorphic figure; *terracotta; height: 79.3 cm (31 1/4 in)*

11 A Tenenku dog figure; *terracotta; height: 37 cm (14 1/2 in)*

10   11

[A] Above and right: **Djenne figures (12th–15th century)**
terracotta; height of the animals and riders: 44 cm (17¹/₄ in);
height of the kneeling figure: 36 cm (14 in)

The two riders, one on a horse and one on a buffalo, are extremely rare and
are of exceptional quality. They reveal the great prestige attached to the
ownership of a horse at the time of the Mali empire. The horse rider wears
a beard and may be a Lord, while the buffalo rider holds a bow and is probably
only a military chief. Unfortunately, it is still not known how these terracotta
figures were used.

The kneeling figure is an archetype of Djenne art. Its hieratic posture
and the attention to detail testify to a refined civilization only known through
its artistic output.

[B] Above, left: **a Djennenke figure (12th–15th century)**
wood; height: 48.5 cm (19 in); private collection

This remarkable Djennenke wooden figure has a typical loincloth and
rectangular temple scarifications which can also be found on Djenne
terracotta figures (*see* A). Its encrusted patina testifies to numerous libations
and offerings which suggest a ritual function.

[C] Above, right: **two Bankoni figures (12th–15th century)**
terracotta; height: 76 cm (30 in)

The elongated features of these two terracotta figures are characteristic of some
Bankoni statues. The extraordinary beaded earrings, numerous bracelets and
anklets may indicate the representation of a noblewoman.

[D] Right: **an equestrian Bura figure (14th–16th century)**
terracotta; height: 45 cm (17³/4 in)

Only two examples of Bura terracotta horses and riders are known to exist. Set
on top of funerary urns, they indicate the prestige of owning a horse, which
is found throughout the Mali empire.

Dogon

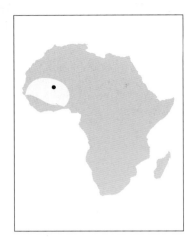

The 250,000 Dogon people live on a large plateau, with most of the villages situated on cliffs to the north and the east. According to Dogon oral tradition, the tribe settled in this area between the 14th and the 15th centuries, after escaping from the Mande kingdom. Legend has it that a snake led them to the cliff at the southern end of the plateau, where they overwhelmed and usurped the local Tellem and Niongom populations. The Dogon livelihood is based on agriculture concentrated in fields at the edge of the cliff, where water is scarce, but enough for occasional irrigation. Dogon social and religious organizations are closely interlinked and out of these arose four principal cults which accounts for the richness and diversity of Dogon culture.

1

1 A *Kanaga* mask;
   wood; height: 103.5 cm (40⁵/₈ in)

2 A 'Master of Ogol' figure;
   wood; height: 61 cm (24 in)

3 A Tintam figure;
   wood; height: 97.1 cm (38¹/₈ in)

4 A Komakon figure;
   wood; height: 68 cm (26³/₄ in)

5 A Bombou-Toro figure;
   wood; height: 71 cm (28 in)

6 A Wakara figure;
   wood; height: 72.2 cm (30 in);
   Schindler collection, New York

7 A Niongom figure;
   wood; height: 73.5 cm (29 in);
   private collection

8 A bird mask;
   wood; height: 65 cm (25¹/₂ in)

9 A trough;
   wood; length: 164 (64¹/₂ in)

Dogon art is extremely versatile, although common stylistic characteristics – such as a tendency towards stylization – are apparent on the statues.

MASKS

Seventy-eight different types of mask have been identified by the French scholar Marcel Griaule. All of them have large geometric eyes and stylized features. Dogon masks evoke the form of animals associated with their mythology, yet their significance is only understood by the highest ranking cult members whose role is to explain the meaning of each mask to a captivated audience.

In the West, the most famous of these masks is certainly the *Kanaga* mask (1). Its stylized face is set beneath two pairs of geometric arms directed towards the sky and the earth. The crocodile mask [B], carved with a long jaw, is thought to protect the Dogon from the *Nyagma* or vital fluids which emanate from a slain crocodile. Bird masks (8), known as *Dyodyomini*, evoke the captured bird in Dogon mythology.

STATUES

Dogon figures are predominantly associated with the ancestor cult. They are carved either for personal or family use or, if they commemorate the foundation of a community, are worshipped by the village.

The artistic influence of Niongom and Tellem traditions on Dogon statues is apparent. The **Niongom** people occupied the southern part of the cliff during the 10th century and carved elongated statues (7) with arrow-shaped noses, lozenge eyes and arms hanging at their sides. The form of Niongom carvings also characteristically followed the shape of the wood. It is thought they were placed on altars which, when later abandoned, were left untouched. With the passing of time, the figures gained a weathered patina.

The **Tellem** people settled at the same time and in the same area as the Niongom, and carved abstract figures in a symmetrical frontal pose with their arms raised [A]. This gesture, thought to represent a plea

2

3

4   5   6

7

9

8

10

11

12

for rain, is presumably an important part of Tellem ceremonies. The figures were regularly sprinkled with chicken blood and were later buried with their owners. The blood patina mineralized over the centuries which accounts for the present condition of the statues.

The **Dogon** people subsequently settled in the same territory and several regional styles of figure emerged. They have been identified in a detailed study by Hélène Leloup.

• Kambari-style figures are associated with the southern end of the cliff and have round heads. Some have a flat surface carved above the head which may have served as a receptacle for libations; others which are rarer are carved with their hands covering their face, thought to symbolize a gesture made by the *Binu* priest during his inauguration ceremony [C].

• Komakon-style statues have raised arms – like the figures carved by their predecessors, the Tellem – and have oblique scarifications on the face, a rectangular mouth and tubular eyes. They are thought to date from the 15th to the 16th centuries (4).

• Bombou-Toro-style figures are associated with an area in the centre of the cliff. They are carved as hermaphrodite figures or couples and are thought to illustrate events in the complex Dogon mythology (5). A group of twenty figures from the same region carved in the 'Master of Ogol' sub-style have been collected and have a typical horizontal chin (2).

• The Wakara style originates from the northern end of the cliff. The figures show typical elongated features, crossed scarifications on the body, angular features and a crested coiffure incised with chevrons (6).

• On the north-eastern side of the plateau, the Tintam style encompasses figures influenced by the Djennenke style (see the Djenne chapter, pp. 56–59). Tintam figures have naturalistic features, a typical smooth coiffure divided into three parts at the front, a loincloth, and an apotropaic Islamic *Korte* necklace. Tintam statues tend to portray people taking part in everyday activities, for instance, maternity figures, female figures carrying water or medicine pots, male figures with raised arms (3) and equestrian figures.

• Nduleri-style figures emerged from the western side of the plateau. They date from between the 16th and 20th centuries, but the most sophisticated

figures were carved during the 18th century. This style is a hybrid of northern rounded features and the more geometric southern cliff styles. Nduleri-style figures have elongated naturalistic features and a typical elaborate coiffure incised with chevrons. The corpus of Nduleri statues is extensive and includes standing and equestrian figures (12).

• On the plain to the west of the cliff, the Dogon mixed with the Bambara and the Bobo populations and as a result, two styles of figure evolved. The first style, known as Tomo-ka (13), is associated with the plain of the Seno River and includes statues with Dogon and Bambara features, such as angular stylization, a crested coiffure and typical semi-circular ears pierced with metal rings. The second style, called Kibsi (11), is almost restricted to just the Yatenga plain, in Burkina Faso, and comprises sculptures characterized by a red patina and geometric features.

EVERYDAY OBJECTS
Historically, the foundation of a village was consecrated by ceremonies headed by the Hogon which included human sacrifice. The human meat was mixed with millet in large zoomorphic troughs carved with a horse's head at the end (9).

Carved animal figures, such as dogs (10) and more rarely ostriches, are placed on village foundation altars to commemorate sacrificed animals, while granary doors, stools and house posts (15) are also adorned with figures and symbols.

Dogon blacksmiths forge iron objects in the shape of small figures with raised arms which are used as part of the rain-making ceremonies. Bronze rings (14), adorned with symbols of Dogon life, and iron necklaces, worn by *Binu* priests, are also made by blacksmiths.

10 A dog figure;
   wood; length: 32 cm (12⅝ in)

11 A Kibsi figure; *wood; height: 20.5 cm (8 in); private collection*

12 A Nduleri figure;
   wood; height: 65.4 cm (25¾ in)

13 A pair of Tomo-ka figures;
   wood; height: 60 cm (23⅝ in); private collection

14 A group of four rings; *bronze; height of the tallest: 7 cm (2⅝ in); private collection*

15 A pair of house posts;
   wood; height of the taller: 280 cm (110 in); private collection

13

14

15

BIBLIOGRAPHY
BEAUDOIN, GÉRARD, *Les Dogons du Mali*, Paris, 1984
Dogon, Exh. Cat., Musée Dapper, Paris, 1994
EZRA, KATE, *Art of the Dogon, Selections from the Lester Wundermann Collection*, New York, 1988
GRIAULE, MARCEL, *Masques Dogon*, Paris, 1938
LAUDE, JEAN, *African Art of the Dogon, The Myth of the Cliff Dwellers*, Exh. Cat., The Brooklyn Museum, New York, 1973
LELOUP, H., *Statuaire Dogon*, Strasbourg, 1994

[A] Left: **a Tellem figure**
wood; height: 37.5 cm (14¹/2 in);
private collection

This figure's arms are raised in a
gesture which is thought to represent
a call for rain and is seen on most
Tellem statues, some of which date
from as far back as the 10th century.

[B] Above: **a crocodile mask**
wood; height: 33 cm (13 in)

With its abstract features and
thick encrusted patina, this Dogon
crocodile mask is typical of the
artistic output of this tribe. It
was worn by dancers during
ceremonies that protected the tribe
from the malevolent influences
of slain crocodiles.

[C] Right: **a Kambari-style Dogon figure**
wood; height: 34 cm (13¹/2 in)

A typical example of Kambari-
style Dogon sculpture, this figure
symbolizes an important episode
in the inauguration ceremony of
a *Binu* priest. Its abstract features
are reinforced by the thick encrusted
patina left by numerous libations
of chicken blood and eggs.

Bambara

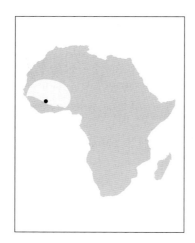

The 2,500,000 Bambara people, also called Bamana, form the largest ethnic group within Mali and occupy the central part of the country, in an area of savannah. They live principally from agriculture, with some subsidiary cattle rearing in the northern part of their territory. The Bambara people are predominantly animists, although recently the Muslim faith has been spreading among them. The Bambara kingdom was founded in the 17th century and reached its pinnacle between 1760 and 1787 during the reign of N'golo Diarra. N'golo Diarra is credited with conquering the Peul people and in turn claimed the cities of Djenne and Timbuktu. However, during the 19th century, the kingdom began to decline and ultimately fell to the French when they arrived in 1892. For the most part, Bambara society is structured around six male societies, known as the *Dyow* (sing. *Dyo*).

1

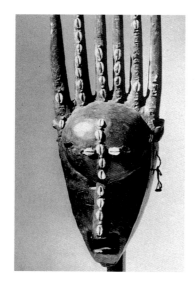

2

The stylistic variations in Bambara art are extreme – sculptures, masks and headdresses display either stylized or realistic features, and either weathered or encrusted patinas. Until quite recently, the function of Bambara pieces was shrouded in mystery, but in the last twenty years field studies have revealed that certain types of figures and headdresses were associated with a number of the societies that structure Bambara life. During the 1970s a group of approximately twenty figures (7), masks and Tji-Wara headdresses belonging to the so-called 'Segou style' were identified. The style is distinct and recognizable by its typical flat faces, arrow-shaped noses, all-over body triangular scarifications and, on the figures, splayed hands.

MASKS

There are three major and one minor type of Bambara mask. The first type (2), used by the *N'tomo* society, has a typical comb-like structure above the face, is worn during dances and may be covered with cowrie shells.

The second type of mask (11), associated with the *Komo* society, has a spherical head with two antelope horns on the top and an enlarged, flattened mouth. They are used during dances, but some have a thick encrusted patina acquired during other ceremonies in which libations are poured over them.

The third type has connections with the *Nama* society and is carved in the form of an articulated bird's head, while the fourth, minor type, represents a stylized animal head and is used by the *Kore* society.

Other Bambara masks are known to exist (3), but unlike those described above, they cannot be linked to specific societies or ceremonies.

Bambara carvers have established a reputation for the zoomorphic headdresses worn by Tji-Wara society members [B, 1]. Although they are all different, they all display a highly abstract body, often incorporating a zig-zag motif, which represents the sun's course from east to west, and a head with two large horns. Bambara members of the Tji-Wara society wear the headdress while dancing in their fields at sowing time, hoping to increase the crop yield.

STATUES

Bambara sculptures are primarily used during the annual ceremonies of the *Guan* society. During these ceremonies, a group of up to seven figures, measuring from 80 to 130 cm in height, are removed from their sanctuaries by the elder members of the society. The sculptures are washed, re-oiled and sacrifices are offered to them at their shrines. These figures – some of which date from between the 14th and 16th centuries – usually display a typical crested coiffure, often adorned with a talisman.

1 Two Tji-Wara headdresses;
wood and metal; height: 92 and
115 cm (36 and 45 in)

2 A mask;
wood and cowrie shells;
height: 52 cm (20¹/₂ in);
H. Rubinstein Collection, Paris

3 A mask;
wood; height: 16.8 cm (6⁵/₈ in)

4 An equestrian figure;
iron; height: 22 cm (8⁵/₈ in)

5 A puppet;
wood and metal;
height: 80 cm (31¹/₂ in);
H. Rubinstein Collection, Paris

6 A maternity figure, 'Bambara queen'; *wood; height: 123 cm*
(48.5 in); Schindler Collection

7 A pair of Segou-style figures; *wood*
and metal; height: 56 cm (22 in)

8 A *Guannyeni* figure of an attendant;
wood; height: 91.5 cm (36 in)

3

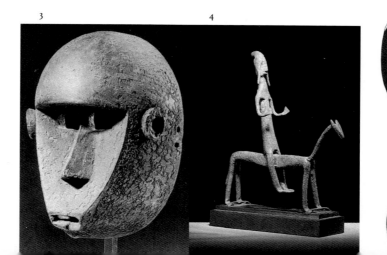

4

5   6

7 8 9 10

Two of these figures were ascribed great significance: a seated or standing maternity figure called *Guandousou* (6) – known in the West as 'Bambara Queen' – and a male figure called *Guantigui*, who usually appears holding a knife. The two figures were surrounded by *Guannyeni* attendant figures (8) – standing or seated in various positions, holding a vessel, or a musical instrument, or their breasts. During the 1970s, numerous fakes from Bamako which were based on these sculptures entered the market. They were produced in Bamako.

Other Bambara figures, called *Dyonyeni* [A], are thought to be associated with either the southern *Dyo* society or the *Kwore* society. These female or hermaphrodite figures usually appear with geometric features such as large conical breasts (9) and measure between 40 and 85 cm in height. The blacksmith members of the *Dyo* society used them during dances to celebrate the end of their initiation ceremonies. They were handled, held by dancers and placed in the middle of the ceremonial circle.

Among the corpus of Bambara figures, *Boli* sculptures (12) are perhaps the best known. These statues represent a highly stylized animal or human figure, and are made of wood which is repeatedly covered in thick layers of earth impregnated with sacrificial materials such as millet, chicken or goat blood, kola nuts and alcoholic drinks. They were employed by the *Kono* and the *Komo* societies and served as receptacles for spiritual forces, and could in turn be used for apotropaic purposes.

EVERYDAY OBJECTS

Iron staffs and figures play an important role in the ceremonies of the *Gouan* and *Dyo* societies. They were used during the funeral rites of either the head of the *Dyo* society – called the *Dyo Sia* – or when the female leaders of the Gouan society died. The iron staffs, constructed with bells, or figures with typical

enlarged hands were placed either under or upon branches of a *Bana* tree. According to Bambara beliefs, the soul of the deceased ascends this sacred tree in order to gain access to the seven heavens and the after-life. These iron staffs and iron equestrian figures (4) were also used during *Gouan* and *Dyo* initiation ceremonies, where they were placed upright near the sanctuary in which large figures were kept.

In certain initiation rites, the dancers used wood cephalomorphic puppets (5).

The Bambara also produced anthropomorphic door locks which, unlike the Dogon variety, were made with a pair of legs (10). They were given as gifts to young brides and symbolized sexual intercourse: a vertical female figure with a moving 'male' horizontal bolt.

RELATED TRIBES

The **Warka** (also known as Marka) and **Bozo** tribes occupy the northern region of the Bambara territory. Although they speak different languages, they share a number of institutions and are famous for their masks and puppets. Similar to Bambara *Ntomo* society masks, Warka masks are generally carved with a comb on top of the head, but unlike Bambara masks they are often covered with metal plaques [C]. Bozo masks (13), similar to those of the Warka, are covered with metal sheets, but have more rounded features.

BIBLIOGRAPHY
EZRA, KATE, *Figure Sculptures of the Bamana of Mali*, Northwestern University, 1983
EZRA, KATE, *A Human Ideal in African Art: Bamana Figurative Sculpture*, Washington, D.C., 1986
GOLDWATER, ROBERT, *Bambara Sculpture from the Western Sudan*, New York, 1960, p. 17
IMPERATO, P. J., *Buffoons, Queens and Wooden Horsemen: The Dyo and Gouan Societies of the Bambara of Mali*, New York, 1985
ZAHAN, DOMINIQUE, 'Antelope Headdress: Female (Chi Wara)', in *For Spirits and Kings: African Art from the Tishman Collection*, New York, 1991

9 A *Dyonyeni* figure; wood; height: 55 cm (22 in)

10 A door lock; *wood and metal inlay; height: 47 cm (18 1/2 in)*

11 A mask; *wood; length: 84.3 cm (33 1/4 in)*

12 A *Boli* figure; *wood covered with vegetal substances; height: 54.6 cm (21 1/2 in)*

13 A Bozo mask; *wood and metal; height: 23.9 cm (9 3/8 in)*

11

12

13

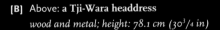

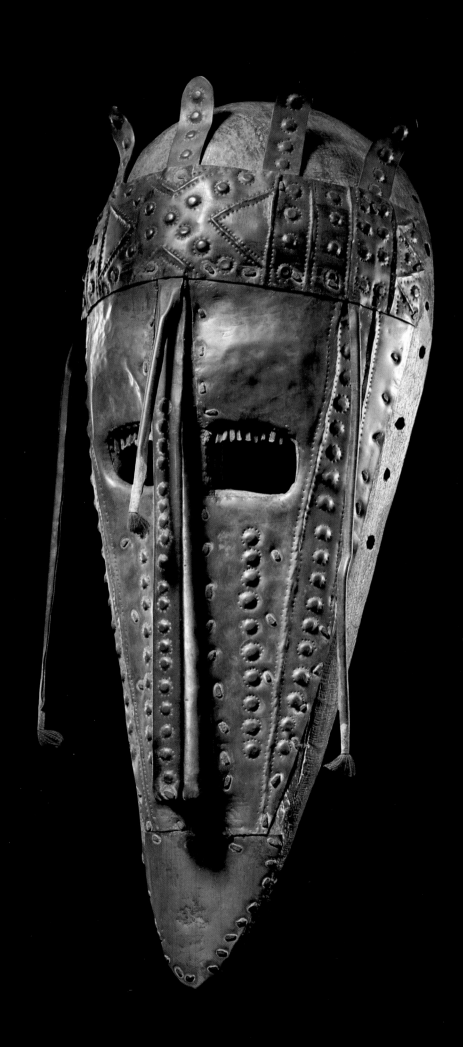

[B] Above: a **Tji-Wara headdress**
wood and metal; height: 78.1 cm (30³/4 in)

Elegant headdresses like this one were worn
during ceremonies related to agricultural rites.
The stylized antelopes are set one on top
of another, which may allude to the idea
of maternity and therefore of fertility.

[C] Right: **a Warka mask**
*wood covered with copper sheet and fibres;
height: 45 cm (18 in); private collection*

Warka masks are typically covered with copper
sheet. This elongated one was probably worn
during dances related to the numerous societies
that regulate the people of Mali.

Lobi-Mossi

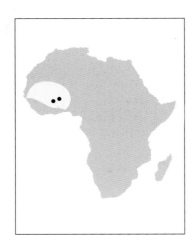

The various tribes living in Burkina Faso (formerly Upper-Volta), Ghana and Togo cultivate millet and cotton, and rear cattle in the northern savannah regions. Their religious activities are dictated by the rhythm of the seasons – during the dry season in particular, when the fields are fallow, large festivals and ceremonies are organized.

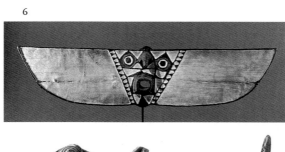

1

2

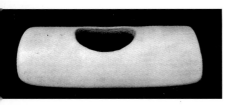

3

1 A Lobi seat;
wood; length: 58.4 cm (23 in)

2 A Lobi *Bateba* figure;
wood; height: 22.2 cm (8³/4 in)

3 A Gurunsi bracelet; *ivory; height: 25 cm (10 in); private collection*

4 A Gurunsi flute; *wood; height: 33 cm (13 in); private collection*

5 A Kurumba headdress;
wood; height: 60 cm (23⁷/8 in);
Courtesy Entwistle, London

6 A Bwa hawk mask;
wood; height: 30.5 cm (12 in);
Courtesy Entwistle, London

7 A Bobo zoomorphic pendant;
bronze; length: 18 cm (7 in);
private collection

The **Lobi** people number 250,000 and live across Burkina Faso, the Ivory Coast and Ghana. They revere spirits known as *Thil*. Shrines are built to these spirits under the instruction of a sorcerer and placed either on the roof or inside the home and are filled with objects such as vessels, abstract iron figures, and stone and wood figures known as *Bateba*, which are believed to embody the *Thil* spirits.

Lobi *Bateba* figures are between 5 and 60 cm high and typically have slightly bent legs with roughly carved feet and an enlarged head with a high smooth or grooved coiffure. They are classified into two main categories – the first includes apotropaic *Bateba* figures, known as *Bateba Duntundora*, which are generally around 60 cm high and are characterized as standing figures with powerful features, showing a readiness to avert curses. The second type of *Bateba* figure embodies *Thil* spirits and includes wooden or clay figures with different postures corresponding to various *Thil* (2), e.g, statues with a single raised arm symbolize a dangerous *Thil*, while copulating couples or maternity figures are believed to enhance the fertility of women living in the house (13).

Lobi people produce seats supported by three feet, and occasionally decorate them with a human or animal figure (1). They wear apotropaic bronze or ivory pendants and bracelets with either geometric designs or with human and animal figures with globular eyes. Unlike other tribes living in this part of Africa, the Lobi do not wear wooden masks during their ceremonial dances.

The first **Mossi** empire was founded during the 15th century by invaders from northern Ghana. Today, the Mossi are the largest tribe living in Burkina Faso. They number 2,200,000 and are the only tribe discussed in this chapter who have a centralized governing body, in addition to clans and professional corporations led by elders known as *Zaksoba*.

Mossi sculptors are famous for their polychrome masks which are worn during funeral ceremonies and to guard the crop. These masks – which have a totemic role – are stored carefully when not worn and are given libations in exchange for help in everyday Mossi life.

There are three main styles of mask, thought to correspond stylistically to the indigenous population living in the area before the 15th-century invasion.

The first style is found in the south west and includes masks with small animal figures or stylized human faces. The second style, from the east, includes semi-cylindrical masks painted with white pigments and represents beneficent spirits associated with the savannah. The third style of Mossi mask, found in the north, is called *Karanga*. These masks characteristically have a stylized face surmounted by a plank, or a human figure representing a totemic animal, or an important ancestor (14).

4

5

6

8

9

7

Mossi statues – which measure between 60 and 100 cm in height – represent deceased chiefs (12). They stand on slightly bent legs, with arms set apart from their bodies, and have rounded heads bearing flattened faces [A]. They were symbolically buried in place of the chief's corpse during sumptuous ceremonies, while the actual corpse was secretly inhumed immediately after death. Mossi fertility dolls, with abstract flattened faces, were given to newly circumcised girls (15).

The 300,000 **Bwa** people are scattered across Mali and Burkina Faso. They are classified into three endogamous professional castes: farmers, blacksmiths and musicians.

The Bwa carve polychrome animal masks in horizontal shapes which symbolize butterflies or hawks (6). The butterfly mask is decorated with concentric circles, while the hawk mask has a plain white surface. Another mask called *Nwantantay* has a circular face with triangular decoration below the mouth and is surmounted by a large plank with a crescent-shaped motif at the end. It was worn during dances accompanying funerals and for entertainment festivities on market days.

Bwa figures are relatively rare and are associated with divination ceremonies and human and agricultural fertility rites. They are paraded through villages and are offered sacrifices (11).

The 100,000 **Bobo** live in eastern Burkina Faso. They are primarily farmers whose lives are regulated by a council of elders. The Bobo cast bronze pendants (7) and carve large masks. The masks symbolize animals or spirits and are worn during ceremonies associated with new crops, initiations and funerals [C].

A number of tribes who speak dialects of the Gur language have been grouped together under the name **Gurunsi**. They number 200,000 and spend the dry season hunting and fishing.

Gurunsi masks (10) represent bush spirits and are characterized by eyes set within concentric circles. They are worn by dancers during funerals, initiation ceremonies, fertility rites and market-day festivities.

Gurunsi figures (16) are less well known in the West, but have a role in divination rituals.

Gurunsi people wear ivory (3) and bronze bracelets (9) and like other tribes in the region, carve wooden flutes (4).

The **Kurumba** people live in the north of Burkina Faso. Their artistic reputation rests on their antelope headdresses which are worn during funeral ceremonies and are believed to represent the soul of the deceased (5).

The 22,000 **Tussian** people of south-west Burkina Faso carved masks called *Loniake* – a square plank of wood pierced with two eyes surmounted by the clan's emblem: a pair of horns or a bird's head. These masks were worn during initiation ceremonies (8).

Tussian headdresses, called *Kable*, are stylistically influenced by the Senufo [B]. They are used during rites associated with the purification of villages and at funerals. Often they have an oily patina resulting from numerous libations of palm oil.

10

BIBLIOGRAPHY

CAPRON, J., *Communautés villageoises Bwa*, Paris, 1973
DUPERRAY, A. M., *Les Gourounsi de Haute Volta*, Stuttgart, 1984
LE MOAL, G., *Les Bobos: nature et fonction des masques*, Paris, 1980
MEYER, P., *Kunst und Religion der Lobi*, Zurich, 1981
ROY, CHRISTOPHER, *Mossi Masks and Crests. The Regional Stylistic Distribution and Function in Society of Traditional Mossi Sculpture*, Bloomington, 1979
ROY, CHRISTOPHER, *Art of the Upper Volta Rivers*, Paris, 1987
SCANZI, GIOVANNI, *Lobi Traditional Art*, Milan, 1986
Skulptur in West Afrika: Masken und Figuren aus Burkina Faso, Exh. Cat., Duisburg, 1995

8 A Tussian *Loniake* mask; wood; height: 65 cm (25¹/2 in); Archives Monbrison, Paris

9 A Gurunsi bracelet; bronze; height: 19 cm (7¹/2 in); private collection

10 A Gurunsi mask; wood; height: 33 cm (13 in)

11 A Bwa figure; wood; height: 88.9 cm (35 in)

12 A Mossi figure; wood; height: 59.7 cm (23¹/2 in)

13 A Lobi *Bateba* figure; wood; height: 18.5 cm (7 in)

14 A Mossi *Karanga* mask; wood; height: 110 cm (43 in)

15 A Mossi doll; wood; height: 30.5 cm (12 in)

16 A Gurunsi figure; wood; height: 46.5 cm (18¹/4 in)

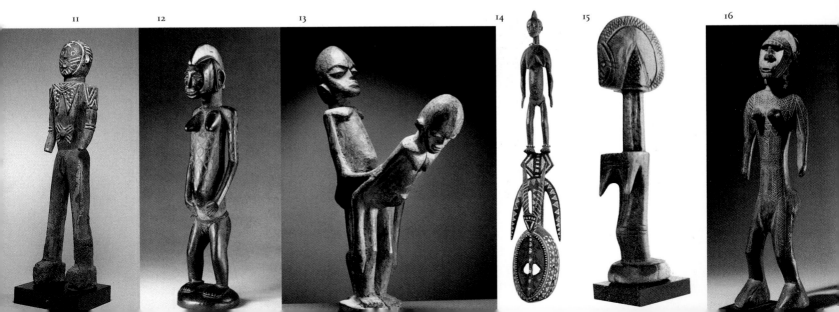
11 12 13 14 15 16

[A] Left: **a pair of Mossi figures**
*wood; height of the taller: 41.5 cm
(16 in); private collection*

Mossi figures are usually associated
with the concept of fertility. The
dynamic posture, resonating with
movement, of this couple is rare
among African sculpture where
static positions are more common.

[B] Above: **a Tussian *Kable* helmet mask**
*wood with oily patina; height: 57 cm
(225/8 in)*

A highly stylized buffalo head
surrounded by horns and set under
four bird figures is displayed on this
cap headdress. Its heavy oily patina is
due to renewed libations of palm oil,
believed to reinforce its power.

[C] Right: **a Bobo mask**
wood, pigments; height: 63.5 cm (25 in)

This mask appeared during
important communal ceremonies.
It is covered with a geometric
decoration also found on body
scarifications. Bobo masks are
usually set under a pair of horns
or, as in this example, a huge crest
symbolizing a bush animal.

Senufo

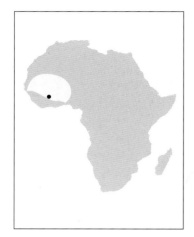

Scattered across the Ivory Coast, Mali and Burkina Faso, the million and a half Senufo tribespeople live principally off the fruits of agriculture and occasionally hunting. They inhabit villages governed by a council of elders, who in turn are led by a chief elected from their number. Tribal cohesion is reinforced through the rituals of the *Poro* society who initiate and educate the men from the age of seven onwards. Senufo theology is based on Koulotiolo, a powerful god, and Katieleo, a goddess mother, who through the rituals of the *Poro* society, regenerates the world.

The Senufo were among the first tribal artists to be admired by the Western world. Their artistic output has been prolific – statues and masks characterized by realistic features or highly geometric shapes which emphasize rhythm and the opposition between void and full spaces.

MASKS

Senufo people use different types of mask depending upon the occasion. Face masks **[B]**, known as *Kpeliyee*, are worn during *Poro* society ceremonies. They display a typical heart-shaped face surrounded by 'wings'. Among the helmet masks is a Janus buffalo mask **(1)** worn during funeral ceremonies and at times of crisis. Their principal purpose is to destroy malevolent spirits – their power comes from

a small cup located at the top of the helmet-head which holds magical substances; sometimes their mouths issue sparks conferring on them the name, 'firespitter'. Another type of helmet mask used during *Poro* initiation ceremonies displays the head of a buffalo topped with a pair of antelope horns **(5)**. The Senufo have also produced three types of headdress. One is a small wooden cap which supports a female figure and is worn during celebrations to honour the most productive village farmer. A second type of wooden cap is worn by healers and issues a pair of animal horns **(3)**. Lastly, a headdress supporting a vertical, open-worked panel is worn during *Poro* society initiations.

STATUES

Senufo figures vary a great deal, but nevertheless can be identified by their heart-shaped faces, arrow-shaped noses and crescent coiffures. Their height varies from 15 to 120 cm. Among the most famous statues of African art are a series known as the *Pombibele*, 'those who give birth'. These are large figures, 120 cm high, used during the funeral ceremonies of *Poro* society members **[A]**. In the central Senufo area they are left standing in the middle of the ceremonial ground, while in the southern Senufo area, they are carried and then pounded on the ground, providing rhythm for the dancers.

6   7   8   9

This ceremonial led to the calling of these statues by the popular name of 'rhythm pounders'. Smaller statues representing divination figures or nature spirits have also been made **[D]**. They are given offerings, which are sometimes made through a cup at the top of their head, thus giving the entire figure a rich black oily patina **(8)**. When carved in pairs, they symbolize the primordial couple – an ideal Senufo nuclear family who respects its ancestors **(6)**.

Secret societies also used figures, referred to as a *Kafigelejo*, which personify spirits with judiciary and punitive powers. These are completely covered with a piece of cloth and bear a thick encrusted patina **(11)**.

Large bird figures can also be seen during *Poro* ceremonies. They stand on the ground or are carried on the heads of new male initiates **(7)**. During ceremonies related to the upper grade of the *Poro* society, dancers incorporate stylized horse figures.

EVERYDAY OBJECTS

A vast array of Senufo everyday objects are adorned with figures – heddle pulleys **(10)**, ointment boxes **(9)**, doors **(14)** and pieces of monoxyle furniture, such as stools, chairs and beds **(13)**. The most pro-

ductive farmers are rewarded with decorated canes bearing small human figures **(2)** or birds. Senufo metalworkers produced refined jewelry and ornaments, usually in copper, such as finger rings **(12)** and foot rings adorned with bovine heads or chameleons, symbolizing their genesis, and small figurative masks and amulets with apotropaic purposes.

RELATED TRIBES

The Senufo have influenced neighbouring tribes stylistically. The **Diula** tribespeople produce metal objects, such as masks and daggers adorned with a face **(4)**, large pipes and food-related vessels. The **Ligbi** tribespeople make typical face masks with pointed chins, semi-closed eyes and raised scarifications framed by wings like Senufo *Kpeliyee* masks **[C]**.

BIBLIOGRAPHY

Art of the Ivory Coast, Musée Barbier-Mueller, Geneva, 1993
CONVERS, MICHAEL, 'Masques en Etain Senufo', *Arts d'Afrique Noire*, 16, winter 1975, pp. 24–36
GLAZE, ANITA, 'Senufo Ornament and Decorative Arts', *African Arts*, 12, no. 1, November 1978
GOLDWATER, ROBERT, *Senufo Sculpture from West Africa*, New York, 1964

6   A Senufo primordial couple; *wood; height of the taller: 47 cm (18 1/2 in)*

7   A bird figure; *wood; height: 170 cm (66 3/4 in)*

8   A figure; *wood; height: 34.9 cm (13 3/4 in); private collection*

9   An ointment box; *wood; height: 18 cm (7 in)*

10   A heddle pulley; *wood; height: 18 cm (7 in); private collection*

11   A *Kafigelejo* figure; *wood, cloth and feathers; height: 56 cm (22 in)*

12   A 'silence' ring; *bronze; height: 8 cm (3 in)*

13   A bed; *wood; length: 177 cm (69 3/4 in)*

14   A door; *wood; height: 115 cm (45 1/4 in); private collection*

10   11   12   14

13

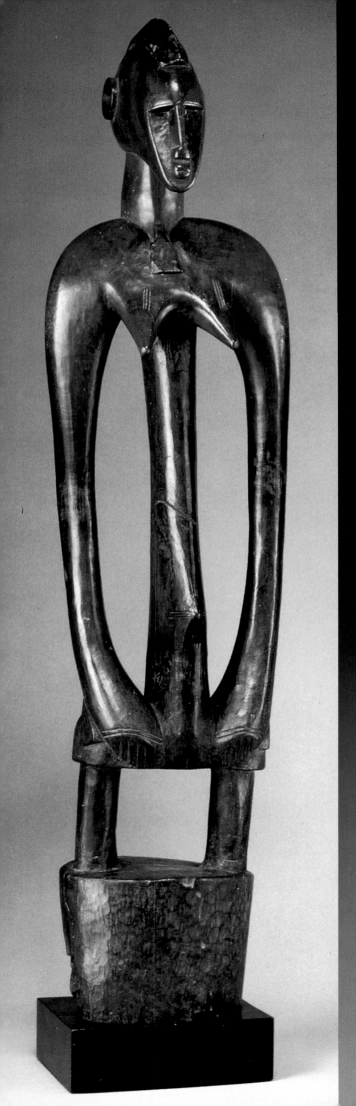

[A] Left: **a rhythm pounder**

wood; height: 90.8 cm (35³/₄ in); provenance: Emile Storrer, Zurich; Werner Munsterberger, New York; William Rubin, New York; location: Arman Arman, New York

Due to its elegant lines and majestic expression, this figure is one of the most famous of all African sculptures. Also called *pombibele*, it was used during the funerals of members of the Poro society.

[B] Below: **a *kpeliyee* mask**

wood; height: 38 cm (15 in); provenance: H. Rubinstein, Paris; private collection

This classical mask displays all the stylistic characteristics of Senufo art: a heart-shaped face, a T-shaped nose and globular eyes. It was worn during ceremonies related to the Poro society.

[D] Below: **a figure from the Sikasso area**
wood; height: 34 cm (13¹/₂ in)

This small figure is from the Senufo area and represents a Nature Spirit. Its surface has a shiny patina due to oil libations.

[C] Above: **a Ligbi mask**
wood and blue pigment; height: 31 cm (12 in)

With its lateral wings, this mask shows the influence of the Senufo *kpeliyee* mask on neighbouring tribes. Nevertheless, the downcast curved eyes and the use of pigments are typical of Ligbi masks.

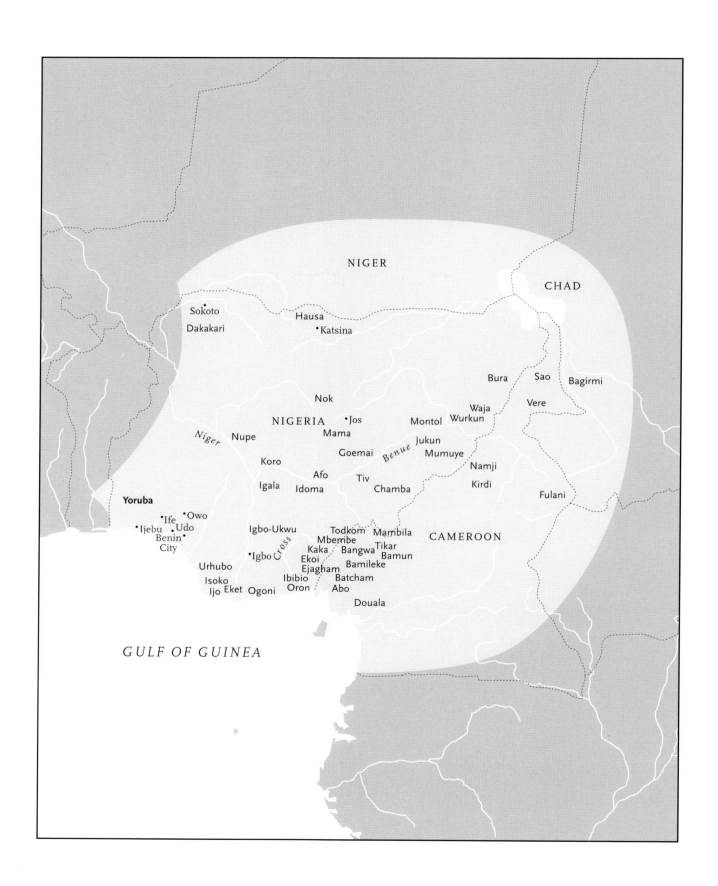

NIGER

CHAD

Sokoto
Dakakari

Hausa

Katsina

Bura   Sao   Bagirmi

Nok

Vere

NIGERIA   Jos   Montol   Waja
Mama   Wurkun
Niger   Nupe   Goemai   Benue   Jukun
Koro   Mumuye
Afo   Namji
Igala   Idoma   Tiv   Chamba   Kirdi
Fulani

Yoruba

Ife   Owo   Igbo-Ukwu   Todkom   Mambila   CAMEROON
Ijebu   Udo   Mbembe   Tikar
Benin   Cross   Kaka   Bangwa   Bamun
City   Igbo   Ekoi   Bamileke
Urhubo   Ejagham
Isoko   Ibibio   Batcham
Ijo   Eket   Ogoni   Oron   Abo
Douala

GULF OF GUINEA

III

NIGERIA
AND CAMEROON

Nok

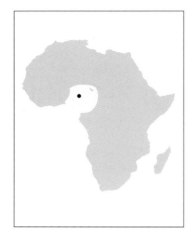

The Nok civilization was only discovered recently. In 1943, a terracotta head was excavated from a tin mine near the town of Nok on the Jos plateau, in central Nigeria. A number of fragmentary terracotta sculptures, stylistically related to the Nok civilization, which are of great artistic quality, were also discovered in further excavations in northern Nigeria. In 1992, a group of eleven complete figures excavated in the town of Sokoto appeared on the Western art market. Since then, other pieces originating from the northern town of Katsina have found their way onto the market, but because Nok pieces come from clandestine excavations, information is scarce.

There are many different styles of Nok figure, but they all date from between 400 BC and AD 200. At this point it is difficult to know whether the styles correspond to distinct civilizations or to different regional workshops. Moreover, these stylistic variations are not exclusive to any particular area. For instance, a number of terracotta heads in the 'classical' Nok style have been excavated in Katsina, 200 miles north of the town of Nok. Further field research may help unravel the mystery of early Nigerian civilizations.

'Classical' Nok style terracottas include full-size figures [B] with elongated heads, high smooth foreheads, elaborate coiffures and eyes with linear upper and curved lower brows (4, 5). Their bodies are usually adorned with numerous rows of terracotta necklaces suggesting stone beads (1).

The terracottas originating from the Sokoto area are cruder [C] and lack the detail of the 'classical' Nok figures. They are identifiable by their heavy upper brows that tend to weigh over the eyes. Most of the Sokoto terracottas are fragmentary, but reconstructions suggest a cone-shaped body which may have phallic connotations. They have been dated to around 400 BC by thermoluminescence tests.

Katsina terracotta figures display typical globular eyes with a curved lower eyelid [A] which convey a distinctive subtle expression (3). They appear not to be as old as the other groups of terracottas and can be dated to between the 1st and the 4th century AD. Another group of terracottas which originate from the central Nok area have an exaggerated, elongated

head adorned with an elaborate coiffure and jewelry (2, 6). This so-called 'elongated style' is thought to be related to the 'classical' Nok style because of the shape of the eyes and the coiffure and the fact that they date from the same time.

It is only possible to speculate about the use of these terracotta figures. When complete, they stand on a spherical base (9). Interestingly, this type of base also appears under contemporary roof finial figures in the town of Bwari in the Nok region. The extreme range in size and shape of Nok terracottas may indicate various uses, for instance, as grave markers or funerary-urn tops.

Several types of terracotta figure can be identified: The first suggests portraiture with highly individualized faces. The second includes statues of standing women. The third is comprised of figures, probably hunters, decorated with all-over animal motifs. The fourth group is made up of men with their chins resting on their right knee [D] or on their upper arms. The last category includes terracottas of half-human, half-animal figures or people with extremely distorted features (11).

Official excavations in the town of Igbo-Ukwu, in south-eastern Nigeria, have uncovered a group of objects which suggest a burial site. The majority of these bronze vessels and bracelets are made from an alloy of copper and tin and were produced by the 'lost wax' process. Technical tests have dated them to the 10th century AD. Although officially excavated, the age of these objects and uncertainty of their

1

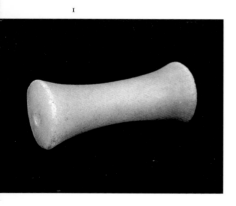

2   3   4   5   6

7

8

9

usage render it difficult to understand these pieces in relation to other finds.

Small terracotta and bronze heads and figures, as well as bronze bells (10), representing either dignitaries or kings have been excavated or found in and around the town of **Ife**. They all date from the 12th to the 15th century and display typical face scarifications and naturalistic features (7, 8). The site of Ife was traditionally revered by Benin kings as their town of origin and the decapitated heads of Benin kings were buried there. It is therefore possible to see a correlation between Ife artistic production and the royal art of Benin, which began during the 16th century.

Once again, the function of these terracotta and bronze heads remains a mystery. Some bronze heads have holes around the base of the neck suggesting an attachment to a wooden pole or a now lost body. However, the great majority of terracotta heads are relatively small in size and may have had a more ritualistic significance.

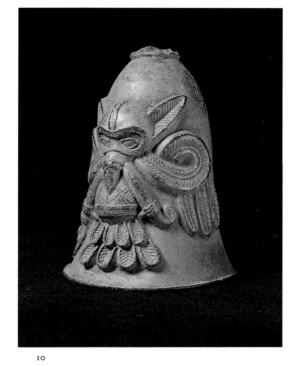

10

BIBLIOGRAPHY

FAGG, WILLIAM, *Nok Terracottas*, Lagos and London, 1977

EYO, EKPO, *Two Thousand Years of Nigerian Art*, Lagos, 1977

SHAW, T., P. SINCLAIR, B. ANDAH and A. OKPOKO, *The Archaeology of Africa*, London, 1993

SHAW, C. T., *Igbo-Ukwu: An Account of Archaeological Discoveries in Eastern Nigeria*, 2 vols, London, 1978

Treasure of Ancient Nigeria, Exh. Cat., Detroit Institute of Arts, 1980–83

Vallées du Niger, Exh. Cat., Musée National des Arts d'Afrique et d'Océanie, Paris, 1993–94, pp. 393–413

WILLET, FRANK, *Ife in the History of West African Sculpture*, London, 1967

WILLET, FRANK, *Ife, une civilisation Africaine*, Tallandier, 1971

1   A Nok stone bead;
    terracotta; length: 9 cm (3¹/₂ in)

2   A Nok elongated-style head;
    terracotta; height: 22 cm (8⁵/₈ in)

3   A Katsina head;
    terracotta; height: 23 cm (9 in)

4   A classical Nok head;
    terracotta; height: 33 cm (13 in)

5   A classical Nok head;
    terracotta; height: 35 cm (13³/₄ in)

6   A Nok elongated-style head;
    *terracotta; height: 21 cm (8¹/₄ in);
    Courtesy Entwistle, London*

7   An Ife head;
    *terracotta; height: 12 cm (4³/₄ in);
    Courtesy Entwistle, London*

8   An Ife head;
    *terracotta; height: 19 cm (7¹/₂ in);
    Courtesy Entwistle, London*

9   A Nok figure;
    *terracotta; height: 73 cm (28³/₄ in);
    Courtesy Entwistle, London*

10 An Ife bell;
    *bronze; height: 13 cm (5¹/₈ in);
    private collection*

11 A Nok figure;
    terracotta; height: 45 cm (17³/₄ in)

11

[A] Far left: a Katsina figure (1st–4th century AD)
terracotta; height: 29.5 cm (11⁵/8 in)

Katsina terracotta figures are characterized by
globular eyes and rounded features. The elongated
neck of this female figure emphasizes her head.

**[B] Left: a 'classical' Nok figure (4th century BC–
2nd century AD)**
terracotta; height: 66 cm (26 in)

This kneeling terracotta figure has all the
characteristics of the 'classical' Nok style – an
enlarged haughty head, cast-down eyes and
intricately carved jewelry. It shows the great
degree of sophistication achieved by Nok artists
two thousand years ago.

[C] Below left: a Sokoto figure (c. 400 BC)
terracotta; height: 74 cm (29 in)

With its overhanging heavy eyebrows, this
impressive terracotta figure is typical of the
figures found in the northern Sokoto area. Its
use is unknown, but its conical body suggests
it may have been the lid of a funerary urn.

**[D] Below: a Nok figure (4th century BC–2nd
century AD)**
terracotta; height: 18 cm (7 in)

The elongated face and features of this stunning
terracotta figure allow it to be classified as being
of the so-called 'elongated style'. The symbolism
of the sculpture's posture of chin on knee is
unknown, but it can also be seen in the work
of the 20th-century French sculptor Rodin.

Benin

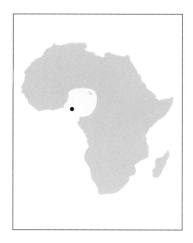

The Benin kingdom was founded by the son of an Ife king in around 1300, but it was not until the 15th and the 16th centuries that the kingdom reached its maximum size and attained its highest artistic standards. Towards the end of the 15th century the Benin made contact with Portuguese traders living along the coast and it is likely that these traders introduced previously unknown techniques such as brass gilting to Benin craftsmen [B]. Following the British punitive expedition to Nigeria in 1897, about three thousand brass, ivory and wooden objects were consigned to the Western world. They were later sold to underwrite the expenses of the expedition and to provide payments for the widows of soldiers killed in the war with Nigeria. At the time, Western scholars were stunned by the quality and magnificence of these objects.

1

2

Benin art is best described as a court art since it was associated with the king, known as the *Oba*. He held the monopoly on ivory and coral beads within the kingdom, and the brass, ivory and wooden objects referred to above were usually displayed during parades or were placed on top of ancestor altars.

STATUES

The numerous brass heads and figures cast by Benin metalworkers were created for the royal palace, where a new *Oba* would dedicate an altar to his predecessor. This rectangular altar was surmounted by brass heads, figures, carved ivory tusks, bells and wooden rattle staffs. It functioned as a tribute to the deceased and a point of contact with his spirit. Using the bells and rattle staffs to call the ancestor's spirit, the *Oba* offered sacrifices to him and to the earth on the altar.

Benin figures are rare. The majority date from the 17th to the 18th century and were carved to represent court officials (11), equestrian figures (9), queens (recognizable by their high coiffure) and roosters

(10). The latter two were seen on the altar of the queen mother.

Benin brass (4), terracotta (8) and wooden (5) heads are relatively more common and were placed respectively on the altars of kings, of brass caster corporation chiefs and dignitaries. Occasionally, a brass head was surmounted by a carved ivory tusk engraved with a procession of different *Obas* (2). For a long time, these heads were thought to represent an *Oba*, but today some Western scholars believe that a number of the 16th-century heads may be representations of prisoners.

The style of Benin brass heads evolved from thin casts with prominent chins dating from the 16th century [C] to thicker casts showing a high collar extending to the mouth and a coiffure framed by two vertical 'wings' (3).

At least two other styles of brass head dating from the 16th century can be distinguished. The first – called the Udo style (7), from the Udo chiefdom where three of these heads were found – includes eight rougher-looking heads, the backs of which were

3   4   5   6   7   8

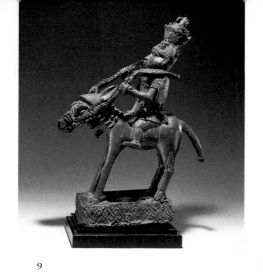

9

10

11

pierced with rectangular holes. The second style also dates from the end of the 16th century and has a rounded head with semi-circular eyes and a flat coiffure (6).

During the British punitive expedition, more than 1,000 brass plaques [A] were appropriated from the *Oba*'s palace. Dating from the 16th and 17th centuries, these plaques were secreted in a storage room. It is thought that in fact they were nailed to palace walls and pillars as a form of decoration or as references to protocol. They show the *Oba* in full regalia along with his nobility, warriors and some Portuguese traders (12). The most elaborate ones display a procession of up to nine people, while others depict only fish or birds.

EVERYDAY OBJECTS

The majority of everyday Benin objects were made for and associated with court ceremonies. They tended to be used by the *Oba* or by his nobility.

Aquamanile in the shape of a leopard (1) was the sole property of the *Oba* – the leopard was the royal animal. Pectorals, hip and waist ornaments in the shape of human or animal heads were worn either by the *Oba* or by major dignitaries (14).

Brass staffs and clappers surmounted by birds appeared during commemorating ceremonies.

After brass, Benin craftsmen favoured ivory as an artistic medium. The *Oba* was given a tusk belonging to each elephant killed and had the right to purchase the other. Bracelets and sceptres (13) were carved from the tusks and usually engraved with court festival scenes. The *Oba* and important court dignitaries

wore them during festivals and religious ceremonies. Brass, ivory and wooden boxes were used for secular and religious purposes and were decorated with animals or courtiers.

Seventy miles north of Benin city lies **Owo**, the ancient capital of Yorubaland. Its rulers, called *Olowo*, claim descent from the Ife royal house and were probably conquered by the Benin kingdom since their court ceremonies and institutions resemble those of the Benin. Owo ivory boxes, bracelets, leopard and human figures (16) date from between the 17th and 19th centuries. Their style is recognizable by the mouth carved as two parallel lips, semi-closed eyes with inlaid pupils and a flattened T-shaped nose.

A number of brass figures have been found in the **Lower Niger River area**. Their appearance suggests they date from the 16th century. They have typical globular eyes and body scarifications (15), but their function is unknown.

BIBLIOGRAPHY

Antique Works of Art from Benin, London, 1900
BLACKMUN, B., in D. ROSS, ed., *The Elephant and its Ivory in African Sculpture*, Los Angeles, 1992
BRADBURY, R. E., in P. MORTON-WILLIAMS, *Benin Studies*, Oxford, 1973
DARK, PHILIP J. C., 'Benin Brass Heads/Styles and Chronology' in *African Images/Essays in African Iconology*, New York, 1975
EZRA, KATE, *Royal Art of Benin, the Perls Collection in the Metropolitan Museum of Art*, 1992
VON LUSCHAM, FELIX, *Die Altertümer von Benin*, Berlin and Leipzig, 1919

1 A leopard shape aquamanile; *brass; length: 48 cm (18⁷/₈ in)*

2 A Benin head under an ivory tusk; *brass and ivory; total height: 199 cm (78 in)*

3 A 19th-century Benin head; *brass; height: 50 cm (19³/₄ in)*

4 A queen's head, middle period; *brass; height: 54.6 cm (21¹/₂ in)*

5 A Benin head; *wood; height: 52.4 cm (20⁵/₈ in)*

6 A 16th-century head; *brass; height: 21.2 cm (8³/₈ in)*

7 An Udo style head; *brass; height: 20.5 cm (8¹/₈ in)*

8 A Benin head; *terracotta; height: 24.5 cm (9⁵/₈ in)*

9 An equestrian figure; *brass; height: 58.4 cm (23 in)*

10 A figure of a rooster; *brass; height: 44 cm (17¹/₄ in)*

11 A figure of a court official; *brass; height: 62.5 cm (24⁵/₈ in)*

12 A plaque with Portuguese traders; *brass; height: 32.8 cm (13 in)*

13 A sceptre; *ivory; height: 36 cm (14¹/₈ in)*

14 A hip mask; *brass; height: 17.1 cm (6³/₄ in)*

15 A Lower Niger River figure; *bronze; height: 20.6 cm (8 in)*

16 An Owo maternity figure; *ivory; height: 14.9 cm (5⁷/₈ in)*

12

13

14

15

16

[A] Right: **a Benin plaque**
brass; height: 49 cm (19 in)

Benin plaques were placed on the walls of the king's palace and refer to court ceremonies. In this example, the main protagonist – in the centre – is probably the king himself who is surrounded by war chiefs and palace courtiers.

[B] Left: **a Benin cup (16th–17th century)**
gilt brass; height: 23 cm (9 in)

The Portuguese trader's head found on this unique cup shows the impact of the first contact between the Benin Kingdom and the Europeans. It has been suggested that the gilt-brass technique was introduced into Africa by Portuguese traders.

[C] Right: **a Benin head (16th century)**
brass; height: 22 cm (8⅝ in)

Sixteenth-century Benin heads characteristically have their necks covered with stylized coral beads leaving the chin exposed. The thinness of the cast and the refined skill demonstrated by these heads have astonished Western scholars since their appearance on the market at the turn of the century.

The Benue Area of Nigeria

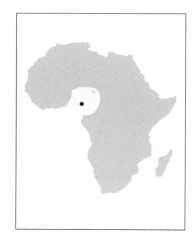

The people living on the banks of the Niger and Benue Rivers share many social and artistic traditions. They are thought to have common ancestors known as the *Akpoko* people. Traditionally, they principally make their money by acting as trade intermediaries between the inland people and the people who inhabit the Niger River Delta.

Living at the confluence of the Benue and Niger Rivers, the 500,000 **Idoma** people are predominantly farmers and traders. Artistically, they have achieved a reputation for their female fecundity figures showing an open mouth with carved teeth and vertical keloids on the temples. The face is usually painted with white pigments – a stylistic characteristic also shared with the Igbo people.

At least two types of female figure can be distinguished. The first, known as *Anjenu*, is used during fertility cults and is revered in small shrines. Once a year they are worn by dancers and paraded through the village. The second type, called *Ekwotame*, is carved as a seated woman (3) and may be painted with black pigments. These figures represent ancestors and thus the idea of lineage, so they are set near the body of the deceased.

Headdresses with a conical base supporting a round human head **[B]** and helmet masks belong to the *Oglinye* society which was originally a warrior society. Nowadays, however, it retains only the idea that its members are strong and courageous. Janus or multi-headed headdresses also exist and are used during entertainment festivities and funerals (7).

Face masks, called *Okua*, are generally found among the southern Idoma people. They are worn by dancers during funerals and display typical keloids, an open mouth and a smooth coiffure (9).

The **Afo** people settled north of the junction of the Niger and the Benue Rivers. Their *Okeshi* figures are used by members of the *Alanya Beshi* society during annual festivities related to fertility rites. They are carved as seated or standing female figures with overall linear body and face scarifications **[A]**. Caryatid stools (6) were also made. Recent studies have suggested that these sculptures, attributed to the Afo, may, in fact, have been carved by northern Nigerian tribes, themselves influenced by the Fulani people.

The **Igala** people live near the end of the Niger River. Every year they participate in important ceremonies celebrating the power of their king. During these festivities, nine types of royal helmet mask, called *Agba*, appear. They display typical facial scarifications and slanted eyes (10). Non-royal helmet masks are covered with linear scarifications and are used during festivals related to the *Egu* cult, which celebrate the spirit of the dead, and during the *Yam* festival when Igala ancestors are evoked. Their features are also found on staffs (8). Headdresses and statues carved in the Akpa area show a typical flattened face with two oblique scarifications on each cheek topped by a crested coiffure (2).

The 1,000,000 **Tiv** people live from farming fields on the left bank of the Benue River and take their name

1

2

3

4

5

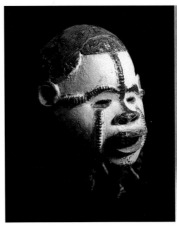

6   7   8   9   10

from their eponymous ancestor. They carve figures which are either large and elongated or naturally proportioned with round heads and occasionally scarification at the corners of the mouth and a crested coiffure. Some of these figures were used as posts for reception huts (1), while others, called *Ihambe*, are linked to the concept of fecundity and marriage (5). Tiv blacksmiths have achieved notoriety for their 'prestige' adzes in which the handle ends in a stylized human head with a blade sprouting from it. These are used during festivities and important meetings (12). Their metal output also includes small copper figures with splayed legs and rounded heads (4).

The **Nupe** people have lived along the banks of the Niger River since the 15th century and were conquered in around 1830 by the Muslim Fulani people. Their art is therefore non figurative and mostly decorative.

Nupe houses are decorated with doors (11) and posts carved with geometric designs, although there are some rare examples of animal designs. Circular stools (13), supported by varying numbers of feet, are presented by grooms to their brides. Traditionally they are used as 'prestige' objects on market days and during important meetings.

BIBLIOGRAPHY

ABRAHAM, ROY C., *The Tiv People*, Lagos, 1933 (1968)
ARMSTRONG, ROBERT G., *The Igala, Peoples of the Niger-Benue Confluence*, London, 1955, pp. 77–90
Art du Nigeria, Collections du Musée des Arts d'Afrique et d'Océanie, Exh. Cat., Paris, 1997
BOHANNAN, L. AND P., *The Tiv of Central Nigeria*, London, 1972
KASFIR, SIDNEY L., *Idoma Art and Culture*, unpub. manu., 1980
LEUZINGER, ELSY, 'Die Schnitzkunst im Leben der Afo von Nord-Nigeria', *Geographica Helvetica* 21, 4, 1966, pp. 152–61
NADEL, S. F., 'Nupe State and Community', *Africa*, 8 (3), 1933
NEYT, FRANÇOIS, and ANDRÉE DÉSIRANT, *Les Arts de la Bénue aux racines des traditions*, Editions Hawaiian Agronomics, 1985
RUBIN, ARNOLD, and MARIA BERNS, *The Arts of the Benue River Valley*, Los Angeles

1 A Tiv figure; *wood; height: 69 cm (27 in); private collection*

2 An Igala figure; *wood; height: 53 cm (21 in)*

3 An Idoma *Ekwotame* figure; *wood and pigment; height: 65.1 cm (25⁵/₈ in)*

4 A Tiv figure; *bronze; height: 33 cm (13 in)*

5 A Tiv figure; *wood; height: 73 cm (28³/₄ in); Dr Michel Gaud, St Tropez*

6 An Afo caryatid stool; *wood; height: 47.3 cm (18⁵/₈ in)*

7 An Idoma Janus headdress; *wood; height: 34 cm (13¹/₄ in)*

8 An Igala staff; *wood and horn; 21 cm (8¹/₄ in)*

9 An Idoma *Okua* mask; *wood and pigment; height: 29 cm (11³/₈ in); private collection*

10 An Igala royal mask; *wood; height: 34 cm (13³/₈ in)*

11 A Nupe door; *wood; height: 164 cm (64¹/₂ in)*

12 A Tiv adze; *metal; height: 43.2 cm (17 in)*

13 A Nupe stool; *wood; height: 41 cm (16 in)*

11

12   13

[A] Left: **an Afo maternity figure**
wood; height: 29 cm (11¹/₂ in); private collection

Facial scarifications, typical among the Afo
tribespeople, can be seen on this maternity
figure. The exaggerated breasts, the baby on
the back and the gesture of holding a pot on
top of the head emphasize the idea of fertility.

[B] Right: **an Idoma headdress**
wood; height: 21 cm (8¹/₄ in); private collection

This heart-shaped headdress displays
an extremely high degree of stylization.
It appeared during ceremonies related
to the *Oglinye* warrior society.

The Niger River Delta

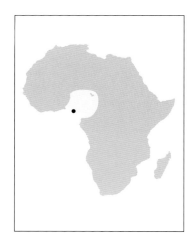

The Niger River Delta area covers the entire southern part of Nigeria from the Benin River in the west to the Cross River in the east. There are two main cultural areas – the first includes the western side of the Niger River Delta and was first populated during the 9th century by migrating tribes who came from the north. The Ijo people were the first to settle in the area and now live on the shore of the Atlantic Ocean. Later, other tribes such as the Urhubo, the Isoko and the Ogoni settled in the northern and western part of this delta area. The second cultural area is centred around the Cross River in eastern Nigeria and is home to the Ibibio, the Igbo, the Ekoi, the Oron and the Eket. The latter shares the same *Ekpo* secret society which was first introduced to the area by the Ibibio people.

1

2

1 An Igbo Janus figure;
  terracotta; height: 31.1 cm (12¼ in)

2 An Ijo headdress;
  wood; length: 71.1 cm (28 in)

3 An Urhubo mask; *wood and
  pigments; height: 44.5 cm (17½ in)*

4 An Ibibio mask;
  *wood; height: 30 cm (11¾ in);
  Dr Michel Gaud, St Tropez*

5 An Ekoi monolith;
  stone; height: 53.3 cm (21 in)

6 An Ibibio *Idiok* mask;
  *wood; height: 35 cm (13¾ in);
  Dr Michel Gaud, St Tropez*

7 An Ogoni mask;
  wood; height: 20 cm (8 in)

The 250,000 **Ijo** people settled in the Niger River Delta where fish are in abundance, providing them with their principal means of subsistence. Ijo carvers produced altar panels and horizontal headdresses (2), called *Otojo*, which represent water spirits. They believe that these spirits are like humans in terms of their strengths and weaknesses and that before their birth, human beings live among the *Otojo*. Once born, the Ijo maintain contact with them through prayers in order to gain their favours.

The **Urhubo** people settled north of the Niger River Delta and live from fishing and farming. They believe that forest spirits, called *Edjo*, influence their everyday lives. They carve *Edjo* figures and ancestor statues – the former is represented as a mythic warrior holding weapons or magical containers, while the latter appears as a Janus or seated figure (8). These ancestor figures are usually kept together in communal houses where they preside over meetings. Smaller standing figures are thought to represent the *Edjo*'s spouse. Masks are worn by young men and used during ceremonies related to the *Edjo* spirits (3). Stylistically, Urhubo figures and masks can be identified by their typical forehead scarifications.

The 180,000 **Isoko** people live north of the Niger River Delta and are stylistically influenced by their north-western neighbours, the Urhubo. They carve small standing figures, known as *Oma* (12), which, in spite of typical Urhubo forehead scarifications, can be distinguished by their protruding mouth and carved teeth. These figures fulfil the same apotropaic functions as Igbo statues.

The rich farming land on the eastern part of the delta sustains the **Ogoni** people. Their carvers produce large puppets and horizontal headdresses, but they are known predominantly for their small human-face masks which are characterized by an articulated jaw with inset teeth (7). These masks are used during Christmas festivities and funerals.

The **Ibibio** and the **Anang** people number around 2,000,000 and live in an area between the Delta and the Cross River. Their main resource is farming maize and iguame. They live in villages led by a chief elected from the most honourable heads of the important families and Ibibio and Anang social life is regulated by three secret societies which incorporate masks into their annual ceremonies. The most important of these societies is the *Ekpo*, which is responsible for the cult of the ancestors, who are in turn responsible for the welfare of the tribe. In Ibibio ceremonies, two main types of mask appear. The first, known as *Mfon*, has an articulated jaw and

3   4   5   6   7

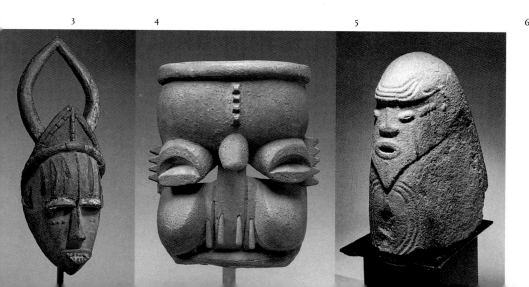

8   9   10   11   12

represents a 'beautiful' spirit who has attained eternal bliss **(4)**. The second mask, called *Idiok*, is thought to represent a hell-dwelling spirit and is carved with a typical emaciated face, possibly alluding to ill-health **(6)**.

The 8,000,000 **Igbo** people – who live primarily from farming – settled in the northern part of the Niger River Delta, in an area of forests and swamps. Village councils composed of the eldest people from each family govern the tribe. Their power is counterbalanced by secret societies.

Igbo artists are famous for their *Ikenga* figures **(10)** which are kept on personal altars and receive prayers and libations before special occasions. They display a typical pair of backward-curving horns which symbolize the strength, power and courage that Igbo men aspire to.

Standing figures represent the numerous Igbo *Alusi* deities **[C]**. They are grouped together in symbolic families and are kept in special houses where they are revered. During annual festivities, these figures are taken out and paraded through the villages. During other ceremonies, women wear large metal anklets decorated with geometric motifs **(14)**. Terracotta figures produced by the women symbolize divination spirits – they are usually designed as Janus figures and are kept on domestic altars **(1)**.

Igbo masks are numerous and are used for initiation ceremonies and entertainment. They all display a typical central crest and an elongated face.

The **Igbo-Izi** people live in the north-eastern part of the Igbo territory and carve an elephant spirit mask, called *Ogbodo*, which has typical tusks and an apotropaic function **(13)**.

Ekoi artists carve cephalomorphic and zoomorphic headdresses, as well as Janus helmet masks, which tend to be covered with antelope skin. This technique, also used by other tribes of the region, consists of applying a fresh skin on top of a wooden core, and then adding hair and details **[A, D]**. The Ekoi and other groups of the Cross River area have produced large monoliths, called *Atal* **(5)**, which are thought to represent ancestors. One of these *Atals* dates from as far back as AD 200.

The **Ejagham** people who belong to the leopard spirit cult meet in a house with magical panels upon which animal skulls and magical substances are attached.

Living on the western side of the Cross River, the **Oron** people carved monoxylous ancestor figures **(11)**. These sculptures, known as *Ekpu*, have a typical coiffure and scarifications, and are kept in the village meeting room and used as mnemonic objects to commemorate tribal history.

To the west of the Oron people, near the sea, live the **Eket** people. They produce panelled and circular masks **[B]** that are used during ceremonies related to their Ekpo secret society. The anthropomorphic headdresses are used in festivities connected with their *Ekong* war secret society **(9)**.

BIBLIOGRAPHY

Art du Nigeria, Collections du Musée des Arts d'Afrique et d'Océanie, Exh. Cat., Paris, 1997

COLE, H. M., and C. C. ANIAKOR, *Igbo Arts, Community and Cosmos*, Los Angeles, 1984

FOSS, PERKINS, 'Urhobo Statuary for Spirits and Ancestors', *African Arts*, IX, 4, 1976

JONES, G. I., *Ibo Art*, Aylesbury, 1989

NEAHER, NANCY, *Bronzes of Southern Nigeria and Igbo Metalsmithing Traditions*, Stanford University, 1976

NEYT, FRANÇOIS, *L'Art Eket, Collection Azar*, Paris, 1979

NICKLIN, KEITH, *The Cross River Bronzes*, in M. T. BRINCARD, *The Art of Metal in Africa*, New York, 1982, pp. 47–52

NICKLIN, KEITH, and JILL SALMONS, 'Cross River Art Styles', *African Arts*, XVII, 1, 1984

13

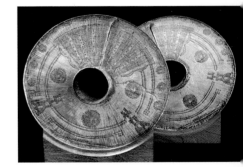

14

8 An Urhubo figure;
wood; height: 152.4 cm (60 cm)

9 An Eket anthropomorphic headdress;
wood; height: 99 cm (39 in)

10 An Igbo *Ikenga* figure;
wood and pigments; height: 76.2 cm (30 in)

11 An Oron figure;
wood; height: 82 cm (32¼ in)

12 An Isoko *Oma* figure;
wood; height: 35 cm (13¾ in)

13 An Igbo-Izi elephant spirit mask;
wood and pigments; length: 59 cm (23¼ in)

14 A pair of Igbo anklets;
copper; diameter: 35 cm (13⅝ in); private collection

[A] Above: **an Ekoi zoomorphic headdress**
wood, vegetal fibres, hair, skin; height: 25 cm (10 in); private collection

The stylized features on this zoomorphic headdress probably refer to a bush animal – they were often associated with spirits. Its power is enhanced by added paraphernalia, including magical substances.

[B] Above, right: **an Eket circular mask**
wood; diameter: 24 cm (9¹/₂ in); private collection

Eket circular masks are usually worn during Ekpo secret society ceremonies. The lack of detail contributes to the power of the mask.

[C] Right: **an Igbo *Alusi* figure**
wood; height: 170 cm (67 in)

The pantheons of the Igbo people are represented by large wooden sculptures. This particular male figure has typical facial and abdominal scarifications and was paraded during annual ceremonies.

[D] Above: **an Ekoi cephalomorphic headdress**
wood, vegetal fibres, hair, skin, ivory; height: 25 cm (10 in); private collection; provenance: P. Harter Collection, Paris

This disturbing headdress bears features typical of those of the Ekoi tribe of Nigeria. Starting with a wooden template, the face is then covered with the hide of an antelope and further embellished with applied human hair, teeth and eye sockets.

Inland Nigeria

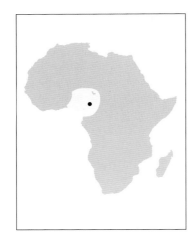

The area lying to the north of the Niger and Benue Rivers includes a range of mountains covered by a savannah. Archaeological excavations have revealed traces of human activity on the Jos plateau and in the Benue River valley dating from the Stone Age – 39,000 years ago.

Over time, the indigenous Benue-Kongo and Adamawa-speaking people of this area were infiltrated by Chad-speaking tribes who migrated from the east and north. This created a mosaic of people with different social and religious traditions. Nevertheless, common artistic conventions can be found among the majority of the people who live in this area. For example, shoulder masks are worn by the Mumuye, the Jukun and Waja people and red seeds are often applied on the surface of headdresses and masks.

Tribes such as the Mumuye, the Chamba, the Jukun, the Wurkun, the Goemai and the Montol live along the Benue River in eastern Nigeria, while the Waja, the Mama, the Hausa, the Koro and the Dakakari people settled in the northern part of the country.

1   2

Living on the left bank of the Benue River, the 400,000 **Mumuye** people intensively farm an area of plains. Socially, they are divided into small family groups called *Dola*, which are headed by a council of elders with an elected leader. The *Vabong* secret society, of which there are seven grades, regulates Mumuye religious life. Entry into the society is achieved through initiation ceremonies which include flagellation and an explanation of the meaning of masks and other magical objects.

Mumuye artists are famous for their wooden statues known as *Iagalagana* (4, 5). These figures vary from 30 to 160 cm in height and display elongated features and exaggerated ear lobes. Carved by blacksmiths or weavers, they are kept in a separate hut located on a family compound, and are entrusted to the family member who has magical powers. The *Iagalagana* have divination, apotropaic and rain-making functions, and serve as prestige objects.

Two principal types of mask are found among the Mumuye. The first is a face mask displaying two large hollowed eye sockets which may have been used during initiation rites (13). The second type is a shoulder mask, known as *Sukwava*, which displays an elongated neck set under a diminutive head with large ears (3). Traditionally, they were used during pre-war ceremonies, but nowadays they are worn during rain-making and healing practices.

The 20,000 **Chamba** people live south of the Benue River, near the Jukun people. They are socially divided into small kingdoms, each headed by a king assisted by a council of elders whose powers are regulated by male and female secret societies.

The Chamba use a type of mask that symbolizes a bush spirit. It has a rounded head with a flattened open mouth and two large backward-sloping horns. It is worn during funerals, circumcisions and inauguration ceremonies (11).

Chamba figures are rare and their function is uncertain [E]. They are usually covered with an encrusted patina. Another type of Chamba figure is thought to be a medium for communication with the spirit world [C]. Small figures were used to cure or protect an individual from snake bites and were attached to iron spikes and inserted into the ground.

The king of the **Jukun**, known as the *Aka Uku*, lives in the town of Wukari from where he rules his 30,000 people. He leads the cult of the ancestors who are in turn responsible for the welfare of the tribe.

Statues are found predominantly among the Jukun people in the north west and represent ancestors, as well as wives and slaves [A]. They are displayed during funerals, agricultural ceremonies and in times of danger. During these rites, the figures serve as an intermediary between the priest and

3   4   5   6   7   8

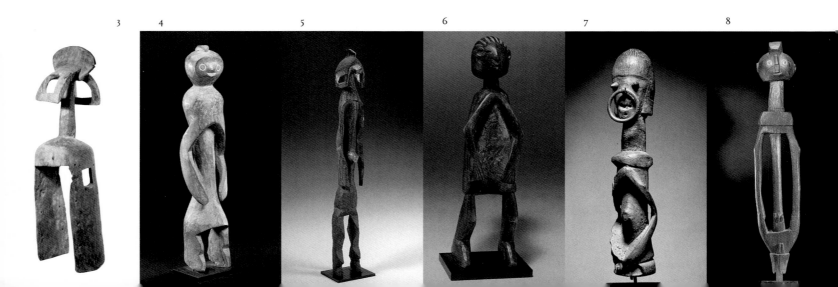

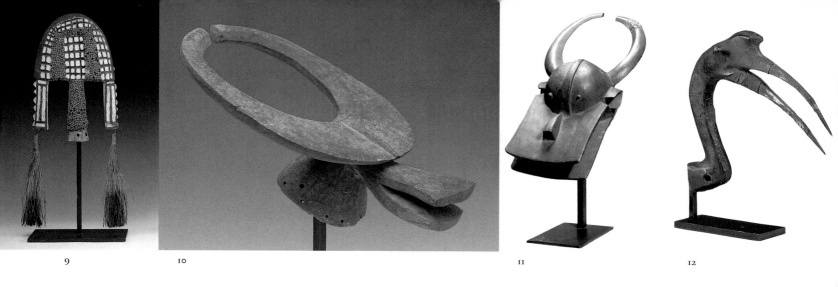

9   10   11   12

the ancestor's world. In the south-western part of the Jukun territory, the role of intermediary is held by male dancers who wear shoulder masks (2) that have a round head, a flattened face and a smooth coiffure.

The **Wurkun** people live on the right bank of the Benue River, between the Jukun and the Mumuye people, in an area of mountains and hills. Their artistic reputation rests on their columnar figures which tend to be covered in a thick encrusted patina and have a rounded head, often with a crested coiffure. These figures are usually pierced with an iron spike, allowing them to be inserted into the ground (7). Known as *Wundul*, these statues have apotropaic functions and are often seen in pairs, protecting field crops, or in house shrines. A group of other statues with highly stylized bodies supporting round heads have been found (8), although their purpose is still unknown.

The **Waja** people settled on the northern part of the Benue River and carve large shoulder masks with a columnar neck set under a small head (1). Little is known about them.

The **Goemai** and **Montol** people live on the right bank of the Benue River and are known for their small figures with splayed legs and hands (6). Members of the *Komtin* male secret society employ these ancestor representations in divination and curative ceremonies.

The **Mama** people, also known as the Kantana, live north of the Jos plateau and carve headdresses in the form of highly stylized animal heads (10). They are worn with a thick fibre costume and symbolize a bush spirit. Worn by energetic dancers, they are thought to bring prosperity to the tribe. There are a number of rare Mama sculptures carved in a rough style with a red weathered patina.

The **Hausa** people live in northern Nigeria in an area of savannah. Before major communal hunts, known as *Bago*, the hunters gather wearing a typical head-dress over a black cloth. This headdress is carved in the shape of a bird's head and is usually constructed from a wooden core covered with antelope skin (12).

The **Koro** people settled north of the junction of the Niger and Benue Rivers. They carve abstract head-dresses embellished with red seeds (9), which are thought to symbolize ancestor spirits and are used during agricultural rites and important social or family events. Anthropomorphic cups are used for drinking and pouring beer or palm wine during ritual sacrifices or secondary funerals [D].

The **Dakakari** people inhabit part of north-west Nigeria and produce terracotta grave markers with a standing human or animal figure set on top of a sphere [B]. Graves of important Dakakari men are surrounded by low stone walls and then filled with earth. Every year, the family of the deceased honour the dead by pouring libations onto these grave markers or into nearby vessels.

13

BIBLIOGRAPHY

ADELBERGER, J., 'The Problem of "Wurkun": New Evidence and a Solution to an Enigma' in *Northern Nigerian Ethnography and Linguistics, African Languages and Cultures*, 5 (1), 1992
Art du Nigeria, Collections du Musée des Arts d'Afrique et d'Océanie, Exh. Cat., Paris, 1997
BASSING, A., 'Grave Monuments of the Dakakari', *African Arts*, VI (3), 1973, pp. 36–39
FRY, P., 'Essai sur la Statuaire Mumuyé', *Objets et Monde*, Brussels, X, 1, 1970, pp. 3–28
MEEK, C. K., *Tribal Studies in Northern Nigeria*, London, 1931
RUBIN, A., *The Arts of the Jukun-Speaking Peoples of Northern Nigeria*, Bloomington, 1969
SIEBER, R., *Sculpture of Northern Nigeria*, New York, 1961
SIEBER, R., and T. VEVERS, *Interactions: The Art Styles of the Benue River Valley and East Nigeria*, Indianapolis, 1974
STRYBOL, J., 'Poterie domestique et poterie sacrée en pays Mumuyé', *Africa-Tervuren*, XXXI, Brussels, nos 1–4, 1985

1   A Waja shoulder mask;
    wood; height: 175 cm (69 in)

2   A Jukun shoulder mask;
    wood; height: 104 cm (41 in)

3   A Mumuye *Sukwava* shoulder mask;
    wood; height: 109.8 cm (43¼ in)

4   A Mumuye *Iagalagana* figure;
    wood; height: 77 cm (30¼ in);
    Dr Michel Gaud, St Tropez

5   A Mumuye *Iagalagana* figure;
    wood; height: 137 cm (54 in)

6   A Montol figure;
    wood; height: 39.4 cm (15½ in)

7   A Wurkun figure; *wood and metal;*
    height: 41 cm (16¼ in)

8   A Wurkun figure from the village of Karim Lamido;
    wood and metal; height:
    95 cm (37½ in)

9   A Koro headdress; *wood and seeds;*
    height: 39 cm (15¼ in)

10 A Mama headdress;
    wood; length: 43 cm (17 in)

11 A Chamba mask;
    wood; length: 85 cm (33½ in)

12 A Hausa headdress;
    wood, skin and bird's beak;
    height: 36 cm (14 in)

13 A Mumuye face mask;
    wood; height: 39 cm (15⅜ in);
    private collection

[A] Left: **a pair of Jukun figures**
wood, metal, vegetal fibres; height:
45 cm (17³/₄ in); private collection

These solid ancestor figures were
paraded through the village during
times of danger and important
communal ceremonies. Their design
and execution suggest they are at
least two centuries old. The ropes
entwined around the forearms
may at one time have been bound,
suggesting their unity as a couple.

[B] Above, left: **a Dakakari grave marker
figure**
terracotta; height: 73 cm (28⁵/₈ in);
private collection

Set on top of the grave of important
people, this grave marker was
honoured every year with libations.
Typical facial scarifications, found
also among the Afo people, adorn
the face of this figure.

[C] Above, right: **a pair of Chamba
figures**
wood; height of the taller: 56 cm (22 in);
private collection

Chamba figures display seemingly
non-human features which
may relate to their function as
intermediaries between the spirit
and human realms.

[D] Below, left: **a Koro libation
anthropomorphic cup**
wood, cowrie shells, seeds; height:
61 cm (24 in); private collection

The applied red seeds on the face,
neck and navel are characteristic of
the northern part of Nigeria. This
anthropomorphic cup was used to
drink from and to pour palm wine
and oil.

[E] Below, right: **a Chamba figure**
wood; height: 45 cm (17³/₄ in);
private collection

In spite of the lack of facial detail,
this figure is still powerful. It is one
of a series of figures which are all
covered in a thick reddish libation-
based patina.

Yoruba

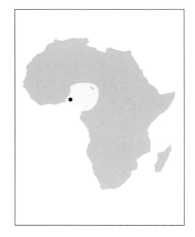

The word 'Yoruba' describes both a language and a tribe living across Nigeria and the Popular Republic of Benin, in an area of forest and savannah. Their origins can be traced back to the end of the first millennium like the civilization of Ife (surveyed in the Nok chapter). Following the collapse of the Ife civilization, a number of kingdoms such as the Ijebu and the Oyo emerged. They, in turn, disintegrated during the 18th and 19th centuries, but were revived by the colonial powers at the end of the 19th century and today still form the political structure of the Yoruba people. The enormous scale of the slave trade in Nigeria contributed to the diaspora of the Yoruba people and informed spiritual practices in countries such as Haiti.

1   An *Ose Sango* staff;
    *wood; height: 42 cm (16¹/₂ in);
    private collection*

2   An *Onile* figure;
    bronze; height: 58 cm (23 in)

3   A pair of Ibeji figures;
    wood; height: 23 cm (9 in)

4   A pair of Ogboni pendants;
    bronze; height: 33.8 cm (13¹/₄ in)

5   A Sango figure;
    wood; height: 52 cm (20¹/₂ in)

6   An *Esu* staff;
    wood; height: 47 cm (18¹/₂ in)

7   Colonial figures by Thomas Ona;
    *wood; height of the tallest:
    27 cm (10¹/₂ in)*

8   A metal staff;
    iron; height: 48.9 cm (19¹/₄ in)

9   An Ijebu bell;
    bronze; height: 25 cm (10 in)

10 A cup; *wood; height: 18 cm (7 in)*

11 Two Gelede masks;
    *wood and pigments; height of
    the taller: 37 cm (14¹/₂ in)*

12 An Egungun headdress by
    Orriyide Adugbologe;
    wood; height: 50.8 cm (20 in)

Yoruba people are prolific artists and craftsmen. Most of the Yoruba art objects date from between the end of the 19th century and the middle of the 20th century and can often be attributed to a specific carver known by name – an exception in African art.

During the 16th century, the **Ijebu kingdom** (1500–1750) dominated Nigeria's coastal region. Portuguese copper was traded between the Ijebu and Portuguese sailors and the Ijebu cast brass objects that demonstrated an influence derived from the Benin kingdom. However, their bracelets, bells **(9)** and office staffs were usually decorated with half-human/half-animal figures with globular eyes and often curved forehead scarifications.

The **Oyo kingdom** (1680–1830) was in the northern part of the Yoruba-speaking territories. It was ruled by a king, called *Alafin*, who served as ultimate judge. His power was counterbalanced by a council of seven chiefs, each of whom was head of a non-royal family. From the 17th century, the Oyo expanded their territory, helped largely by their cavalry, which was, in turn, immortalized by carved figures seen on Epa masks. The two most important cults created by the Oyo centred on the *Egungun* and *Sango* societies who are still active today, leading to the generation of masks, headdresses and sculptures.

Egungun masked ceremonies involve dancers who represent heavenly creatures, known as *Ara Orun*, capable of bringing good fortune or punishing the guilty. Egungun headdresses are worn at ceremonies related to the annual Egungun masquerade, but also

appear during festivities following the death of a dignitary or during initiation ceremonies. Egungun headdresses **(12)** show considerable stylistic variation and, indeed, the principal characteristic element of the Egungun dancer is his loose body-covering costume rather than a unique headdress.

The name **Sango** allegedly belonged to the fourth Yoruba king who was deified and became associated with thunder, symbolized by a double-axe motif on the head of the sculptures associated with his cult. During annual Sango cult ceremonies, women devotees sing and dance holding the *Ose Sango* (dance wand) **(1)**. His cult is also associated with a number of large figures, typically either kneeling in devotion, holding a cup **(5)**, or standing with a musical instrument or holding the *Ose Sango*.

Sango shrines, known as *Ojubo Sango,* are often framed by anthropomorphic caryatid figures.

Today, Nigeria is structured by a number of cults – the following are a few of the important ones:
Among the western Yoruba-speaking kingdoms, the **Gelede** cult pays homage to the power of elderly women. During Gelede festivities, helmet masks carved in the form of a human face are worn. On top of the head there is either an elaborate coiffure or a carved representation of a human activity **(11)**.

The **Epa** cult (also known as *Elefon*) is found predominantly in the north-eastern kingdoms of Yorubaland. *Epa* masks vary enormously according to the town in which they appear. Generally, they are worn during funerals or rites of passage ceremonies

1

2

3

4

5

6

7

8

and characteristically they are composed of many elements – usually a human-face helmet mask topped by an elaborate standing figure **[C]**. When not worn, these masks are kept in shrines where they are honoured with libations and prayers.

The **Ogboni** society (also known as *Osugbo*) is pervasive among Yoruba-speaking people, but probably originates from the Ijebu. At its head are the wisest man and woman from the community whose role is to adjudicate. Ogboni brass figures, called *Edan*, are cast in pairs and attached to spikes and a chain runs from head to head to join the pair (4). They are worn over the shoulders of Ogboni members as sign of office or as an amulet.

Large brass figures, called *Onile*, are carved as a pair and represent the male and female aspects of *Ile*, the earth Goddess (2).

The **Esu** cult centres around a divine male messenger, who mediates between humans and spirits and brings wealth or punishment. He is revered in shrines where staffs carved with his figure are placed on his altar or carried by dancers during the Esu annual festivities (6). The figure is characterized by an enlarged backward-swept coiffure, symbolizing the shape of his club and can be covered by strings of cowrie shells representing wealth and fecundity.

Yoruba sculptors were commissioned to decorate palace and shrine doors and the posts supporting roofs and verandas. Among the most famous of all these artists was Olowe of Ise who carved posts in a recognizable angular style for the palace located in southern Ekiti **[B]**.

EVERYDAY OBJECTS

Divination trays are found all over Yorubaland. They are either rectangular or oval and the edges are decorated with faces, animals and geometric motifs. During divination ceremonies, Yoruba diviners cover the centre of the divination tray with saw dust, and the diviner evokes the spirits with the help of an ivory or wooden taper and then throws sixteen palm nuts, *Ikin*, or a chain, called *Opele*, onto the tray. Their position reveals the answer to the question asked. Following the divination ceremony, the *Ikin* and *Opele* are stored in ceremonial figurative cups (10).

Iron staffs decorated with up to sixteen birds play a part in ceremonies related to *Osanying*, the God of medicine (8).

Yoruba beadwork is undertaken for royal commissions and appears on crowns and tunics. They are sometimes given to foreign dignitaries as a welcoming gift **[A]**.

Among the most famous Yoruba carvings are the Ibeji figures which represent deceased twins. According to Yoruba belief, they influence the daily lives of family members and hence are honoured with libations and prayers (3).

Thomas Ona, a famous Yoruba artist, carved anecdotal figures for the tourist trade. They feature colonials in daily activities such as polo playing or crossing a river in a boat (7).

BIBLIOGRAPHY

Art du Nigéria, Collection du Musée des Arts d'Afrique et d'Océanie, Exh. Cat., Paris, 1997

DREWAL, HENRY H., JOHN PEMBERTON III and ROWLAND ABIODUN, *Yoruba, Nine Centuries of African Art and Thought*, New York, 1989

FAGG, WILLIAM, and JOHN PEMBERTON, *Yoruba Sculpture of West Africa*, New York, 1982

9

10

11

12

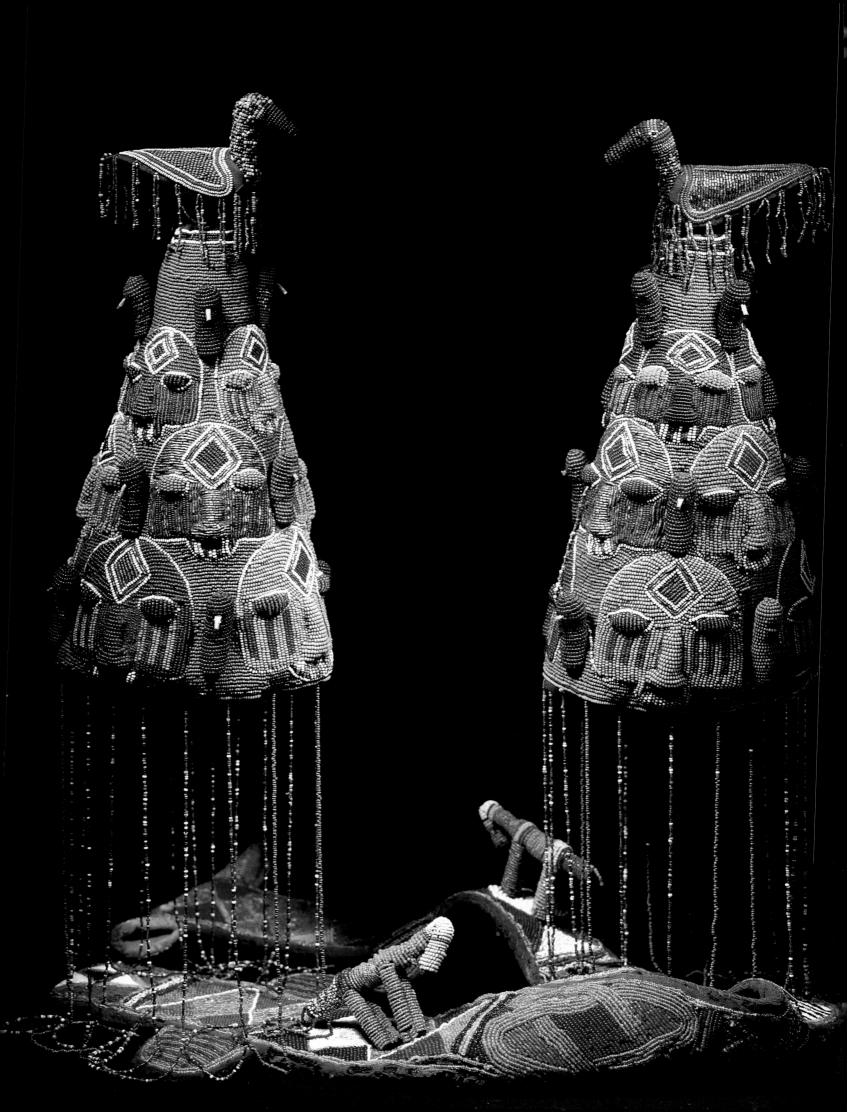

[A] Far left: **two beaded crowns**
beads on vegetal fibres; height: 38.6 cm (15¹/₄ in)

Yoruba beaded crowns are among the most colourful African works of art. They were worn by the king and his courtiers and were often given as presents to important visitors.

[B] Left: **a house post by Olowe of Ise**
wood; height: 180 cm (71 in)

The elongated and dynamic characteristics of the Olowe of Ise art are shown in this complex veranda post. The theme of the equestrian figure, prevalent in Yoruba art, is also found in the artistic output of the 13th-century Mali empire and shows the status attached to the ownership of horses.

[C] Above: **an *Epa* mask**
wood; height: 128 cm (50¹/₂ in)

This *Epa* mask has most of the characteristics of Yoruba art – its face is emphasized, it has globular eyes, a high coiffure and a complex statue on top of its head. When not worn by dancers during ceremonies related to rites of passage, the mask was reverentially kept and honoured with libations.

Cameroon

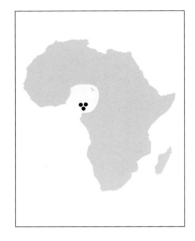

By convention, Cameroon is divided into four cultural and artistic areas – the Forest Zone, the Grassland area in the south-western corner, the Nigerian border region and the north. The Grassland area, traditionally rich in works of art, is discussed in the following chapter, while the three other regions, which are known to have a less prolific artistic output, are treated together here.

The **Forest Zone** is a fertile area in the southern part of Cameroon which supports a population whose ancestors were the first people to make contact with the European colonials at the end of the 19th century. The tribes mix together, so the art of this area is more or less stylistically uniform, although the precise origin and function of pieces cannot be identified with certainty. Nevertheless, a rare anthropomorphic figure can be ascribed to the **Abo** people **[C]**. It is covered with a rich encrusted patina which suggests that regular offerings and libations were poured over it.

Carvers living in the **Duala** area produce zoomorphic masks (4), chiefs' stools and canoe prows showing polychrome decoration. It is thought that most of these sculptures were produced for the tourist trade, although a number of ivory objects were manufactured in this area prior to contact with westerners.

Masks found in the western part of the Forest Zone are thought to have been used in male secret society ceremonies and echo Nigerian stylistic traditions.

Artistically, the people living in the area lying along the **Nigerian border** (e.g., the Kaka, the Mbembe, the Todkom, the Mfumbe, the Banyang and the Anyang) have been strongly influenced by their Grassland neighbours to the east and their Nigerian neighbours to the west.

Kaka masks (2) and figures **[B]** are characterized by a heavily encrusted patina which suggests numerous libations. These figures – all with open,

screaming mouths – appeared on the Western market in the early 1970s. It is thought they were used during funerals and initiation ceremonies, but owing to the scarcity of field research, this is merely speculative.

The majority of **Mbembe** people occupy an area that borders Nigeria, although some actually live in Nigeria. They are renowned as traders and for the fact that they include palm wine in their festivities and ceremonies. Mbembe carvers worked large basalt columns which were erected above the graves of the nobility and also carved large slit drums which had the figure of a chief holding a prisoner's head at the end **[A]**. The drums were beaten to call the tribe in an emergency. The particular type of drum illustrated was carved by the Igala people of Nigeria and other tribes living on the border, who share a similar artistic tradition.

The artistic output of the **Todkom** and **Mfumbe** people further demonstrates the amalgamation of Cameroon and Nigerian artistic traditions. Both tribes live in autonomous villages and carve masks and figures (5) with extremely distorted features characteristic of the Grassland Tikar people and the Cross River tribes of Nigeria.

The territory in the **north of Cameroon** is vast and is home to the Mambila and the Namji in the west, the Wute and Vere in the south, the Fulani in the east and the Kirdi in the north.

The 25,000 **Mambila** people produced a considerable number of masks and figures that are

1

2

3

4

5

6
7
8
9

characterized by a heart-shaped face; red and white pigments were often applied later. Mambila figures **(3)** are thought to embody ancestors who, according to Mambila beliefs, are responsible for the clan's wealth. The figures appear with bent legs and a typical enlarged head outlined in wooden pegs.

Dances celebrating the end of the planting seasons are led by a tribesman wearing a cephalomorphic helmet mask **(6)**. In turn, he is followed by a retinue of assistants wearing secondary masks in the shape of a dog's head **(8)** and a crow's head. Janus masks **(7)** are rare and may reflect the artistic influence of the Bamileke Janus masks which symbolize lineage.

Namji people are famous in the West for their wooden dolls carved with geometric features and adorned with numerous multi-coloured necklaces **(9)**.

The **Wute** and the **Vere** people are decreasing in number – in 1890 they numbered 60,000, in 1915, 30,000 and today they are a fraction of that number. They live in round huts grouped in fortified cities and their artistic output is limited to basketry and rare metal objects such as necklaces **(11)**.

The 450,000 **Fulani** people live a nomadic life and consequently have not produced many large works of art. They are known mostly for their carved bowls and utilitarian objects, although Fulani women wear gold earrings during significant gatherings **(12)**.

The **Kirdi** people, numbering 80,000, are primarily farmers and live in small autonomous hamlets. Their artistic production is largely confined to small leather or metal objects, among which are iron 'cache-sexe' garments used by women during important ceremonies **(10)**. The Kirdi also make small terracotta figures which are stylistically related to Sao figures and are thought to be their precursors.

In an area covering the north of Cameroon, Chad and Nigeria archaeologists have discovered numerous bronze and terracotta objects **(1)** belonging to the **Sao civilization** (12th–19th centuries). They are known for their terracotta anthropomorphic and zoomorphic statuettes which are up to 35 cm high and appear with numerous scarifications and rough features. Some were excavated from sanctuaries, while others were found in burial sites. Pierced zoomorphic figures are thought to have been used either as currency or as ritual objects. The Sao also made bronze jewelry – bronze bracelets and pendants were often decorated around the edges with an undulated motif.

BIBLIOGRAPHY
HARTER, PIERRE, 'Kaka or Keaka', *Tribal Arts*, 3, 1994
LEBEUF, JEAN-PAUL and ANNIE, *Les Arts des Sao*, Paris, 1977
NORTHERN, T., *The Art of Cameroon*, Washington, D.C., 1984

1 A Sao figure; *terracotta; height: 7.5 cm (3 in)*
2 A Kaka mask; *wood; height: 125 cm (49 1/4 in)*
3 A Mambila figure; *wood; height: 48.3 cm (19 in)*
4 A Duala mask; *wood and pigments; height: 84 cm (33 in)*
5 A Todkom/Mfumbe figure; *wood; height: 16 cm (6 1/4 in)*
6 A Mambila mask; *wood; height: 28.9 cm (11 3/8 in)*
7 A Mambila Janus mask; *wood; height: 41.9 cm (16 1/2 in); private collection*
8 A Mambila dog's head mask; *wood and pigments; height: 67.3 cm (26 1/2 in)*
9 Two Namji dolls; *wood, vegetal fibres and cowrie shells; height: 29.8 cm (11 3/4 in)*
10 A Kirdi 'cache-sexe'; *iron and leather; length of the claws: 11 cm (4 3/8 in); private collection*
11 A Vere necklace; *brass; length: 23 cm (9 in); private collection*
12 A Fulani earring; *gold; height: 12 cm (4 3/4 in)*

10
11
12

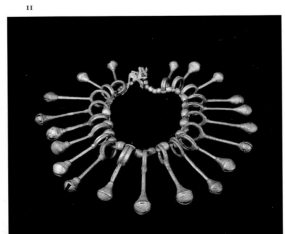
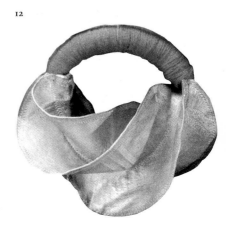

[B] Left: **a Kaka figure**
wood; height: 100 cm (39¹/₄ in)

Paternity figures such as this one are rarely found in African art. The aggressive expression of the mouth enhances the protective function of such a figure towards the child it carries and the tribal people who made it.

[C] Below: **an Abo figure**
wood; height: 47 cm (18¹/₂ in)

Made by an Abo artist from south Cameroon, this mysterious-looking figure has an encrusted patina which suggests it was revered with libations. Unfortunately, little is known about its function.

[A] Left: **a Mbembe-style drum**
wood; height: 93 cm (36⁵/₈ in); private collection

Drums were used by the Mbembe people and their neighbours to rally the men during times of emergency. The facial scarifications on this end-of-drum figure, probably carved by Igala artists, have been strongly influenced by the Mbembe style.

The Grassland of Cameroon

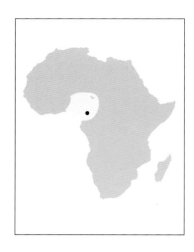

The grassland region, in south-west Cameroon, is a hilly and mountainous area covered by an equatorial forest in the south and a savannah in the north. Politically, the area is divided into numerous small independent kingdoms and chiefdoms, whose powers are counterbalanced by male and female societies. Since its colonization by the Germans in 1884, this entire region, in particular the Bamileke, Bamun and Tikar territories, has attracted the attention of Western scholars because of its artistic heritage. The Bamileke area is occupied by approximately 700,000 people. They are ruled by kings, whose funerals are organized by the powerful *Troh* society. The most artistically prominent kingdoms in this area are the Batcham, the Bafang and the Bafoussan. The sultanate of Bamun is ruled by a single, sacred king, known as the *Fon*, who resides in the capital Fumban. He is assisted by three officials and seven hereditary councillors to rule the 80,000 people. The Tikar area is occupied by around 250,000 people who speak different languages, but yet claim common ancestors. It is divided into two main geographical sub-groups – the first includes village-dwelling people who live in round huts covered by conical roofs and whose artistic output is largely associated with 19th-century bronze pipes. The second sub-group occupies the north-west highlands and they predominantly carve statues and masks.

1

The artistic production of the people living in the Grassland of Cameroon is closely associated with royal and societal ceremonies. Large figures, thrones and prestige paraphernalia are used by the king to assert his power. Masks are primarily worn during ceremonies related to the societies that structure each kingdom.

Each autonomous kingdom has developed a specific artistic style – for example, Bangwa figures [B] display an encrusted patina and filed teeth typical of the fashion of this kingdom, Northern Grassland kingdom masks and figures have a deeply grooved coiffure [C], and Bamun masks are often covered by a sheet of metal (6).

MASKS

In spite of the ethnic and stylistic variations found in the Grassland area, similar types of mask have been produced. They are usually worn during state ceremonies such as the funeral of an important dignitary, or during annual festivities. During these ceremonies, the leading dancer wears a *N'kang* mask which bears a false beard, a coiffure split in two

symmetrical parts and is often covered in royal paraphernalia such as cowrie shells and beads.

The *N'kang* mask is followed by other masks representing a woman, a man or an animal. The female mask (7), called *Ngain*, has a typical oval-shaped coiffure and embodies the idea of femininity and fertility. There are several types of male mask which can be carved with different coiffures such as two large buns, or an open-worked coiffure with spider motifs symbolizing the ancestral wisdom, or even with various carved faces appearing in the coiffure. The latter sometimes displayed two opposing faces. Another mask with a large, open-worked coiffure was specifically worn during the royal festivities held within the king's palace (8).

There are two Bamileke zoomorphic masks that have slightly different functions. One is an elephant mask (2) constructed of beaded cloth and is only used during ceremonies related to the *Kuosi*, an association that unites members of the royal family with members of the warrior class. The second mask is a helmet mask which represents a buffalo's head (9) and is thought to be the property of the king.

2   3   4

5   6   7   8   9

A cephalomorphic headdress, representing a face with two large vertical eyebrows over the eyes and a horizontal mouth **[D]**, is frequently found within the Bamileke region. It was incorrectly attributed to the Batcham people, but little is known about its use, although it is thought to be closely associated with the king.

Tikar people carve a headdress characterized by a flattened human head on top of a conical base (5). Since the Tikar people do not structure themselves around any form of society, it is thought that these headdresses, owned by each lineage, are only worn during funeral and harvest ceremonies.

STATUES

Statues representing ancestors are found all over the Bamun and Bamileke areas. They can be life size and can be incorporated into the backrest of an elaborate throne (see p. 15). These figures (13), representing the king's wives and his attendants, are usually stored in a secret part of the palace and are displayed when a foreign dignitary visits or during important ceremonies headed by the king.

Beaded figures (4) are among the better-known sculptures of the Grassland area. They come from the Bamileke area, but in particular from the Bamun sultanate. Carved with a wooden core and covered by a raffia cloth, the figure itself is hidden by a layer of multi-coloured beads.

Regal figures from the Bangwa kingdom have also achieved fame in the West. One of the more famous African sculptures is a statue of a dancing queen **[B]** carved in a dynamic, asymmetrical pose which is a rare feature in African art. It appears only during the funeral ceremonies of kings.

Smaller figures, called *Mu Po*, are used by Bamileke healers during curative rites (12) or for anti-witchcraft purposes and serve as representations of their patients. They are often characterized as women with rounded features, which is likely to suggest the general idea of fertility. This idea is also embodied in maternity figures.

The royal palaces were often decorated with open-worked panels bearing human figures and symbols which referred to royal heritage and power (1).

EVERYDAY OBJECTS

A large number of prestigious items of paraphernalia were produced within the Grassland area, including thrones, stools and tables decorated with small heads and figures (3), large bowls, carved horns for royal feasts, anthropomorphic terracotta and bronze pipes (11), ivory bracelets worn by royal princesses (10) and elaborate coiffures made from red feathers and worn during important ceremonies. Musical instruments such as anthropomorphic **[A]** and zoomorphic drums, as well as metal gongs, were played during royal and state ceremonies.

BIBLIOGRAPHY

GEBAUER, PAUL, *Art of Cameroon*, New York, 1979
HARTER, PIERRE, *Arts anciens du Cameroun*, Arnouville, 1986
JOSEPH, M. B., 'Dance Masks of the Tikar', *African Arts*, vol. VII, no. 3, spring 1974, pp. 46–52
NORTHERN, T., *The Sign of the Leopard, Beaded Art of Cameroon*, Storrs, 1975
NORTHERN, T., *The Art of Cameroon*, Washington, D.C., 1984

10

1   An architectural panel; *wood; height: 170 cm (67 in); Archives Monbrison, Paris*

2   An elephant mask; *cloth and beads; height: 75.5 cm (29³/4 in)*

3   Two stools and a table; *wood; height of the tallest: 44 cm (17¹/2 in)*

4   A beaded figure; *wood, vegetal fibres, cowrie shells and beads; height: 119 cm (47 in)*

5   A Tikar headdress; *wood; height: 65.1 cm (25⁵/8 in)*

6   A Bamun mask; *wood, hair and metal sheet; height: 45 cm (17³/4 in)*

7   A female *Ngain* mask; *wood; height: 36.2 cm (14¹/4 in)*

8   A mask with open-worked coiffure; *wood; height: 45.7 cm (18 in)*

9   A buffalo Bamileke mask; *wood; height: 40 cm (15³/4 in); Dr Michel Gaud, St Tropez*

10 A bracelet; *ivory; diameter: 10.5 cm (4³/8 in); private collection*

11 A pipe; *bronze; height: 22.5 cm (9 in)*

12 A small *Mu Po* figure; *wood; height: 28.5 cm (11³/8 in)*

13 A Bamileke seated figure; *wood; height: 78 cm (30³/4 in); private collection*

11   12   13

[A] Above, left: **an anthropomorphic drum used by the *Alaling* society in the Fontem area of the Bangwa kingdom**
wood; height: 66 cm (26 in); private collection

Although rare, this drum is typical of objects from the Grassland of Cameroon with its overall black patina, fierce expression and the absence of detail.

[B] Top right: **a Bangwa Queen figure**
wood; height: 82 cm (32^1/$_2$ in); provenance: collected in 1898 by G. Conrau

One of the most famous African sculptures, this figure achieved its notoriety through its dynamic pose which is uncharacteristically African. It represents a dancing queen who is wearing carved rather than applied jewelry.

[C] Above, right: **a Bamileke mask**
wood; height: 28 cm (11 in); private collection

The complex construction of this Bamileke mask illustrates the remarkable skill of its carver. This mask was used on, among other occasions, the death of a society member.

[D] Right: **a Batcham headdress**
wood; height: 96 cm (37^5/$_8$ in); private collection

The highly original treatment of the facial features on this headdress gives it a striking power. The rarity of such a mask is explained by its association with a specific Batcham king.

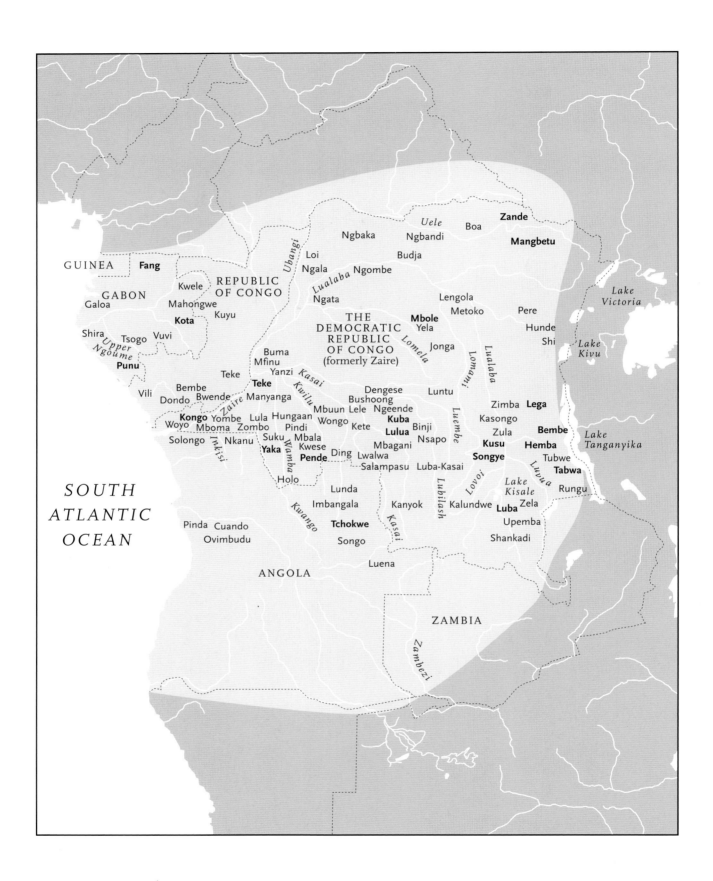

GUINEA

GABON

Fang

Galoa

Shira

Tsogo   Vuvi

Kwele

Mahongwe   Kuyu

Kota

Upper
Ngoume

Punu

Vili

Bembe

Dondo   Bwende

Manyanga

Woyo

Kongo

Yombe   Lula   Hungaan

Solongo   Mboma   Zombo   Pindi

Nkanu   Suku   Mbala

Yaka   Kwese

Pende   Ding

Holo

Pinda   Cuando

Ovimbudu

Lunda

Imbangala

Tchokwe

Songo

Luena

ANGOLA

REPUBLIC
OF CONGO

Buma

Mfinu

Teke

Yanzi

Teke

Loi

Ngala

Ngata

Ubangi

Lualaba   Ngombe

Ngbaka

Uele   Boa

Ngbandi

Budja

THE
DEMOCRATIC
REPUBLIC
OF CONGO
(formerly Zaire)

Kasai

Kwilu

Mbuun   Lele

Wongo   Kete

Dengese

Bushoong

Ngeende

Lomela

Kuba

Lengola

Metoko

Mbole

Yela

Jonga

Lomami

Zande

Mangbetu

Pere

Hunde

Shi

Lake
Victoria

Lake
Kivu

Lualaba

Lualaba   Lega

Zimba

Kasongo

Zula

Bembe

Luena

Luembe

Lubilash

Lovoi

Kalundwe

Luba

Upemba

Shankadi

Kanyok

Luba-Kasai

Salampasu

Lwalwa

Mbagani

Nsapo

Binji

Lulua

Kusu

Songye

Hemba

Lake
Kisale

Zela

Tubwe

Tabwa

Rungu

Luvua

Lake
Tanganyika

SOUTH
ATLANTIC
OCEAN

Inkisi

Wamba

Kwango

Kasai

Zambezi

ZAMBIA

IV

GABON
AND ZAIRE

PUNU
KOTA
FANG
KONGO
TEKE
MIDDLE LUALABA RIVER AREA
MANGBETU
MBOLE
LEGA
BEMBE
LUBA
HEMBA
TABWA
SONGYE
KUBA
PENDE
LULUA
YAKA
TCHOKWE

Punu

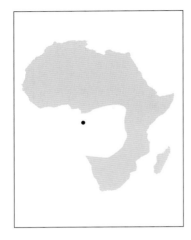

The Punu reside on the left bank of the Upper Ngoume River and belong to a group of tribes known as *Shira* which were originally part of the Luango kingdom of Angola. With the Eshira, the Lumbo, the Vili, the Galoa and the Vungu people, the Punu migrated northwards during the 18th century and settled where they are now. They live in independent villages divided into clans and families and social cohesion is ensured by a society, known as *Moukouji*, whose primary role is to subjugate harmful forest spirits. During ceremonies related to the society, small statues and masks appear which are often covered in white pigments, alluding to their anti-witchcraft functions.

MASKS

Punu masks are thought to represent ancestors' faces. They are worn during funerals and by a *Moukouji* initiate who stands on stilts. The masks have realistic, usually white, faces with protruding pursed lips, T-shaped noses, globular protruding eyes incised with a curve, high-domed foreheads and characteristic ridged high coiffures (5), which reflects the Punu women's style (15).

Some Punu masks have raised lozenge scarifications on the temples (2) which are thought to be associated either with a female ancestor, or with a southern sub-group of the Punu tribe. Black face masks [B] have exactly the same stylistic characteristics as the white masks, but they are believed to have a judiciary function.

Sub-groups of the Punu tribe carved their masks with stylistic variations – for example, the Njabi people of the Upper Lola River carved masks with a double coiffure and a square chin, while the Tsangui people, in the Republic of Congo, adorned their masks with linear face scarifications (3).

STATUES

Punu artists carved small statues (10), amulets and everyday objects (8) showing faces similar to those found on masks. It is thought they were used as prestige objects, during magical ceremonies, or were kept alongside the ancestral bones in a reliquary box.

The **Galoa** people settled in the lakes area, near the Atlantic shore, and carved rectangular masks bearing triangular motifs designed with pigments (1). These masks are worn during important ceremonies such as the death of a prominent chief or the birth of twins. Through the power and authority believed to be inherent in them, the bearer of the mask can regulate the social life of the Galoa villagers.

Lumbo artists carved figures influenced by Punu and Kongo styles. Typically, they include reliquary figures which served as guardians of ancestors' bones kept in baskets [A] and are decorated with pigments and have inset mirror eyes.

Living in a remote region of dense forest lying on the right bank of the Upper Ngoume River, the **Mitsogho** people make their living from agriculture and fishing. Each family lives independently and the social cohesion of the tribe is ensured by the *Bwiti* society. Initiation into this society involves the use of hallucinogenic plants and being told the meaning of sacred objects such as bust figures (11). These figures were usually stored in baskets, known as *Bumba Bwiti*, together with ancestor bones and other magical substances. Carved by certain initiates, these bust figures were alleged to have therapeutic powers and to act as reliquary guardians. They are characterized by an arched body framed by two diminutive arms with hands resting on the chest, while their enlarged

1 A Galoa mask; *wood, pigments and vegetal fibres; height: 33 cm (13 in)*

2 A Punu mask; *wood and pigments; height: 28 cm (11 in)*

3 A Tsangui mask; *wood; height: 33 cm (13 in)*

7   8   9   10   11   12

head shows an open mouth with eyes inset with copper. The entire statue is covered in red pigments.

Mitsogho masks (4), when not worn during funeral ceremonies, were kept at the back of the *Ebanza* house, where the men's cult met. They were covered in white pigments and were carved with an open mouth, a small triangular nose, and typical slanted eyes set under M-shaped brows.

The **Vuvi** live near the Mitsogho and carved masks which were stylistically influenced by their neighbours (6). They are flat, covered with white pigments, display a triangular chin, and are often more elongated than those of the Mitsogho, but like the Mitsogho, they were worn during funeral ceremonies.

The Vuvi cast metal bells with cephalomorphic handles, while their carvers decorated the *Ebanza* cult house with doors (13) and posts (9). They were covered with white pigments, leaving the raised geometric and figurative motifs plain.

The **Ambete** live on the frontier with Gabon and the Republic of Congo, and are related to the Kota population. They carved three types of sculpture: heads, busts and full figures with a hollowed back. The latter have short legs, an elongated columnar torso and a flattened face with a triangular chin, an open mouth showing teeth and a triangular nose, all resting under a ridged coiffure. They are thought to have a connection with the ancestor's cult – they were either used as reliquaries (7) or placed alongside ancestor bones in a basket [D].

Heads and busts were probably positioned on poles and placed in front of the chief's house. They may have had an apotropaic and emblematic purpose.

Living in the Republic of Congo, the **Kuyu** people are divided into two clans whose totemic animals are the snake and the panther. They achieve cohesion through a secret male society called *Ottote*. Kuyu artists carved light wood figures (12), known as *Okue*, who carry an emblematic animal on their heads. Very little is known about their function, but they are thought to be used during *Ottote* ceremonies. Kuyu carvers also produced wooden heads [C] with rounded features and complex or conical coiffures (14). These heads were inset with feathers and carried on top of long poles during ceremonies at the end of the *Ottote* initiation period.

BIBLIOGRAPHY

BENEZECH, ANNE-MARIE, *L'Art des Kouyou-Mbochi de la République Populaire du Congo*, Paris, 1989
FOURQUET, ANDRÉ, 'Chef d'oeuvre de l'Afrique: les masques Pounou', *L'Oeil*, no. 321, April 1982
GOLLNHOFER, O., P. SALLÉE and R. SILLANS, *Art et artisanat Tsogho*, Paris, 1975
NICKLIN, K., 'Kuyu Sculpture at the Powell-Cotton Museum', *African Arts*, XVII, I, 1983
PERROIS, LOUIS, 'Arts du Gabon, les arts plastiques du Bassin de l'Ogooué', *Arts d'Afrique Noire*, 1979
PERROIS, LOUIS, *Art Ancestral du Gabon dans les collections du Musée Barbier-Mueller*, Geneva, 1985

4   A Mitsogho mask;
    wood; height: 28 cm (11 in)

5   A Punu mask;
    *wood; height: 28 cm (11 in);
    Courtesy Entwistle Gallery, London*

6   A Vuvi mask;
    wood; height: 35 cm (13³/₄ in)

7   An Ambete reliquary figure; *wood,
    beads and snakes' vertebrae; height:
    70 cm (27¹/₂ in); private collection*

8   A Punu spoon; *wood; height: 15 cm
    (6 in); Archives Monbrison, Paris*

9   A Vuvi post; *wood; height: 149 cm
    (59 in); private collection*

10 A Punu figure; *wood; height: 59 cm
    (23¹/₄ in); Epstein Collection, London*

11 A Mitsogho bust figure; *wood and
    metal; height: 42.5 cm (16³/₄ in)*

12 A Kuyu figure; *wood; height: 93 cm
    (36⁵/₈ in); private collection*

13 A Vuvi door;
    wood; height: 147 cm (58 in)

14 A Kuyu head;
    *wood; height: 100 cm (39¹/₄ in);
    Dr Michel Gaud, St Tropez*

15 A photograph of two Punu women;
    c. 1880

13   14

15

[A] Left: **a Vuvi/Mitsogho reliquary figure in a basket**
wood, vegetal fibres, mirrors, bones;
height: 66 cm (26 in); private collection

Reliquaries are receptacles for ancestors' bones.
Baskets were often used for such purposes and
were guarded by reliquary figures as here. The
vivid features correspond to the statue's function.

[B] Below: **a black Punu mask**
wood; height: 30 cm (12 in); provenance: Vlaminck
Collection, Paris; private collection

The refined features and elaborate coiffure of
this Punu mask mirror the dress and adornment
of the tribal women. In contrast to the abstracted
features that are usually found on African masks,
Punu artists have achieved a high degree of
naturalism in their art.

[C] Above: **a Kuyu head**
wood; height: 65 cm (26¹/₂ in); provenance: A. Courtois, Paris; M. Rousseau, Paris;
P. Verité, Paris; private collection

The elaborate coiffure carved with recurring mouth motifs creates an
extraordinary effect enhanced by the insertion of feathers, which are now
missing. The wooden head was supported by a pole and paraded through
the village at the end of initiation ceremonies.

[D] Right: **an Ambete figure**
wood, cowrie shells; height: 79 cm (31 in); A. Courtois, Paris; C. Ratton, Paris;
M. Rousseau, Paris; R. Rasmussen, Paris; private collection

This is another example of a reliquary figure – the ancestor bones were
inserted into the back of the statue. A curious feature of the statue is the
contrast between the powerful, solid body and legs and the diminutive
and rather frail arms.

Kota

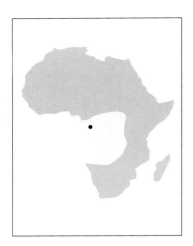

1 A Sango-style reliquary figure;
   wood and metal sheet;
   height: 29 cm (11 1/2 in)

2 A Kota/Kwele helmet mask;
   wood; height: 47.5 cm (19 in)

3 An Obamba-style reliquary figure;
   wood and metal sheet;
   height: 49.5 cm (19 1/2 in)

4 A Kwele mask;
   wood; height: 36 cm (14 in)

5 A reliquary basket;
   wood, metal, vegetal and bones;
   height: 49 cm (19 1/4 in)

6 A Mahongwe reliquary figure;
   wood and metal; height: 25 cm (10 in)

Living on the eastern side of Gabon, on the frontier with the Republic of Congo, the Kota people comprise a number of small tribes such as the Mahongwe, the Sango, the Obamba and the Shamaye, who all practise similar ceremonies. It is thought they migrated southwards during the 18th century and settled in the upper valley of the Ogooué River, in a forest environment. Their main resources come mostly from hunting and agriculture.

Historically, the Kota left their dead unburied in the forest, far from the village. Under the influence of neighbouring tribes, they then began to bury their dead. Chiefs were always buried, but often their bones (especially the skull) were later exhumed and placed with magical objects (shells, seeds, fruits) in a bark box or a basket called a *Bwete*, in which a carved figure was inserted. These reliquary baskets were kept for generations, but during the 20th century, when religious beliefs changed, they were abandoned or even destroyed. Between 1940 and 1964, a movement referred to as the 'culte des demoiselles' was responsible for the destruction of most of these traditional objects. This movement was based on the idea that mimicking Western values and lifestyles, as well as abandoning the old cults and idols, would help them to gain what they perceived as Western power.

The reliquary baskets, *Bwetes* (5), were kept in a special cupboard at the back of the chief's house. The *Bwetes* were the focus of offerings and prayers aimed at bringing good fortune to the clan. During boys' initiation ceremonies, several of these boxes – representing different families and clans – were grouped together, reinforcing the unity of the various components of the tribe. On top of the *Bwete* basket a figure (8) was placed with a highly stylized body in the shape of a lozenge, which supports an enlarged, stylized copper-plated head. The back of the head is usually undecorated, except for a geometrical shape. Some rare examples display two faces. Even rarer are a few figures displaying a stylized body on a four-footed stool (10). Their function is unknown.

MASKS

Kota masks are scarce. They are principally helmet masks and have simplified features such as tubular eyes, large incised brows and a crested coiffure. They are often covered with pigments and were used in initiation ceremonies [B, 2].

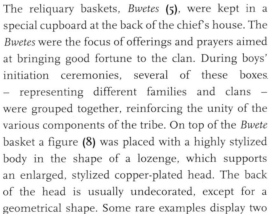

7   8   9   10

STATUES

Six different regional styles of Kota figure have been identified:

• Mahongwe (also called Ossyeba) figures have a truncated almond-shaped face covered with metal wires **[A, 6, 11]**.

• Shamaye figures have an almond-shaped face covered with metal wires and sheets and framed by two lateral flanges **(8)**.

• Obamba figures have an oval face partly covered with metal sheet, lateral flanges and a curved coiffure **[D, 3]**.

• Kota figures have an oval face, curved coiffure and lateral flanges ending in horizontal line **(9)**.

• Upper Ogooué figures have an oval face, sometimes a curved coiffure and S-shaped lateral flanges **(7)**.

• Sango figures have a small elongated head without any flanges or coiffure **(1)**.

EVERYDAY OBJECTS

The Kota adorned copper bells with figures probably used during ancestors' cult ceremonies. Moreover, they produced deeply grooved large anklets, intended as dowry objects, given their excessive weight, and throwing knives, evoking birds' heads **(12)**. The Kota also produced seats featuring four concave legs supporting a concave circular seat which was covered with copper sheets.

RELATED TRIBES

The **Kwele** tribe live on the northern frontier of the Republic of Congo, and have produced a famous type of mask called *Ekuk*. It displays a flat surface **[C, 4]** and often has a whitened heart-shaped face, a triangular nose and coffee-bean eyes. These masks were hung in their houses and rarely worn during dances related to the initiation ceremonies of the *Bwete* cult. Their function was to 'warm up' the village atmosphere in order to activate the beneficial forces resident in the *Bwete* box.

7   An Upper Ogooué-style reliquary figure;
wood and metal sheet;
height: 38.7 cm (15 in)

8   A Shamaye-style reliquary figure;
wood and copper;
height: 41.5 cm (16 3/8 in)

9   A Kota-style reliquary figure;
wood and metal sheet;
height: 40 cm (16 in)

10   A Kota figure on a stool;
wood and copper;
height: 63 cm (25 in)

11   Two Mahongwe reliquary figures;
wood and copper; height of the larger:
27 cm (11 in)

12   A Kota bird knife;
iron and copper; height: 34.5 cm
(13 1/2 in)

11

BIBLIOGRAPHY

CHAFFIN, A. AND F., *L'Art Kota, les figures de reliquaires*, Meudon, 1979

Culturas primitivas de la Guinea Ecuatorial, Museu Arqueológico, Barcelona, Spain, 1965/66

LEHUARD, RAOUL, 'Statuaire du Stanley Pool', *Arts d'Afrique Noire*, Supplement T.I., Villiers-le-Bel, 1974

PERROIS, LOUIS, 'L'Art Kota-Mahongwe', *Arts d'Afrique Noire*, no. 20, pp. 15–37, 1976

PERROIS, LOUIS, *Arts du Gabon, les arts plastiques du bassin de l'Ogooue*, Arnouville, 1979

PERROIS, LOUIS, *Art Ancestral du Gabon dans les collections du Musée Barbier-Mueller*, Geneva, 1985

SIROTO, LEON, *Masks and Social Organization among the Bakwele People of Western Equatorial Africa*, Ph.D. Dissertation, Columbia University, Ann Arbor

12

[A] Left: **a Mahongwe reliquary figure**
*wood and copper sheets; height: 43.2 cm
(17 in); provenance: O. Lecorneur,
Paris; R. Nash, London; M. and D.
Ginzberg, New York*

Mahongwe artists were able to
make highly stylized and abstract
representations of the human face
as in this guardian figure. The
figures were covered with copper
sheet and wires which gave them
a shiny appearance.

[B] Above: **a Kota helmet mask**
*wood; height: 61 cm (24 in); location:
private collection*

This mask, called *emboli*, may
have been used during initiation
ceremonies. It has been suggested
that the dotted motifs recall
a panther's skin, which is the
emblem of chiefs and warriors, but
unfortunately the meaning of the
decoration is no longer known.

[C] Below: **a Kwele mask**

wood; height: 36 cm (14 in); provenance: Aristide Courtois, Paris; Charles Ratton, Paris; Madeleine Rousseau, Paris; Charles Lapicque, Paris; location: private collection

With its three pairs of eyes, this mask would have been hung in houses rather than worn – an uncommon practise in black Africa. This piece has often been used to exemplify the black African artist's superb ability to stylize the human form.

[D] Right: **an Obamba-style Kota reliquary figure**

wood and copper sheets; height: 56 cm (22 in); provenance: brought back to France between 1905 and 1910 by Alfred Larsonneur; private collection

Made of different copper sheets, this Janus Kota figure gives a fearful impression. The metal used on the figure has been taken from imported European dishes. The face on the reverse side is concave.

Fang

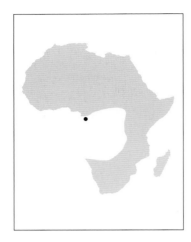

Fang tribespeople migrated from the north-west during the 18th and 19th centuries and are today scattered across southern Cameroon, Equatorial Guinea and Gabon. They are principally hunters, but also farm. Fang social structure is based on the clan, a group of individuals with a common ancestor, and on the family. They also maintain tribal cohesion through the *So* and *Ngil* societies. Each family possessed a *Byeri*, or reliquary box, in which the bones of famous ancestors were kept. The box was kept by the *Esa*, the eldest man in the family.

1

1   A choker;
    *copper; diameter: 23 cm (9 in);
    private collection*

2   A Mabea-style figure; *wood and
    metal; height: 65 cm (25⅝ in)*

3   A *Byeri* figure with a peg;
    wood; height: 46 cm (18 in)

4   A Mvai-style figure;
    *wood; height: 45 cm (17¾ in);
    Paul Guillaume, Paris;
    private collection*

5   A Betsi Nazman-style figure;
    *wood, metal and leather strap; height:
    49.2 cm (19⅜ in); Mendes-France
    Collection, Paris; M. Pinto Collection*

6   A Ngouma-style figure;
    *wood and metal; height:
    57.8 cm (22¾ in)*

7   A Ntoumou-style figure; *wood and
    copper; height: 55 cm (21⅝ in)*

The Fang's naturalistic treatment of human features and the distinctive oily patina was instantly appealing to collectors and artists alike. The great majority of Fang wood sculptures were related to the cult of the *Byeri*. The box was surmounted by a figure or a head who acted as a guardian [D] and it was kept in a dark corner of the house and had an apotropaic function. It was used during the *So* initiation ceremonies for young men – the guardian figure was removed from its box and paraded around. However, from the 1920s on, these customs were abandoned.

MASKS

One of the important Fang societies is the *So*. Its initiations took place every three years and were financed by a powerful chief. During these initiations, masks, *Byeri* statues and large clay figures (3 metres high) were presented to the candidates.

Important masks [B] are associated with the *Ngil* society. They are characterized by elongated features and a heart-shaped face and were thought to have judiciary powers and so were worn when sentences were handed down by the society. *Ngil* masks were outlawed in 1910 by the French colonials following a series of ritual murders. In around 1920, a new mask

was created, the *Ngontang* [C], which symbolizes a 'young white girl'. It is a helmet mask, generally coloured with white pigments, with either two or four faces and was used during funeral ceremonies and births. The symbolism of the many faces is not clear – they have been interpreted as a representation of the male–female, or as an allegory of death, life, birth and disease. Among the Fang people, the colour white is associated with the ancestors' world.

STATUES

Fang *Byeri* figures (i.e., the guardian statue that surmounts the *Byeri* box) are usually characterized as a seated male figure. He has bent legs, an elongated torso, hands which are usually joined holding a cup and a head with stylized features that may have feathers inset into it. The figure is carved with a stalk coming out under his buttocks, allowing it to be placed on top of the *Byeri* box (3). Some *Byeri* figures are in the shape of a human head (12), suggesting that these are earlier versions of the full figures when the *Byeri* box symbolically represented the ancestor's body.

The Fang occupy such a large geographical area that numerous sub-styles have emerged. There are,

2

3

4

5

6

7

8

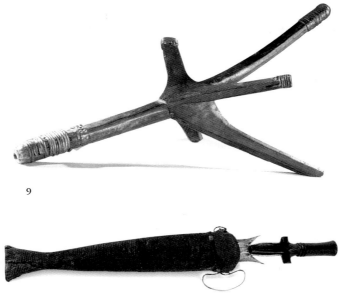

9

10   11

however, two main stylistic groups – the northern and the southern. In addition, each of these has three sub-styles.

Northern Fang figures usually have elongated features and are often adorned with copper strips. European trade had little impact in this area, so copper was rare and was considered to have magical powers.

• The Ngouma figures (6) have a protruding navel and mouth and, sometimes, a typical square beard. The figure usually holds an animal horn referred to as a *Nlakh*, which, in Byeri cult ceremonies, contains magical substances.

• The Mabea figures (2) display more realistic features. Their eyes are usually inset with metal.

• Ntoumou figures (7) have rounded features, especially the forehead and skull, and their eyes are inset with rounded copper sheets. They do not have any applied metal decoration, but do have a heavy oily black patina. Most of the Fang *Byeri* heads are thought to belong to this sub-style.

Southern Fang figures have shortened features and give an impression of robustness.

• Betsi Nazman figures (5) have an oily patina, a rounded massive head with a triangular nose, a well-defined coiffure and shortened arms with hands usually resting on the navel. Some *Byeri* heads have also been carved in this sub-style.

• Okak figures [A] have an oily dark patina, a rounded smooth forehead and a typical small triangular face with a prognathous jaw. The eyes are often inset with metal sheets.

• Mvai figures (4) have a typical coiffure divided into three crests.

EVERYDAY OBJECTS

The Fang adorn their everyday objects. They often use harps (11), seats (9) and spoons (8) during initiation ceremonies.

Fang daggers (10) have a typical flared handle and a sheath, often decorated with copper wire.

Metal chokers decorated with geometric designs (1) were worn by both men and women. The women's are distinguished by their heaviness and were only removed following their death.

BIBLIOGRAPHY

BINET, J., *Sociétés de danse chez les Fang*, Paris, 1972
Byeri Fang, Sculpture d'ancêtres en Afrique, Exh. Cat., Musée d'arts Africains, Océaniens, Amérindiens, Centre de la Vieille Charité, Marseille, France, 1992
Fang, Exh. Cat., Musée Dapper, Paris, 1992
FERNANDEZ, R. and J., 'Fang Reliquary Art: its Quantities and Qualities', *Cahiers d'Etudes Africaines*, 60, XV, 4, 1976, pp. 723–46
MCKESSON, JOHN, 'Réflexions sur l'évolution de la sculpture des reliquaires Fang', *Arts d'Afrique Noire*, 1987, no. 63, pp. 7–20 and no. 64, p. 28
OKAH, M., *Les Beti du sud-Cameroun et le rituel So*, Paris, 1965
PERROIS, LOUIS, *La Statuaire Fang (Gabon)*, Paris, 1973
PERROIS, LOUIS, 'Arts du Gabon, les Arts plastiques du bassin de l'Ogooue', *Arts d'Afrique Noire*, 1979
PERROIS, LOUIS, *Art Ancestral du Gabon dans les collections du Musée Barbier-Mueller*, Geneva, 1985
PERROIS, LOUIS, and SIERRA DELAGE, *L'Art Fang, Guinée Equatoriale*, Barcelona, 1991
TESSMANN, G., *Die Pangwe*, 2 vols, Berlin and New York, 1913 and 1972

12

8   A spoon;
    wood and beads;
    height: 14.6 cm (5³/₄ in)

9   A seat;
    wood and metal;
    height: 47 cm (18¹/₂ in)

10 A dagger;
    wood, iron and skin;
    length: 71 cm (28 in);
    private collection

11 A harp;
    wood, metal and skin;
    height: 58 cm (22³/₄ in)

12 A Fang head;
    wood and metal;
    height: 40 cm (15³/₄ in);
    Paul Guillaume, Paris

[A] Left: **an Okak-style Fang figure**
wood and metal; height: 58 cm (23 in);
Paul Guillaume collection, Paris;
private collection

The rich oily patina on this
powerful figure is the result of
continual libations of palm oil.
The eyes inlaid with copper
enhanced such a figure's
presence.

[B] Right: **a Fang *Ngil* mask**
wood, white pigment and vegetal
fibres; height: 63.5 cm (25 in);
provenance: René Whittofs,
Brussels; Schindler Collection

It would be hard to find a more
simplified version of the human
face, yet the power behind the
abstraction remains intact.
Not surprisingly, this mask had
a role in the judiciary activities
of the tribe.

[C] Right: **a Fang *Ngontang* mask**
wood; height: 45 cm (17⁵/₈ in); private
collection

The meaning of the four faces
carved on this helmet mask is
uncertain, although the white
pigments applied on the surface
may refer to the ancestor's world.
The mask appeared during birth and
death ceremonies.

[D] Far Right: **a Byeri figure on a bark box**
wood, metal and bark; height: 88 cm
(35 in); collected at the end of the 19th
century by the Mission of the Holy
Spirit Fathers; private collection

Southern Fang sculptures
commonly feature a compact
body. This figure is set on top of
a bark box containing the bones
of ancestors and acts as their
guardian.

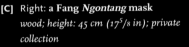

Kongo

During the 13th century, the Kongo people were led by their king, *Ne Kongo*, to a vast area across three frontiers, where they settled. Their kingdom expanded rapidly and, by the end of the 16th century, it engulfed the Atlantic Coast of present-day Gabon, the Republic of Congo, the Democratic Republic of Congo (formerly Zaire) and Angola. In 1482, Portuguese sailors arrived at the royal court in Mbanza Congo and eventually converted the Kongo king to Christianity in 1491. By the end of the 16th century, the kingdom was weakened and its demise came with the death of the last Kongo king, Dom Antonio II, in 1957. Today, the Kongo people number three million.

Originally, the Kongo kingdom comprised a number of separate tribes – the Vili, the Yombe, the Beembe, the Bwende and the Woyo, among others – which were led by a king, the *Ntotela*, who was elected by a council of governors. The *Ntotela* controlled the nominations for official positions at court and in the provinces. The main economic resources of the empire were ivory, copper and the slave trade.

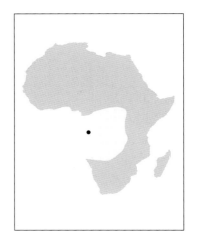

1. A Woyo mask; *wood and pigments; height: 44.5 cm (17¹/₂ in)*
2. A Woyo lid; *wood; diameter: 18 cm (7 in); private collection*
3. A Kongo cross; *bronze; height: 18 cm (7 in); E. Anspach Collection, New York*

Kongo artists carved numerous figures and objects generally characterized by naturalistic features, although minor stylistic tribal variations do occur.

MASKS

Masks found within the Kongo empire were worn during initiation ceremonies and the funerals of important personalities, but also appeared to be embodied with a judiciary power. Yombe masks **[A]** have realistic features such as carved ears and filed teeth, while Woyo masks **(1)** are often painted with a variety of pigments to form a geometric pattern.

STATUES

Nail fetishes **[C]**, called *Nkondi*, were revered throughout the Kongo kingdom. They are 'carriers' for a variety of magical objects called *Nkissi* which can be bags, roots or leaves and are spectacularly carried on the head or abdomen of the *Nkondi* figure. The *Nkissi* are manipulated by their owner or by a specialist, known as the *Nganga*, in order to please the different spirits and forces who are believed to regulate the world. In order to 'activate' these forces and provoke

the *Nkondi*, the *Nganga* insults it, sings or creates an explosion in front of it, or may even hammer a blade or a nail into its body. Some *Nkondi* represent an anthropomorphic spirit holding a spear, ready to strike and punish a person or a spirit responsible for a curse. Other *Nkondi* figures characterize a woman carrying a baby – embodying a gentler power than the male figure – or a dog, called *Koso*, who mediates between the living and the dead **(14)**.

EVERYDAY OBJECTS

Wooden bells **(15)**, known as *Dibu*, were used for activating the *Nkissi*, but were also attached to a breed of Kongo hunting dogs that did not bark. The *Dibu* are circular in shape and are generally carved with geometric motifs and occasionally with a human face.

Ivory was carved to make prestige objects, such as fly-whisks, depicting a chief seated on a throne, holding the sacred root, called *Munkwiza*, which bestows supernatural powers **(11)**. Cane tops with kneeling female figures, suggesting the idea of submission, were also popular.

4 5 6 7 8

9 10 11 12 13

Under the influence of the Christian missionaries, Kongo blacksmiths cast bronze crucifixes which integrated a European image with an African style (3).

RELATED TRIBES
Within the Kongo kingdom, a number of tribal styles evolved.

• Stretching across the coasts of Gabon and the Democratic Republic of Congo (formerly Zaire), the **Vili**, also called Loango, are famous for their artistic diversity. Vili artists carved figures with naturalistic features, often carrying mirrors, *Nkissi* or nails **[C, 8]**.

• The **Beembe** reside within the territory of the Republic of Congo. Their artists carve small figures, thought to represent their ancestors, which have typical geometric abdominal scarifications. There are two sub-styles – the 'western style' includes figures with a columnar torso and flat shoulders, while the 'eastern style' is more realistic and includes numerous representations of hunters (4).

• Occupying regions across the Democratic Republic of Congo (formerly Zaire) and the northern bank of the Zaire River, **Bwemde** artists carved figures artistically informed by the style of their north-western neighbours, the Beembe. However, they did place an emphasis on large shoulders, numerous body scarifications and the statues often have a complex, asymmetrical coiffure swept to the side (7).

• On the shore of the Atlantic Ocean, the **Woyo** and **Kakongo** territories lie between the Democratic Republic of Congo (formerly Zaire) and the Republic of Congo. Their artists carved wooden lids with high-relief objects or figures illustrating proverbs (2). Their statues, often adorned with *Nkissi*, have a triangular-shaped jaw and enlarged eyes.

• The **Dondo/Kamba** occupy the frontier between the Republic of Congo and the Democratic Republic of Congo (formerly Zaire). Their figures can be identified by their elongated features and by their lozenge scarifications on the temples or forehead (9).

• **Zombo** artists work from Angola and are stylistically influenced by the Yaka, their eastern neighbours. Although they are politically part of the Kongo kingdom, their artistic output is examined in the Yaka chapter (pp. 184–87).

• Living on the right bank of the Zaire River, **Manyanga** artists are famous for their elongated nail fetishes with a typical lozenge scarification set on the temples (5).

• The 300,000 **Yombe** people are artistically prolific. Their maternity figures **[B]**, nail and mirror fetishes have typical shoulder scarifications and a high, pointed or rounded coiffure incised with geometric motifs (12). Mirror and nail fetishes have an aggressive expression characterized by an open mouth usually showing filed teeth.

• The Angolan **Solongo** style is characterized by statues with an oval face (6). Solongo artists are predominantly known for their *Nkondi* nail fetishes, but from the 1850s they carved ivory tusks to sell to Europeans (13). They are often adorned with a frieze of indigenous people engaged in everyday activities.

• The **Mboma** people settled on the left bank of the Zaire River and produced soft-stone grave figures known as *Mintadi* (10). It is thought that these figures were carved after 1825, when the wealth of the Mboma increased dramatically following the ban on slave trading imposed by the English in the neighbouring Ngoyo region.

BIBLIOGRAPHY
Astonishment and Power, Exh. Cat., National Museum of African Art, Washington, D.C., 1993
CORNET, JOSEPH, *Pictographies Woyo*, Milan, 1980
The Four Moments of the Sun: Kongo Art in Two Worlds, Exh. Cat. National Gallery of Art, Washington, D.C., 1981
HABI BUGANZA, MULINDA, *La Société Woyo, Structures Sociales et religieuses*, Brussels, 1985–86
LEHUARD, RAOUL, *Les Phemba du Mayombe*, Arnouville, 1976
LEHUARD, RAOUL, 'Art Bakongo, Les centres de Style', *Arts d'Afrique Noire*, 1989
LEHUARD, RAOUL, *Art Bakongo: Les Masques*, Arnouville, 1993
MACGAFFEY, W., *Religion and Society in Central Africa: The Ba-Kongo of Lower Zaire*, Chicago and London, 1986
Pierre Sculptées du Bas Zaire, Exh. Cat., Institut des Musées Nationaux, Kinshasa, 1978
SODERBERG, B., 'Les Figures d'ancêtres chez les Babembe', *Arts d'Afrique Noire*, 13–14, 1975, pp. 14–37
THIEL, J. F., and H. HELF, *Christiche Kunst in Afrika*, Berlin, 1984
VERLY, R., *Les Mintadi: La Statuaire de pierre du Bas-Congo (Bamboma-Mussorungo), Zaire*, Louvain-la-Neuve, 1955
WIDMAN, RAGNAR, 'Le Culte du Nuiombo des Bwende', *Arts d'Afrique Noire*, 2, 1972, pp. 13–41

14

15

4 A Beembe figure;
   wood; height: 19.5 cm (7³/₄ in)

5 A Manyanga figure;
   wood; height: 44 cm (17¹/₄ in)

6 A Solongo figure;
   wood; height: 58 cm (23 in)

7 A Bwemde figure;
   wood; height: 39 cm (15¹/₂ in)

8 A Vili figure;
   wood; height: 33.5 cm (13¹/₄ in)

9 A Dondo figure; *wood; height: 25 cm (9³/₄ in); Dr Michel Gaud, St Tropez*

10 Three Mboma grave figures; *stone; height of the tallest: 37 cm (14¹/₂ in)*

11 A Kongo fly-whisk;
   ivory; height: 28 cm (11 in)

12 A Yombe maternity figure; *wood and glass eyes; height: 21 cm (8¹/₄ in); private collection*

13 A Solongo carved tusk;
   ivory; height: 71.1 cm (28 in)

14 A *Koso* dog fetish figure;
   wood; length: 35 cm (13⁵/₈ in)

15 A Kongo bell;
   wood; height: 22 cm (8³/₄ in)

[A] Below: **a Yombe mask**
wood; height: 32 cm (12¹/₂ in)

Yombe masks, and more generally Kongo
masks, were worn during important communal
ceremonies. The fearful aspect of the present
example, expressed by its mouth, is in keeping
with the judiciary role of the mask.

[B] Right: **a Yombe maternity figure**
wood; height: 36 cm (14¹/₄ in)

This superb example of Kongo sculpture shows
the emphasis given to the head with its filed teeth
and to the characteristic back scarifications. This
female figure embodied a gentler spiritual force
than the threatening male figures and was used
for fertility rituals.

[C] Right: **a Kongo nail fetish figure**
wood, metal and fetish material;
height: 49.5 cm (19¹/₂ in)

In order to stimulate and obtain
a spirit's protection, Kongo people
hammer nails into its wooden
representation and shout at it.
The contrast between the
delicate treatment of the face
and the roughness of the nails is
particularly striking in this figure.

Teke

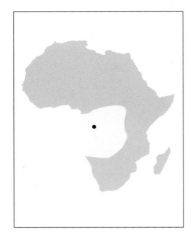

The Teke people settled in a territory lying across the Republic of Congo, the Democratic Republic of Congo (formerly Zaire) and Gabon. During the 15th century, they were integrated into the Tio kingdom, but attained independence in the 17th century. Today, they live in villages led by a clan elder known as the *Mfumu*, who answers to a hereditary land-chief called *Mfumu na tzee*. Their economy is mainly based on farming maize, millet and tobacco, but the Teke are also skilled fishermen and traders. They believe in a supreme God, *Nzambi*, whose favours can be obtained with the help of tutelary spirits.

1   A Teke necklace;
    bronze; diameter: 38 cm (15 in)

2   A *Matomba* Teke figure;
    wood and magical substances;
    height: 44 cm (17¼ in)

3   A *Mutinu Bmamba* Teke figure;
    wood; height: 49 cm (19¼ in)

4   A Teke figure;
    wood; height: 24 cm (9³/₈ in)

5   A *Ikwak* Buma figure;
    wood; height: 29 cm (11½ in);
    Dr Michel Gaud, St Tropez

Teke artists carved figures predominantly surrounded by fetish material, known as *Bilongo* **[B]**. These figures protect and assist the Teke and, if a fetish figure successfully demonstrates its power, its owner may detach its *Bilongo*, break it into several pieces and insert fragments into other figures. He will then sell the new figures to neighbouring families, leaving the original statue with an emaciated body **(4)**.

MASKS

Teke masks are worn by members of the *Kidumu* society either during the funerals of chiefs, or weddings, or important meetings. They are circular in shape, are bisected by a horizontal stripe and are decorated with geometric designs filled with white, black and red pigments **(9)**. Numerous copies of these masks have been made for the Western market.

1

STATUES

The figures carved by Teke artists are characterized by slightly bent legs, a columnar torso framed by arms bent at right angles and an enlarged head with typical linear facial scarifications and a trapezoidal beard. Their height varies from between 15 and 80 cm and these figures can be used either for an individual or for the entire community **[D]**.

The shape of the magical substances attached to the statue's body often indicates its function. For example, figures known as *Mutinu Bmamba* **(3)** are covered by a cylindrical-shaped *Bilongo* and are used to assist women during pregnancy. *Matomba* figures **(2)** carry a barrel-shaped *Bilongo* and have apotropaic functions. *Butti* figures **(6)** representing ancestors have magical substances attached to them, including the finger nails or hair of a dead person, and are kept in special huts. With their shiny patina, they are generally adorned with a metal necklace attesting the importance of the deceased ancestor.

Other figures known as *Iteo* symbolize the spirit of happiness and are characterized by a cone of whitish earth surrounding their bodies **(10)** and are kept within families. During hunting or trading expeditions, the Teke sometimes wear a small anthropomorphic fetish.

Brass figures and maternity figures **[A]** are rare.

EVERYDAY OBJECTS

Teke artists carved neckrests, adzes and fly-whisks adorned with human figures which were used as prestige objects by chiefs and the nobility. They also cast bronze neckrests with geometric decorations **(1)**.

RELATED TRIBES

Like the Teke people, the **Mfinu** were part of the 15th-century Tio kingdom, but gained their independence during the 19th century. Mfinu villages are grouped in small clusters led by an elected chief, known as the *Mbe*. The Mfinu economy is based on hunting, fishing and farming manioc, maize and sugar cane. The corpus of Mfinu objects is similar to the Teke, but differs stylistically. Their figures are often covered with red pigments and their heads are larger and rounder than Teke statues. However, unlike the Teke, they do not have beards, but a characteristic backward-sloping bun coiffure **(8)**. The neckrests are abstract and are thought to represent a highly stylized human figure **[C]**.

The **Yanzi** people, too, once belonged to the Tio kingdom. Today, they number 40,000 and are divided into three castes: the ruling clan, the plebeians and the slaves. As part of the ruling class, chiefs are assisted by the nobility and receive tributes from the

2

3   4   5   6   7   8

Hungana and the Mbala people who live on their territory. Their economy is largely based on trade, but they also hunt and farm.

Yanzi carvers produced Teke-like figures, but their figures are usually more elongated and angular, are made of a light-coloured wood and have a head carved with a sharp angular chin and vertical facial scarifications **(7)**.

During the 16th century, the **Buma** people gained their independence from the Tio kingdom and expanded their influence over the area. Later they fragmented and their number diminished. Today, there are only 15,000 of them and they are organized into small chiefdoms and make their livelihood from hunting and fishing.

Buma artists carved figures known as *Ikwak*, which represent ancestors, or a clan's guardian **(5)**. They also produced hunting fetishes which they kept in baskets. Stylistically, Buma figures are similar to Teke ones, except that their arms form a lozenge on the body and their cheek scarifications run diagonally.

BIBLIOGRAPHY

BIEBUYCK, D., *The Art of Zaire*, Vol. I, Los Angeles, 1985
DE BEAUCORPS, R., *Les Bayanzi du Bas-Kwilu*, Louvain-la-Neuve, 1933
DE PLEIN, G., *Les Structures d'authorité des Bayanzi*, Paris, 1974
Dieu, Idoles et Sorcellerie dans la région du Kwango/Bas-Kwilu, Bandundu, 1968
DUPRÉ, MARIE-CLAUDE, 'A Propos d'un masque Teke de la collection Barbier-Mueller', *Connaissance des Arts Tribaux-Bulletin du Musée Barbier-Mueller*, no. 2, 1979
LEHUARD, R., *Statuaire du Stanley Pool*, Villers-le-Bel, 1974
LEHUARD, R., 'Arts Bateke', *Arts d'Afrique Noire*, 1996
LEMA, G., *La Statuaire dans la société Teke*, Louvain-la-Neuve, 1978
ROULIN, H., *Les Bateke, Bahumbu, etc.*, Province Leo. District Kwilu, Territoire Banningville, 7, 1936

6   A *Butti* Teke figure; wood; height: 34 cm (13 1/4 in)

7   A Yanzi figure; wood; height: 19.7 cm (7 3/4 in)

8   A Mfinu figure; wood; height: 41 cm (16 1/8 in)

9   A Teke mask; wood; height: 35 cm (13 3/4 in); private collection

10   A *Iteo* Teke figure; wood; height: 32 cm (12 5/8 in)

10

9

[A] Left: **a Teke maternity figure**
wood; height: 35 cm (13³/₄ in);
private collection

A carving of considerable
refinement, this Teke maternity
statue has powerful features,
but curiously does not display
the typical facial scarifications
known to have characterized
the corpus of Teke sculpture.

[B] Right, above: **a Teke figure**
wood and copper nails; height:
41.2 cm (16¹/₄ in); private collection

This figure is typical of Teke
artistic output with its arms set
at right angles and its enlarged
head with vertical scarifications.
The abdomen is hollowed so that
the *bilongo* (magical substances),
which gives the figure its power,
can be placed in it. This was
probably removed when Robert
Lehuard took the statue from the
village of M'pila in 1924.

[C] Right, below: **a Mfinu neckrest**
wood and copper nails;
height: 14.8 cm (5⁷/₈ in)

The base and foot of this
anthropomorphic Mfinu neckrest
is a highly stylized carved human
form. The copper nails inset
in the base attest to the wealth
of its owner.

[D] Far right: **a Teke figure**
wood, magical substances and
copper nails; height: 29.5 cm
(11⁵/₈ in); private collection

Seated figures are rare among
the corpus of Teke statues;
this one has kept its *bilongo*.
The asymmetrical coiffure is
reminiscent of Bembe artistic
traditions and demonstrates
that one tribe's artistic output
influenced that of another in
this part of Africa.

Middle Lualaba River Area

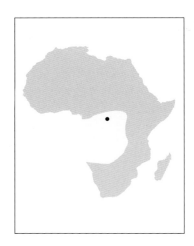

This chapter focuses on a number of different tribes living in an area between the Ubangi and the Middle Lualaba (Zaire) Rivers. Owing to their close contact with one another, their culture and their stylistic output overlaps. The major tribe in the region is the Ngbaka who inhabit the high plains on the left bank of the Ubangi River. They migrated from the north and settled in their present location – an area controlled by the Ngbandi – in the 1920s. Several political chiefs and family patriarchs rule over the 400,000 people. Ngbaka men farm the land which is their main food resource.

1

1 A Budja headdress;
   wood; height: 50 cm (19³/₄ in);
   private collection

2 A Ngala figure; *wood; height: 27 cm*
   (10¹/₂ in); private collection

3 A Ngala figure;
   wood; height: 43 cm (17 in)

4 A Ngbandi figure;
   wood; height: 53.3 cm (21 in)

5 A Ngbaka figure;
   wood; height: 100 cm (39¹/₂ in)

6 A Ngombe stool;
   wood and copper nails;
   height: 70 cm (27¹/₂ in)

7 A Ngombe neckrest;
   wood; height: 18 cm (7 in);
   private collection

8 A Ngata knife;
   iron, wood and copper nails;
   length: 47 cm (18¹/₅ in);
   Van Opstal Collection, Belgium

Large figures and masks feature in the **Ngbaka** initiation ceremonies. They can be recognized stylistically by the scarification line on their foreheads and between the ears and eyes.

MASKS

Ngbaka masks, known as *Dagara*, are worn during and after ceremonies associated with the *Gaza* initiation and the circumcision of young men. They are oval and often have a concave face with an elongated triangular nose with vertical scarification on the forehead (9).

STATUES

Ngbaka figures (5) are often found in pairs and can be as tall as 100 cm. They are believed to represent their two primordial ancestors, *Seto* and *Nabo*, and are placed on altars in houses where they fulfil a protective role. Similarly, small anthropomorphic or zoomorphic fetishes covered in red pigment are believed to bring good fortune.

Spikes surmounted by a stylized head were used to mark off sacred ground.

EVERYDAY OBJECTS

Ngbaka dignitaries smoked anthropomorphic pipes, often covered with copper wire, and cephalomorphic harps were carved to accompany singers **[C]**.

RELATED TRIBES

Located on the left bank of the Ubangi River, the 120,000 **Ngbandi** have lived in this area of forest and plains since the 17th century, mainly surviving from hunting and farming. The artistic style of their statues and masks, which are related to the Ngbaka, is recognizable through their elongated features, a line of vertical scarification on the forehead and sometimes on the sides, and a pointed chin. Figures representing the *Ngbirondo* spirit (4) are kept in special huts where libations are poured over them. They can also be placed at the entrance to a village for apotropaic reasons. Small ivory amulets were carved and worn by hunters, while masks (10) with a concave face and protruding mouth were worn for society ceremonies. Prestige objects such as harps, cups and pipes were also made.

2

3

4

5

The 120,000 **Ngombe** live scattered along the banks of the Lualaba River. They migrated during the 18th century from Lake Victoria and finally settled in their present site during the 19th century. They are led by a chief, accredited by the warrior's society, *Elombe*, who rules over the village and family chiefs. The artistic style of their carvings relates to the Ngbaka and Ngbandi, but is less refined and more geometric. Small standing figures, thought to be hunting fetishes and masks (11), which were possibly worn during *Mani* society ceremonies, are held in a number of collections. Stools inlaid with copper nails (6) and neckrests (7) were used as prestige objects.

Living on the banks of the Lualaba River, the 110,000 **Ngala** share the same political structure as the Ngbaka: a regional chief, village head and family elders collectively control the tribe's social and political life. As traders, they regulate the traffic on the Lualaba River. Their statues (2, 3), carved to represent primordial ancestors, are closely related to the Ngbandi in style, but have a rounded head and horizontal chin. Ngala vegetal-fibre shields are decorated with geometric motifs (12).

9   10   11

The 5,000 **Ngata** (also called Ntomba) live on the banks of the Lualaba River. Historically, the Ngata had an appointed leader, but today they live in autonomous farming communities. Ngata artists carved large anthropomorphic coffins **[A]**, called *Bongange*, covered with painted decoration. They were commissioned by important dignitaries and contained the exhumed bones of the deceased. Later, the sarcophagus and the bones were consigned to the river. Ngata blacksmiths cast iron knives which are used for executions (8).

The 50,000 **Budja** live principally from farming on the right bank of the Lualaba River. Budja artistic output is limited to a number of crested headdresses (1) and face masks characterized by abstract features and worn during agrarian festivities.

Little is known about the **Loi** tribe other than that they live between the Lower Ubangi and the Lualaba Rivers. Loi artists produced zoomorphic slit drums **[B]** which were beaten to transmit information across the forest and were played to evoke *Nyambondoli*, the spirit of war.

6

7

8

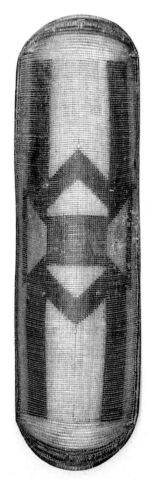

12

BIBLIOGRAPHY
BURSSENS, H., *Les Peuplades de l'entre Congo-Ubangi (Ngbandi, Ngbaka, Mbandj, Ngombe, et gens d'eau)*, London, 1958
BURSSENS, H., 'Sculptures in Ngbandi Style', *Kongo-Overzee*, Antwerp, 1958
HULSTAERT, G., 'Les Cerceuils anthropomorphes', *Aequatoria*, Coquilhatville, XXIII (4), pp. 121–29
LAURENTY, J. S., *Les Tambours à fente de l'afrique centrale*, Tervuren, 1968
MAES, J., *Les Ngbaka*, Kinshasa, 1984
TANGHE, B., 'Ngombe et Nyi in Ubangi', *Aequatoria II*, Coquilhatville, 1939
THOMAS, J., *Les Ngbaka de la Lobaye, etc.*, Paris, 1963
WEEKS, J., 'Anthropological Notes on the Bangala of the Upper Congo River', *Journal of the Anthropological Institute*, 39, London, 1909
WOLFE, A., *In the Ngombe Tradition*, Chicago, 1961

9 A Ngbaka mask; wood; height: 38 cm (15 in)

10 A Ngbandi mask; wood; height: 44 cm (17 1/2 in); private collection

11 A Ngombe mask; wood and pigments; height: 30 cm (11 5/8 in)

12 A Ngala shield; vegetal fibres; height: 110 cm (43 1/4 in)

[A] Right: **a Ngata sarcophagus**
wood, height: 255 cm (100 in); private collection

The power and dignity of the owner is conveyed in this life-size sarcophagus.
The detail of the face, including the inset teeth, is in sharp contrast to the rather
simply carved body.

[B] Below: **a Loi zoomorphic slit drum**
wood; length: 251 cm (99 in)

The elegance of this drum belies the power of the sound created when it
is beaten. It was predominantly played to rally the tribe in times of emergency.

[C] Far right: **a Ngbaka anthropomorphic harp**
wood and skin; height: 81.5 cm (32¹/₈ in)

This extraordinary harp shows the imaginative skills of African artists.
Anthropomorphic harps are also found among the Mangbetu, yet the
treatment of the face on this example is typical of the Ngbaka people.

Mangbetu

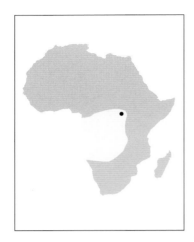

When the Mangbetu tribespeople left the Sudan in the middle of the 18th century, they re-located their kingdom in the north-eastern part of the Democratic Republic of Congo (formerly Zaire). Their social structure is not dissimilar to other Zairean forest-based tribes where the men hunt and fish, while the women are left to cultivate the manioc fields. Ultimate authority over the 40,000 Mangbetu rests with a king whose sons govern the various provinces, which are divided into districts and villages. The Mangbetu tribe have been at war with their neighbours, the Zande, since the 18th century.

1

1 A Mangbetu stool; *wood; height: 22.9 cm (9 in); collected in Zaire in 1926*

2 A Mangbetu drum; *wood and copper nails; length: 70 cm (27¹/₂ in)*

3 A Mangbetu anthropomorphic pipe; *wood; height: 9.5 cm (3³/₄ in)*

4 A Mangbetu anthropomorphic honey container; *wood; height: 51.5 cm (20¹/₄ in)*

5 A Mangbetu knife; *ivory and metal; height: 37 cm (14¹/₂ in)*

6 Two Mangbetu knives; *wood, metal; height of the taller: 28 cm (11 in)*

2

Mangbetu art, famous for its realism, is a court art – objects were displayed in the king's presence as prestige paraphernalia. When Western contact was first made with the Mangbetu at the turn of the century, white explorers were struck by the quality of the architectural and artistic skills of their tribal craftsmen. The king's great hall was alleged to have been 50 metres wide.

Most of the pieces produced by the Mangbetu were made of light wood and date from around the turn of the century, so it has been suggested that the arrival of colonials stimulated the production of artistic objects and a European influence was felt on Mangbetu art.

The physical characteristics of the Mangbetu people are reflected in highly realistic-looking statues. For example, the Mangbetu tradition of compressing an infant's head within raffia in order to obtain an elongated skull is apparent in the statues. This elongation was further enhanced by a high coiffure finishing in a cup-like finial.

Besides wood carvings, the Mangbetu also worked in ivory, the trade of which was controlled by the king.

MASKS

Mangbetu art was produced exclusively to enhance the prestige of the court and therefore it is not surprising that masks, which are usually associated with initiation ceremonies, were not produced.

STATUES

Mangbetu artists have sculpted a series of ancestor figures **[C]**, male and female, about 60 cm high, in light wood with linear scarifications on the body.

EVERYDAY OBJECTS

The Mangbetu adorned many prestige objects with figures, i.e., anthropomorphic harps **[D]**, where the body of the instrument issues arms and legs, although sometimes only a head is carved at the end of the shaft (7). They have carved small anthropomorphic pipes (3), knives (6) and honey containers (4) and have produced a dark grey ceramic adorned with a head **[B]**.

They are also famous for a type of knife with an open-worked curved blade (5), circular stools (1) with an open-work foot and semi-circular drums (2), sometimes inset with copper nails.

3

4

5

6

7

ZANDE

Like the Mangbetu, their neighbours, the Zande (also called Azande) migrated during the 18th century from Sudan to the northern part of the Democratic Republic of Congo (formerly Zaire), settling on the banks of the Uele River. They occupy a region of savannah and forest and in common with the Mangbetu, Zande men hunt and fish while the women tend the fields. In political terms, this tribe of 750,000 people is ruled by a king with succession to the throne passing to his eldest son, while the younger ones govern the kingdom's provinces. This political structure is counterbalanced by the Mani secret society, created at the turn of the century.

Zande art displays great similarities to Mangbetu art, although it is not a court art – rather it is related to the Mani secret society.

MASKS

Zande masks (8) are very rare. They are rounded and flattened, have an opened mouth showing teeth and carved-out rounded eyes. They were used by the Mani society, and for funeral ceremonies.

STATUES

The Zande have produced two main types of statue. The largest, measuring from 30 to 50 cm, are probably ancestor figures (11). Made of light-coloured wood with darker details, they have stylized features and elongated faces. The other type (13), called *Yanda*, is smaller (10 to 20 cm) and typically they represent human or animal figures which are sometimes adorned with metal rings or necklaces. They have an apotropaic function and were also used in divination ceremonies [A]. *Yanda* statues are characterized by simplified features. Often an enlarged head will have a face divided in two planes under a rounded coiffure.

EVERYDAY OBJECTS

The Zande are famous for decorating an array of everyday objects with figures. Musical instruments such as harps or *Sanzas* (finger pianos) (12) are often anthropomorphic in character and design. Neckrests/boxes [F] and knives were also carved. A typical knife, for example, has an elongated blade with grooved geometric decoration (9).

RELATED TRIBE

The **Boa** tribe comprises 200,000 savannah-dwelling people living in the northern part of the Democratic Republic of Congo (formerly Zaire). Each village is headed by a chief from the most prestigious clan. The Boa are mainly farmers and are in frequent contact with the Mangbetu and the Zande. The Boa are known principally for their masks [E], believed to be used in war-related ceremonies, particularly to enhance a warrior's courage or to celebrate victories. They have set-apart ears and are covered with white and black pigments. The Boa also carve statues with apotropaic functions (10). The Mangbetu influence can be seen in the Boa tendency to decorate knives, ceramics, harps and seats with human heads.

BIBLIOGRAPHY

BURSSENS, H., *Yanda-Beelden en mani-sekte bij de Azande*, Tervuren, 1962
FELIX, M., *100 Peoples of Zaire and their Sculpture*, Brussels, 1987
Mangbetu, Art de cour Africain des collections privées belges, Exh. Cat., KreditBank Gallery, Brussels, 1992
Trésors d'Afrique, Exh. Cat., Musée Royal de l'Afrique Centrale, Tervuren, 1995

8

9

7 A Mangbetu cephalomorphic harp; *wood and hide; length: 61.5 cm (24 in)*

8 A Zande mask; *wood and pigments; height: 37 cm (14¹/₂ in)*

9 A Zande knife; *iron; length: 52 cm (20¹/₂ in); Van Opstal Collection, Belgium*

10 A Boa figure; *wood; height: 57.1 cm (22¹/₂ in)*

11 A pair of Zande figures; *wood; height of the larger: 36 cm (14 in)*

12 Three Zande finger pianos, *Sanzas; wood; height of the largest: 28.9 cm (11¹/₄ in)*

13 A Zande *Yanda* figure; *wood with metal rings; height: 18.4 cm (7 in)*

10

11

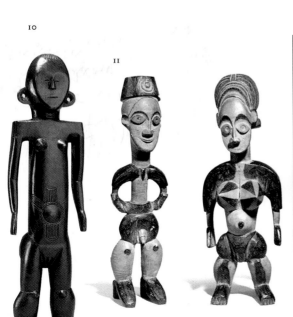

12

13

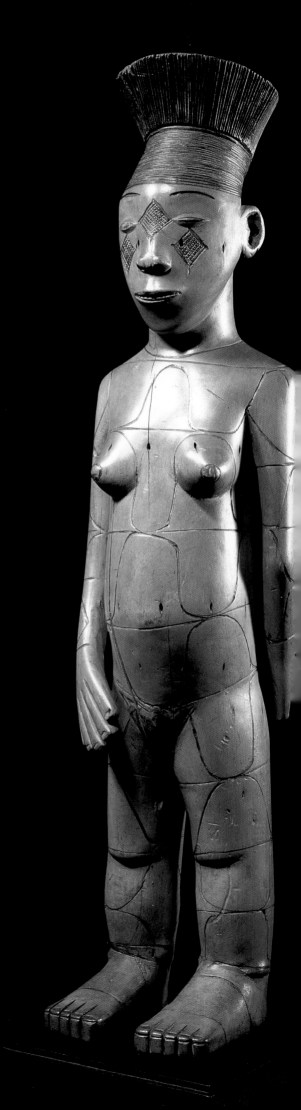

Far left, above: **a Zande figure**
wood and shells; height: 30 cm (11⁵/₈ in);
private collection

Zande figures are extremely rare. This
figure was probably used during divination
ceremonies; the inlaid eyes focus the
attention of the viewer on the face and
reinforce the idea of clairvoyance.

Far left, below: **a Mangbetu**
cephalomorphic ceramic
clay; height: 28 cm (11 in)

This ceramic is another example of
Mangbetu court art in which the human
head is used to adorn an everyday object.
Note how similar this figure's coiffure is to
that of the female figure in illustration C.

Left: **a Mangbetu ancestor figure**
wood; height: 77 cm (30³/₈ in); provenance:
brought back to France by a member of the
'Croisière Noire', a French expedition to
Africa in 1932; J. J. Dutko Archives, Paris

The elongated skull enhanced by an
up-swept coiffure and the overall body
scarifications of this figure are typical
characteristics of the Mangbetu people.
This figure is one of a small group,
numbering less than ten, which date
from the turn of the century.

Above, right: **a Mangbetu**
anthropomorphic harp
wood, snake skin, metal nails and strings;
length: 63 cm (24³/₄ in); provenance: collected
in 1908 by A. Demuenynck, Artillery
Lieutenant (1876–1942)

Music was very important to the Mangbetu
people – they used drums and string
instruments such as this harp during
court ceremonies. This is a typical
example of a 'prestige object'.

[E] Below, left: **a Boa mask**
wood; height: 26.5 cm (10¹/₂ in); provenance: Alberto Magnelli, Paris

Black and white pigments are usually applied to masks used in war-related
ceremonies. The large, set-apart ears and the inset teeth are typical features
on these masks.

[F] Below, right: **a Zande neckrest/box**
wood and bark; length: 43.2 cm (17 in); provenance: collected by M. Heyman,
Ubangi River, Uele Bama area in 1885; Mr and Mrs Kuhn, Los Angeles

Zande nobility used this type of neckrest which also acts as a box when the
lid is removed. The two heads on either side serve to protect the sleeper.

Mbole

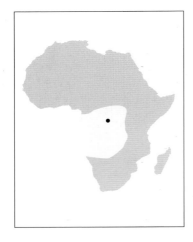

The 150,000 Mbole people (also called Bambole) live on the left bank of the Zaire River, in the heart of the Democratic Republic of Congo (formerly Zaire). They migrated from north of the Lualaba River during the 18th century. Politically each Mbole village is autonomous, headed by a chief chosen from the elders of each family. The tribe's main resources are manioc and rice, which the women farm, and hunting which the men do. Three main societies give the Mbole social structure cohesion: the *Ekanga* is reserved for the healers, the *Otuku* for wives of dignitaries and the powerful *Lilwa* society oversees every aspect of social and religious life, from circumcision to death, through different initiation ceremonies. The head of the *Lilwa* society, known as *Isoya*, is so important that he is buried in a tree and his village hut is kept empty.

The Mbole are known principally for their figures which tend to be characterized by their geometric features, elongated emaciated bodies, enlarged heads with heart-shaped faces, protruding mouths and crown-like coiffures. Yellow and white pigments are usually applied to the whole statue.

MASKS

Mbole masks [B] are rare and are only worn during circumcision ceremonies or for the funeral of a *Lilwa* society dignitary. They are oval-shaped and covered with pigments suggesting a human face.

STATUES

The Mbole are renown for their figures [D], which represent a human figure, with hands on its thighs, legs slightly bent, hunched shoulders and an enlarged head with a typical heart-shaped face. They can be large (up to 100 cm high), but are mostly medium sized. They are thought to represent hanged men, *Ofika*, who have been judged guilty by the *Lilwa* society or sacrificed in order to allow a dignitary to obtain the *Isoya* grade of the *Lilwa* society. The figure is made by a sculptor belonging to the same family as the dead man and is supposed to contain his soul.

They are kept in special huts in the forest and are shown during initiation ceremonies and can be used to inhibit criminal behaviour among new initiates. These statues are carried out of the forest on stretchers and are talked about during meetings, although women and children are not allowed to see them. Other figures, carved in a similar style, are believed to represent ancestors and are characterized by flattened shoulders and horizontal feet (4).

RELATED TRIBES

The 50,000 **Yela** people live to the south of the Mbole in independent villages grouped in *Bonanga*. Each is headed by the leading member of the oldest family. They produce small figures (5) which are strongly influenced by the Mbole, but have rounder heads. Like some Mbole figures, they are presumed to represent a criminal hanged by the *Lilwa* society. The Yela also carve circular masks with oblique scarifications on their cheeks (2). They are worn by members of the diviners society, the *Ekanga*, and stored in baskets in the meeting hut.

Also living on the left bank of the Zaire River are the **Lengola** people, who number 100,000. The

1 A Metoko mask;
   *wood; height: 24 cm (9¹/2 in);
   private collection*

2 A Yela mask;
   *wood; height: 25 cm (10 in);
   private collection*

3 A Lengola mask;
   *wood; height: 32 cm (12¹/2 in);
   private collection*

4 A Mbole ancestor figure;
   wood; height: 23 cm (9 in)

5 A Yela figure;
   wood; height: 40 cm (15³/4 in)

6 A Jonga figure;
   *wood; height: 59 cm (23¹/4 in);
   private collection*

1

2

3

4   5   6   7

Butoka society regulates their social, political and economic activities, and they make their living from elephant hunting and banana farming. They produce large statues **[A]**, called *Butoka*, which are made from six pieces of wood and have apotropaic functions and ensure social stability. These figures are used during initiation into the *Butoka* society. Monoxylous figures **(7)** are related to circumcision ceremonies. Masks **(3)** are rare and are stylistically informed by those of the Lega tribe.

The 15,000 **Metoko** people live surrounded on three sides by the Lengola. They are also regulated by the *Bukota* society and are divided into six clans. Living in deep forests, hunting is their main source of food. The figures produced by the Metoko are large, have either very angular or abstract features, and are often covered with painted or incised dots **(8–10)**. They are used at the beginning of the circumcision ceremonies. Metoko masks are covered with paint

across the cheeks and the forehead **(1)** and are worn during funerals of *Butoka* society members.

The 15,000 **Jonga** people settled south of the Mbole in a forest. They farm and hunt. There is little information about their artistic output. Jonga carvings were produced from a light wood and tend to be covered in red and black pigments and it is thought they represent ancestors and were employed during healing ceremonies **[C, 6]**.

BIBLIOGRAPHY
BIEBUYCK, D., 'Sculpture from the Eastern Zaire Forest Regions', *African Arts* 9 (2), Los Angeles, 1976
BIEBUYCK, D., 'Sculpture from the Eastern Zaire Forest Regions: Mbole, Yela and Pere', *African Arts*, 10 (1), Los Angeles, 1976
BIEBUYCK, D., 'Sculpture from the Eastern Zaire Forest Regions: Lengola, Metoko and Komo', *African Arts*, 10 (2), Los Angeles, 1976
JACK, J., 'De wa Lengola', *Congo*, 2, Brussels, 1939

7 A Lengola monoxylous figure;
   wood; height: 55 cm (22 in);
   E. Anspach Collection, New York

8 A Metoko abstract figure;
   wood; height: 54 cm (21¹/₄ in)

9 A Metoko figure;
   wood; height: 81.3 cm (32 in)

10 A Metoko figure;
   wood; height: 38 cm (15 in)

8   9

10

[A] Left: **a Lengola figure**
wood; height: 194 cm (76 in); private collection

Lengola figures display the same pigments as
Mbole figures. Their role was either to ensure
social stability or to represent the spirits during
the circumcision ceremonies of Lengola boys.

[B] Above: **a Mbole mask**
wood; height: 56 cm (22 in); private collection

This mask is a typical example of Mbole
artistic output. Highly abstract features and
the use of white, yellow and black pigments
are also found on Mbole figures.

[C] Below: **a Jonga figure**
wood and pigments; height:
48 cm (18⁷/8 in); private collection

Less than ten Jonga figures are
known to exist. They all display
a columnar torso and an enlarged
head, characteristically separated
by pigments of different colours.
Unfortunately, no information is
available concerning their function.

[D] Right: **a Mbole figure**
wood; height: 58.5 cm (23 in);
private collection

Mbole figures represent hanged
people. They were carried on
stretchers to the initiation camps
where they served as social
regulators. On this example, the
stretchers are part of the figure and
the curves of the legs and the arms
bring a dynamism to an otherwise
static sculpture.

Lega

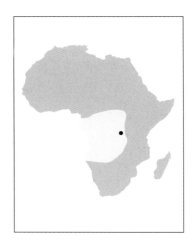

After their exodus from Uganda in the 17th century, the Lega tribespeople eventually settled on the west bank of the Lualaba River in the Democratic Republic of Congo (formerly Zaire). Known also as the Warega, the 200,000 people who constitute the Lega tribe live in autonomous villages, collectively situated at the summit of a hill surrounded by a palisade. The position of chief, referred to as the *Kindi*, is held by the oldest member of the clan who must also hold the highest grade within the *Bwami* society. The function of the *Bwami*, which is open to both men and women, is to regulate the social and political life of the Lega. Progression through the seven male and four female grades is made possible by the giving of presents and the participation in initiations. Division of labour is gender based and akin to the economic patterns of other tribes living in a forest environment: men hunt and clear new land and women cultivate manioc.

I

1 A Janus figure;
   ivory; height: 14 cm (5¹/₂ in)

2 A figure;
   wood; height: 31.1 cm (12¹/₄ in)

3 A figure with a raised arm;
   wood; height: 21 cm (8¹/₄ in);
   private collection

4 A figure;
   ivory; height: 15 cm (6 in);
   Van Opstal Collection, Belgium

5 A figure;
   ivory; height: 13.3 cm (5¹/₄ in)

6 A face mask;
   wood; height: 19 cm (7¹/₂ in);
   private collection

7 A *Lukwakongo* miniature mask;
   wood and vegetal fibres; height:
   17.5 cm (6³/₄ in)

Lega art is exclusively focused on and associated with the *Bwami* society. Each object has a precise role and function within their ceremonies and rituals and is used only by the initiated. These artefacts are numerous and are created from a variety of materials, particularly wood, ivory, bone and elephant hide (8).

MASKS

Two major types of mask figure in Lega ceremonies: the first is a face mask (6), used during initiation ceremonies, which typically has a heart-shaped face with globular coffee-bean eyes, a linear nose and a diminutive mouth usually located in a pointed chin. White pigments are applied to the mask. The second, called *Lukwakongo*, is a mask worn on the arm (7), but it shares the same characteristics as the face masks, except it is smaller and is worn on an initiate's body to indicate his or her rank within the *Bwami* society.

Both types of mask are exhibited on fences during initiation ceremonies. There is also a particular type of ivory mask, called *Lukungu* (9), which is used exclusively by the highest graded of the *Bwami* society (i.e. the *Kindi*).

STATUES

Lega statuettes, called *Maginga*, are rarely taller than 35 cm and were carved principally out of wood (2) and ivory [D, 1, 4, 5]. Employed during initiation ceremonies, they had a mnemonic function insofar as they assisted in the telling of 'ancestor stories' or in the depiction of proverbs. For example, a statuette with several heads [A] would be used in ceremonies to evoke the elephant hunter who sees the animal in front of him while, at the same time, he calls for help behind him. A figure with a raised arm (3) indicates a man acting as a judge. Numerous zoomorphic

2

3

4

5

6   7   8   9

figures, carved either in wood or ivory, in the shape of frogs **(13)**, dogs or snakes, are related to every grade of the *Bwami* society. Finally, ivory heads **[B]** displaying a pointed chin are found among the Lega as well as their neighbour, the Zimba. These are used only during initiation ceremonies of the highest *Bwami* grade. Prior to an initiation ceremony, these statuettes are removed from their storage bags or baskets and are rubbed in oil which accounts for their characteristic patina.

EVERYDAY OBJECTS
Wood, bone and ivory spoons **(11, 12)** decorated with faces, men's bodies or animals were used principally during initiation ceremonies.

RELATED TRIBES
The 50,000 **Zimba** people live between the Lualaba River and Lake Kivu. They migrated from the north and were influenced politically and artistically by the Lega. During the 18th century, they came under Luba domination. They are headed by a chief, referred to as the *Fumu*, who governs an area inhabited by several families. The *Bwami* and *Nsobi* societies counterbalance his power. Historically, they were traders, but nowadays their main economic resource is agriculture.

Stylistically, Zimba statues or ivory heads **[C]** can be recognized by their concave heart-shaped face, upward-pointing coiffure and by the extensive use of the dotted circle motif. They were used during initiation ceremonies. Their masks bear a resemblance to the Lega *Bwami* style. 'Prestige objects' such as staffs and stools demonstrate Luba influence.

The **Pere** and **Nande** tribes, who are mostly farmers, live between the Lualaba River and the Lake Idi Amin. Each is headed by a king, known as the *Mooni*, who acts as the keeper of the regalia displayed during coronation ceremonies. The Pere and Nande tribes are renowned for their wooden trumpets designed in abstract shapes and for their figures decorated with geometric motifs which were part of the royal treasure, the *Makinga*. Nande figures are often carved out of a reddish wood while the Pere are known for their figures used in hunting and fertility rites **[E]**.

Living along the shore of Lake Kivu, between the Democratic Republic of Congo (formerly Zaire) and Rwanda, the **Shi** and **Hunde** tribes are headed by chiefs, known as *Mwami*, who are assisted by three village elders. Their main economic resources are farming and cattle breeding. Although the Shi and Hunde did not produce much art, they are known for their masks **(10)**, influenced by the Lega, which were stored in baskets and used exclusively during *Bwami* initiation ceremonies. They are characterized by a rough aspect and display a domed forehead. Hunde masks are usually triangular in shape and have a reddish patina.

10

8   A face mask; *elephant hide; height: 25 cm (9³/₄ in); private collection*

9   A *Lukungu* mask; *ivory; height: 10 cm (4 in)*

10   A Shi mask; *wood; height: 30 cm (11⁵/₈ in); private collection*

11   A spoon; *ivory; length: 13 cm (5 in); private collection*

12   A spoon; *ivory; length: 14 cm (5⁵/₈ in); Van Opstal Collection, Belgium*

13   A frog; *ivory; length: 8.7 cm (3¹/₂ in); private collection*

BIBLIOGRAPHY
BERGMANS, L., *Les Wonande*, I and II, Brussels, 1970
BIEKBUYCK, D., *Lega Culture*, Berkeley and London, 1973
BIEKBUYCK, D., Sculpture from the Eastern Zaire Forest Regions', *African Art*, 9 (2), 1976
BIEKBUYCK, D., *The Arts of Zaire*, vol. II, Berkeley and London, 1986
BIEKBUYCK, D., *La Sculpture des Lega*, Galerie Leloup, Paris, 1994
DE KESEL, P., 'Der Kunst die Bashi', *Nieuw Afrika*, Antwerp, 1939
FELIX, M., *100 Peoples of Zaire and their Sculpture*, Brussels, 1987
MAES, J., 'Zimba', *Man*, London, 1911
VIAENE, L., 'La Vie domestique des Bahunde', *Kongo-Overzee*, 17, Antwerp, 1951

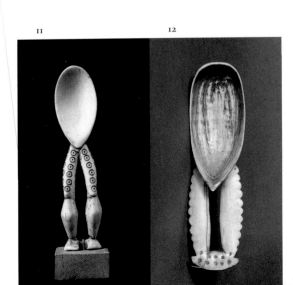

11   12

13

[A] Left: **a figure with several heads**
*wood and feathers; height: 32 cm
(12¹/₂ in); provenance: J. Vanderstraete,
Brussels; Dr Michel Gaud, St Tropez*

This fetish figure was used during
initiation ceremonies related to the
Bwami secret society. It represents
the elephant hunter who calls for
help on seeing an elephant.

[B] Above: **a Lega ivory head**
height: 18.2 cm (7³/₈ in)

Such ivory heads were removed
from their boxes only for initiation
ceremonies of the highest grade
of the *Bwami* society. This one has
inset shell eyes and a shiny patina
from numerous oil libations.

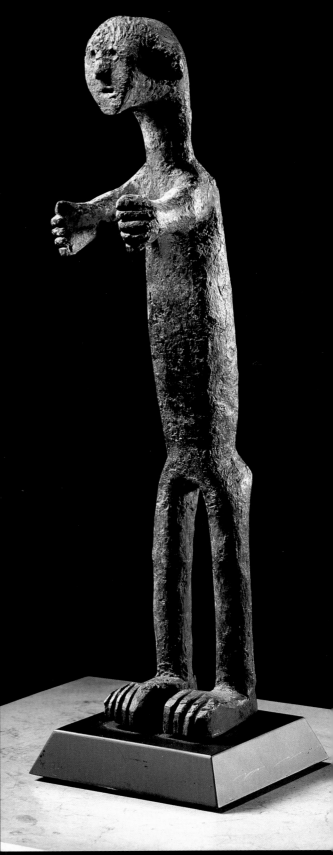

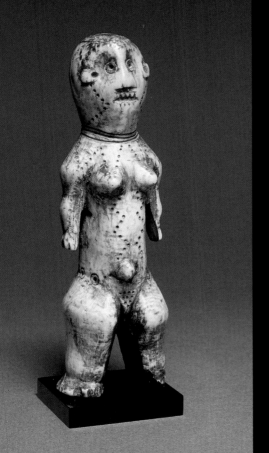

[C] Above: **a Zimba ivory head**
height: 11 cm (4³/₈ in); provenance:
J. Blanckaert, Belgium; Leloup archives

Zimba heads are characterized by
an upward-looking face and are
decorated with a pointed circle.
Here the shell inset at the top of the
head reinforces its magical power.

[D] Left: **an ivory figure**
height: 15.5 cm (6¹/₈ in)

The incised decoration on the body
of this small ivory figure is typical
of Lega figures used during *Bwami*
ceremonies.

[E] Right: **a Pere figure**
wood; height: 41 cm (16 in); provenance:
Jacques Hautelet, Belgium; private
collection

Small Pere figures are extremely rare
and were used for fertility rituals. The
thick patina displayed on the present
example suggests numerous libations
of blood and chicken eggs.

Bembe

The Bembe people migrated from Congo in the 18th century and resettled in the eastern part of the Democratic Republic of Congo (formerly Zaire), near its border with Tanzania and Burundi. A semi-nomadic people, who often settled in forest environments, the Bembe tended to abandon their small villages as the soil became less fertile. The women cultivated the crops and the men hunted and fished.

The 'cult of the ancestor' is an important part of Bembe social and spiritual life. It recalls the history of their respective clans through worship at private and public shrines, which appear in the form of miniature huts, enclosures or tables and are situated either somewhere in the village or on an ancestor's grave. Often food is offered or animals are sacrificed on the shrine and, sometimes, magical stones, horns or blades are left *in situ*. In exchange, the ancestor protects the tribe and increases fecundity. Ancestor figures are rare and appear only in the south-western Bembe territory. They are roughly made and are usually a cylindrical bust surmounted by a large head. Bembe artistic production is, in fact, limited mostly to masks.

Secret societies play an important role in Bembe life. The *Bwami* society, inspired by the neighbouring Lega tribe, exists in a simplified form, but male members are still circumcised and small statuettes and magical objects are handled. The *Elanda* society exercises social control over the tribe and is accessible to men only through a substantial initial subscription paid to the head of the society. The *Alunga* male society is in charge of public dances and is responsible for conducting the ceremonies which precede a hunt.

1 A Bembe face mask;
wood and feathers;
height: 27 cm (10³/4 in)

2 A Basumba figure;
wood; height: 34 cm (13³/8 in);
E. Anspach Collection, New York

3 An eastern-style figure;
wood; height: 69.5 cm (27³/8 in)

4 A Bassikassingo *Misi* figure;
wood; height: 39 cm (15¹/4 in)

5 A Bassikassingo *Misi* figure;
wood; height: 54 cm (21¹/4 in)

6 A Bassikassingo figure;
wood; height: 57.2 cm (22¹/2 in)

The settlement history of the area helps to clarify the variety of artistic styles in this region. Recent studies have attributed many so-called Bembe figures to pre-Bembe hunting groups who migrated from the shores of the Lualaba River prior to the Bembe's arrival in the 18th century. This migration, along with the increasing slave trade controlled by Islamic merchants in the 19th century, forced the indigenous population to scatter and merge with neighbouring tribes such as the eastern Lega, the Hemba, the Boyo and the Holoholo. Thus, when the first scholars arrived in the 20th century they assumed that all the art discovered was attributable to the Bembe.

The pre-Bembe clans, for example, the Bassikassingo, the Basilugezi and the Bahese, were hunters and worshipped their heroic ancestors through cults and figures.

MASKS

There are two types of Bembe mask. The most famous [C], the *Echawokaba*, belongs to the *Alunga* secret society. It is a Janus face helmet mask with two enlarged concave orbits and a central tubular pupil. It represents a spirit from the forest and is kept in a sacred grotto. It is taken out during initiation ceremonies related to the *Alunga* society and is worn during ceremonies related to hunting and the cult of the ancestor. In *Bwami* society circumcision ceremonies, flat face masks (1, 10), showing typically enlarged concave orbits and bulging coffee-bean eyes, are worn.

7   8   9

STATUES

Bembe people never produce large statues, but small statuettes are made in the western part of their territory. These statuettes are used as healing implements and during exorcism ceremonies. It is thought that certain female statuettes may have been used as fecundity figures – they stand on short legs with their hands resting on their abdomen. Characteristically, their heads are enlarged and have almond eyes framing a triangular nose (7).

EVERYDAY OBJECTS

Bembe objects are rarely adorned with figures, but a number of fly-whisks and canes have been found decorated with human figures (9) and faces. Some wooden knives were also made.

RELATED TRIBES

The **Boyo** live in the eastern Democratic Republic of Congo (formerly Zaire), between the Luluaba River and Lake Tanganyika. Their population is declining and their culture disintegrating due to the expansion of the Bembe over the past 60 years into their territories. The Boyo tribe is composed of six clans – the Baniabemba, the Bahutse, the Basonga, the Basumba, the Bahaya and the Bassikassingo. Unlike the Bembe, the Boyo tribe is largely matrilineal (the son belongs to the mother's lineage), but in some instances within the royal family it is patrilineal. Names are inherited from the father (except for the royal family), but the succession to chiefdom within a clan and part of the material inheritance passes through the mother's family.

Among the six clans that form the Boyo tribe, three are known predominantly for their male and female ancestor figures. These figures, which represent several generations of ancestors, are kept in small huts and displayed in series of five to seven, and have either a beneficial or a malefic influence on everyday life, so they require a cult and associated offerings. Within each series, the artistic style varies enormously, reflecting the different periods of manufacture. The art produced by these clans does, however, display common stylistic characteristics – enlarged heads, short legs and a rich encrusted patina. The series is placed in a row, with the tallest figure representing the primordial ancestor, and at the front, a guardian figure, the *Otambilia*. Sometimes bust figures were also left outside the ancestor shrine, either in the village or in the forest.

• The **Bahutse** produced ancestor figures, standing or seated on a typical circular base. Their hands are set away from their abdomen and they have a characteristic head with a horizontal low forehead (8).

• The **Basumba** produced two series of ancestor figures. The first includes figures that stand on enlarged feet, have an angular elongated face and are between 30 and 80 cm in height (2). The second series includes figures which have typical enlarged spherical heads and numerous scarifications on their bodies **[A]**. This second series has traditionally been attributed to the Boyo in general rather than the Basumba clan specifically.

• The **Bassikassingo-Basilugezi** live on Bembe territory unlike the other Boyo clans. They produce ancestor figures called *Misi* (4, 5), which characteristically display bearded triangular faces, triangular noses, globular enlarged eyes and have a cap-like coiffure. The coiffure represents an insignia worn by the highest graded member of the *Bwami* society (6). Face masks **[B]** and helmet masks are very rare and their function is unknown.

Some other clans, connected with the pre-Bembe hunting groups, who presently live on the shore of Lake Tanganyika, also produced ancestor figures. They stand on enlarged, set-apart feet and have a typical cap-like swept-backward grooved coiffure (3).

7   A Bembe figure;
    wood; height: 30 cm (11³/₄ in);
    private collection

8   A Bahutse figure;
    wood; height: 54.6 cm (21¹/₂ in)

9   A Bembe cane;
    wood; height of the figure:
    23 cm (9 in); private collection

10 A Bembe face mask;
    wood; height: 45.7 cm (18 in)

BIBLIOGRAPHY
BIEBUYCK, D., *Statuary from the Pre-Bembe Hunters*, Tervuren, 1981
DE KUN, N., 'L'Art Boyo', *Africa-Tervuren* 26 (1979), pp. 29–44
FELIX, M., *100 Peoples of Zaire and their Sculpture*, Brussels, 1987
HOSTEN, *Les Babuye*, Kabambare, 1955
ZANGRIE, LUC, 'Les Institutions, la religion et l'art des Babuye (groupe Basumba)', *L'Ethnographie* 45 (1947–50), pp. 54–80

10

[A] Below: **a Basumba ancestor figure**
wood; height: 86.4 cm (34 in);
provenance: Mrs Franyo Schindler
Collection, New York

A magnificent example of a Basumba
figure, it has abdominal scarifications
associated with a particular ancestor.
The sculpture's circular motifs are
echoed in the eyes, the wrist bangles
and the numerous scarifications.

[B] Right: **a Bassikassingo face mask**
wood; height: 25 cm (10 in)

Bassikassingo masks are rare. The
bi-coloured pigments can still be
seen on this one. Its characteristic
indented beard is also found on
figures made by the same tribe.

[C] Far right: **a Bembe** *Echawokaba*
helmet mask
wood; height: 49.4 cm (19 1/2 in)

This highly abstract mask represents
the face of a spirit of the forest with
two enlarged orbits and horns. It
was worn during the *Alunga* society
ceremonies.

Luba

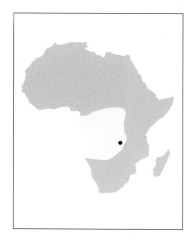

The Luba empire was founded in 1585 in the Upemba depression by King Kongolo. His nephew and successor, Kalala Ilunga, rapidly expanded the kingdom to encompass all the territories on the upper left bank of the Lualaba River. At its peak, about one million people, living in several tribes, were paying tribute to the Luba king. At the end of the 19th century, with the advance of the Ovimbudu people from Angola and the raids of the East African Muslim slavers, the empire weakened and, in fact, collapsed when the Belgian colonials took control.

With the assistance of a court of notables, called *Bamfumus*, the king, known as the *Mulopwe*, reigned over his subjects through clan kings called *Balopwe*. These clan kings could symbolically become the *Mulopwe*'s son which created client states throughout the empire. A secret society, *Bambudye*, kept the memory of the Luba empire alive and permeated throughout Luba territory, bonding the diverse populations together. The Luba empire economy was complex – it was based on a tribute system and the redistribution of resources from agriculture, fishing, hunting and mining. The production of salt and iron was under the king's control.

1

1 A Luba mask;
wood; height: 46.5 cm (18¼ in);
J. Mestach, Brussels; W. Rubin,
New York

2 An Upemba Mitwaba-style
Mboko figure;
wood and beads; height: 33 cm (13 in)

3 A Luba *Bankishi* fetish figure;
wood, fur and feathers; height: 36 cm
(14 in); Spik Collection, Zurich

4 A Luba *Katatora* divination
implement;
wood; height: 10 cm (4 in)

5 An Upemba Mwanza-style *Mboko*
figure; *wood and beads; height:*
47 cm (18½ in)

6 A Shankadi classical-style bellows;
wood; length: 65.5 cm (25¾ in)

7 A Shankadi Sungu
anthropomorphic stool;
wood; height: 43 cm (16¾ in)

8 A Zela figure;
wood; height: 55 cm (21½ in)

9 A Luba neckrest by the 'Master
of the Cascade'; *wood; height:*
15 cm (6 in); private collection

10 A Zula stool;
wood, height: 34.3 cm (13½ in)

11 A Kanyok figure;
wood; height: 20 cm (7⅞ in)

Luba artists created numerous objects that related to the royal court activities. Prestige objects were usually decorated with female figures which are omnipresent in Luba art. As the Luba empire extends over a vast territory, there are a large number of stylistic variations. Luba artists showed their social status through the adze they carry on their shoulders.

MASKS
Luba masks are rare and are primarily found in the eastern Luba kingdoms. Some masks (1) are very similar to the *Kifwebe* mask used by the Songye, although they display more rounded features. Zoomorphic masks (12) are extremely rare and their use is unclear.

STATUES
Luba artists carved kneeling or standing female figures, called *Mboko*, who were usually holding cups for divination purposes (5). Standing figures, believed to represent forest spirits or ancestors, are rare and are usually covered by an oily patina that comes from continuous libations [A]. Smaller figures, called *Bankishi* (3), and friction devices known as *Katatora* (4) are used by Luba diviners.

EVERYDAY OBJECTS
The Luba produced numerous prestige objects – anthropomorphic caryatid stools, bowstands (18), spears, staffs [B], pipes (13), axes and neckrests which were adorned with figures and were used during official ceremonies or to display wealth. Ivory apotropaic amulets were worn by some Luba people. Luba terracotta vessels are often decorated with incised geometric motifs (14).

RELATED TRIBES
The 100,000 Luba people, who live in the **Upemba depression** and along the Upper Lualaba River, form the nucleus of the Luba empire. This area is in a strategic position since from this point the river traffic can be controlled.

There are three regional artistic styles. The first, known as Mwanza (5), emanates from the north, along the Lualaba River, and is characterized by figures carved from a light blackened wood which have enlarged rounded heads. The second style, called Upemba [C], is centred around the homonymous lake, and includes figures carved from a light brown wood. Characteristically, they have an elongated torso and a cascading coiffure. The third

2

3

4

5

6

7   8   9   10   11

style, known as Mitwaba (2), comprises statues carved from black wood that are similar to the Upemba style, but they have less elongated torsos.

The 30,000 Luba **Kalundwe** people have lived on the western side of the Luba empire, on the Luembe River, since the 17th century, and their statues are characterized by a coiffure divided into several buns set on the back of their heads (15).

The 200,000 Luba **Shankadi** people are divided into independent clans under the control of a hereditary chief, known as the *Mulowhe*. The Shankadi artistic style is characterized by a tiered coiffure.

A number of regional stylistic variations occur among the Shankadi: the classical style (6), the Sungu style (7) and the south-western style (17). The 'Master of the Cascade' style is characterized by an exaggerated coiffure divided into large, spreading planes (9).

The 250,000 **Luba-Kasai** people live on the western side of the Luba empire, on the Lubilash River. Their artistic production reflects the influence of their neighbours, the Luba, the Songye, the Lulua and the Kanyok. They carve fetish figures characterized by a typical vertical scarification running under the mouth or on to an elongated neck (19).

The 30,000 **Zela** people live between the Luvua River and Lake Kisale, on the eastern border of the Luba empire. The Zela artistic style is characterized by the use of a light brown wood, a ridged, backward-sloping coiffure and by body scarifications (8).

On the left bank of the Lualaba River, to the north of the Luba empire, **Zula** people have used rare stools (10) and neckrests with seated female figures whose arms and legs are carved in a typical 'W' shape.

The **Kanyok** people, on the eastern side of the Luba empire, are renowned for prestige objects and a series of anecdotal figures, some of which depict erotic couples (11), crouching figures and musicians. They were carved from a black wood and tend to be characterized by a mouth of filed teeth and a coiffure divided into several buns.

The 10,000 **Kasongo** people were colonized by the Luba during the 18th century and occupy the northern border of the empire. Kasongo carvers produced, from a reddish wood, small apotropaic figures with elongated beards which show a typical triangular hollowed head containing fetish material (16).

BIBLIOGRAPHY
DE MARET and ALII, 'The Luba Shankadi Style', *African Art*, 7, 1973
FELIX, M., *100 Peoples of Zaire and their Sculpture*, Brussels, 1987
NEYT, F., *Luba, aux sources du Zaire*, Exh. Cat., Musée Dapper, Paris, 1993–94
NOOTER ROBERTS, MARY, and ALLEN F. ROBERTS, *Luba Art and the Making of History*, Exh. Cat., New York, 1996
VAN CAENEGHEM, R., *Hekserij bij de Baluba van Kasai*, Brussels, 1955
VAN RIEL, F., and G. DE PLATEN, *Données sur les Binja des environs de Kasongo*, Tervuren, 1967
WYMEERSH, P., *Les Bin Kaniok, Culture et tradition*, Bandudu, 1983

12

12   An elephant mask; *wood; length: 85 cm (33^1/$_2$ in); private collection*

13   An anthropomorphic pipe; *wood; length: 54 cm (21 in)*

14   A Luba vessel; *terracotta; height: 32 cm (12^1/$_2$ in); private collection*

15   A Kalundwe figure; *wood and beads; height: 44 cm (17^1/$_4$ in)*

16   A Kasongo fetish figure; *wood and metal; height: 16 cm (6^1/$_4$ in)*

17   A Shankadi south-western style figure; *wood, horn, metal and beads; height: 40 cm (15^1/$_2$ in)*

18   A Luba bowstand; *wood and metal; height: 64 cm (25^1/$_4$ in); G de Miré, R. Mendes-France; private collection*

19   A Luba-Kasai fetish figure; *wood; height: 32 cm (12^1/$_2$ in)*

13   14

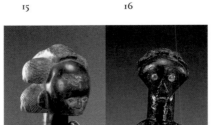

15   16   17   18   19

[A] Left: **a Luba figure**
wood; height: 46 cm (18 in);
private collection

A superb example of Luba sculpture, this figure epitomizes the sensibility of Luba carvers when rendering the image of a woman. Its black oily patina is the result of more than two centuries worth of libations.

[B] Right: **a Luba staff**
wood and metal; height: 170 cm (67 in);
private collection

Within Luba culture, staffs are symbols of authority and power. The female figure set on this one probably represents a spirit. The elegance of this staff is achieved by the balance between figurative representation and plain geometric forms.

[C] Far right: **an Upemba-style Luba figure**
wood; height: 53 cm (21 in)

The body scarifications on this mysterious-looking figure and its general form are typical of the Upemba style of Luba art. The disproportionate body parts enhance its presence and elegance.

Hemba

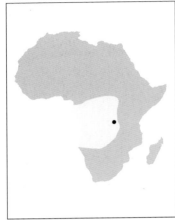

During the 18th century, the Hemba people, led by their chief *Niembo*, migrated from the south-west and settled on the right bank of the Lualaba River, in a region of fertile savannah. Today, they number 80,000 and are divided into large clans which, by definition, are families with a common ancestor. The hereditary chief of each clan is called the *Fumu Mwalo* and is the keeper of the ancestor figures. He renders justice and his status as clan head means that he has the privilege of receiving numerous gifts. The Hemba live mostly from farming manioc, sesame, yams and beans. Secret societies such as *Bukazanzi* for the men and *Bukibilo* for the women counterbalance the *Fumu Mwalo's* power.

Until the 1970s hardly any Hemba figures had entered Western collections. Because they share some stylistic features with Luba figures, they had not been recognized as being significant in their own right, and had been included into the Luba corpus of sculpture. Then, in the mid-1970s several dozen statues and caryatid stools were collected in Africa and brought to Europe. When viewed *en masse*, it became apparent that these figures constituted a distinct tribal style. In 1975, research conducted by François Neyt established that these sculptures had been produced by the Hemba people. Their corpus principally includes ancestor figures and a few masks.

MASKS

Two types of Hemba mask have been identified so far: the first is the rarest and displays a perfectly symmetrical human face with a small mouth and a linear nose set between two slanted eyes (1). The second type of mask imitates a monkey face with a large, pierced, crescent-shaped mouth and a pointed nose [D, 11]. The function and meaning of these masks remains obscure.

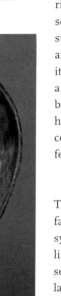

1

STATUES

Hemba ancestor figures [B], called *Singiti*, are between 55 and 90 cm high. They are male figures that stand on a circular base and characteristically have short legs, elongated torsos, hands resting on navels and an enlarged head with a backward-swept coiffure in the shape of a cross. Warrior figures holding weapons (8) are rare. They were kept by the *Fumu Mwalo* and conferred power on him. During ritual ceremonies, he communicated with these figures by recalling significant and heroic events in the ancestor-warrior's life and sacrificed a chicken or some other animal in homage to him. The blood of the animal would be poured over the statue, which gave it an encrusted patina (6, 9).

The 'Master of Buli', a member of the Hemba, was the first tribal carver to be identified by European scholars. He has been credited with producing about twenty figures and anthropomorphic stools [A], all of which are in a characteristic style identified by simian faces. There are also different Hemba regional stylistic traditions. The most famous style emanates from the Central Niembo area and is characterized by perfectly symmetrical and rounded features.

Smaller Janus figures (4), known as *Kabejas*, belong to each *Fumu Mwalo* and have a hollowed skull, which contains magical substances. They represent spirits who protect the clan and, as such, are the beneficiaries of sacrifices.

EVERYDAY OBJECTS

In addition to their statues and masks, the Hemba also adorned everyday objects with human figures. For instance, anthropomorphic caryatid stools (10), which were used by the *Fumu Mwalo* while he presided over meetings, and neckrests, rattles (3) and calabashes containing pigments (2) were adorned and used by diviners.

BIBLIOGRAPHY

DE STRYCKER, L., and B. DE GRUNNE, 'Le Trésor de Kalumbi et le style de Buli', *Tribal Arts*, III, 2, August 1996

NEYT, F., *La Grande statuaire Hemba du Zaire*, Louvain-la-Neuve, 1977

2

3   4

5   6   7   8   9

KUSU

The Kusu population of about 60,000 live on the left bank of the Lualaba River. During their exodus from the north, they passed through Luba, Hemba and Songye territories where they assimilated social and artistic traditions from these respective tribes. They are divided into clans, each headed by a chief, known as the *Wembi*, who is himself assisted by village chiefs, known as *Mwamkana*, and by family chiefs called *Bankumi*. The social structure of the Kusu is relatively complex and varies according to the different regions that they live in. In the southern part of the Kusu territory, a caste system, probably influenced by the Luba social structures, divides the society into categories such as aristocracy, freemen, slaves and foreigners. In the northern territory, only clan and family structures exist. Historically, the Kusu were hunters, but they now farm and raise cattle.

Kusu art is relatively rare and reflects the artistic influences of their neighbours: the Luba, the Hemba and the Songye. Statues are usually carved from a dark red wood which is sometimes covered with an oily patina.

MASKS

No Kusu masks have been identified so far.

STATUES

Influenced by the Hemba, the Kusu carved ancestor figures (5) which differ from Hemba statues with their typical high coiffures and enlarged eyes. Based on Songye tradition, Kusu people also carved magical statuettes **[C]** into whose abdomen or head fetish material was inserted. The ancestor figures were always carved with their hands on their abdomen, whereas the fetish figures are seen either in this position or holding their beard with both hands. The Kusu also produced Janus figures (7) influenced by the Songye *Kalunga* fetish figures.

EVERYDAY OBJECTS

During important celebrations or councils, chiefs often used anthropomorphic caryatid stools based on Luba and Hemba traditions. Adorned rattles

and calabashes were integral components of Kusu divination ceremonies.

BIBLIOGRAPHY

FELIX, M., *100 Peoples of Zaire and their Sculpture*, Brussels, 1987

NEYT, F., *La Grande statuaire Hemba du Zaire*, Louvain-la-Neuve, 1977

1   A Hemba mask;
    *wood; height: 34 cm (13 1/2 in);
    private collection*

2   A Hemba figure on a calabash;
    *wood, fur and calabash; height:
    29 cm (11 1/2 in)*

3   A Hemba rattle;
    *wood and calabash; height:
    24 cm (9 1/2 in); private collection*

4   A Hemba Janus figure;
    wood; height: 24.5 cm (9 3/4 in)

5   A Kusu ancestor figure;
    *wood; height: 75 cm (29 1/2 in);
    private collection*

6   A Hemba ancestor figure;
    *wood; height: 46 cm (18 in);
    private collection*

7   A Kusu Janus figure;
    *wood; height: 32 cm (12 1/2 in);
    private collection*

8   A Hemba warrior figure;
    wood; height: 92 cm (36 in)

9   A Hemba ancestor figure;
    *wood; height: 52 cm (20 3/8 in);
    private collection*

10 A Hemba stool;
    *wood; height: 55 cm (21 1/2 in);
    private collection*

11 A Hemba monkey mask;
    *wood; height: 19 cm (7 1/2 in);
    private collection*

10

11

[A] Left: **a Hemba stool by the 'Master of Buli'**
wood; height: 58 cm (22⁷/8 in)

The artist who created this stool is known as the 'Master of Buli' – a reference to the village where some of his sculptures were found. A great artist, whose work can be recognized by the facial features of his figures, he gave this caryatid stool a lightness and animation.

[B] Right: **a Hemba ancestor figure**
wood; 64 cm (25 in); private collection

This serene Hemba figure epitomizes the art and mystery that carvers from this tribe have imbued in their sculpture. The quiet power of the figure elicits the respect that the tribe owed to their ancestors.

[C] Far right, above: **a Kusu fetish figure**
wood, horn, vegetal fibres, fur and metal; height of the figure: 33 cm (13 in); private collection

Kusu figures are characterized by the use of reddish wood. This fetish figure nearly disappears under the paraphernalia believed to enhance its power.

[D] Far right, below: **a Hemba monkey mask**
wood; height: 18 cm (7 in); private collection

Hemba monkey masks are usually more realistic than this one which, with its mysterious round face and large smile, may evoke a beneficiary spirit. The encrusted patina is the result of numerous libations and offerings.

Tabwa

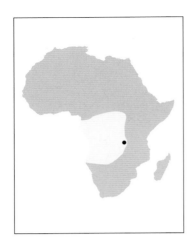

Historically, Tabwa people lived under Luba domination in small autonomous villages scattered within a territory that expanded across the Democratic Republic of Congo (formerly Zaire) and Zambia, along Lake Tanganyika. Interestingly, the verb 'tabwa' means 'to be tied up' and refers to when these people were taken as slaves. During the 19th century, the ivory trade brought wealth to the region and Tabwa people gained their independence. Today, they number 200,000 and are led by chief-sorcerers who rule over village chiefs and family chiefs. Their power is counterbalanced by male societies created on Luba prototypes and by female associations influenced by East African models. Traditionally, Tabwa people made their living from hunting and blacksmithing; nowadays, they farm and fish.

I

1 A Tabwa female mask; *wood, shell and metal; height: 22 cm (8⁵/₈ in)*

2 A Tabwa ancestor figure; *wood; height: 49.8 cm (19¹/₂ in)*

3 A Tabwa double figure; *wood; height: 56 cm (22 in)*

4 A pair of Tabwa ancestor figures; *wood and metal; height of the taller: 32 cm (12¹/₂ in); Archives Monbrison, Paris*

5 A Holoholo figure; *wood; height: 31 cm (12 in); private collection*

6 A pair of Rungu figures; *wood; height: 10 cm (4 in); private collection*

7 A Tabwa stool; *wood; height: 33 cm (13 in); private collection*

8 A Tabwa necklace; *ivory; length: 32 cm (12¹/₂ in); private collection*

The influence on Tabwa art of their eastern Tanzanian neighbours is seen in their use of linear geometric decoration, while their western neighbours, the Luba, influenced the incorporation of prestige objects into Tabwa life. Tabwa figures display typical linear face scarifications and elongated features.

MASKS

Two types of Tabwa helmet mask were used during fertility rites. The first one is a female mask in the shape of a man's head (1) and the second is a male mask in the shape of a buffalo's head [B].

STATUES

Tabwa ancestor figures (4) were carved as prestige objects and their role was to assert the chief's authority – a Hemba tradition. They measure between 20 and 70 cm in height and are carved in the shape of elongated figures and stand on a circular base, with slightly bent legs, their hands resting on their abdomen and have an elongated neck supporting a rounded head with linear scarifications (2). They were placed on dedicated shrines. Statues of dead chiefs and fetishes were usually covered with an oily patina, the result of continuous libations [C]. Rare carvings of one figure carrying another were used during inauguration ceremonies (3).

EVERYDAY OBJECTS

Tabwa everyday objects are characterized by geometric motifs and are often adorned with figures. Spatulas (9), stools (7), thrones, zithers (10) and water pipes were used as prestige objects and for ritual purposes. Ivory necklaces include triangular-shaped elements (8).

RELATED TRIBES

Occupying the western side of Lake Tanganyika, the 60,000 **Tubwe** people live from farming and fishing. They migrated into this area during the 17th century and created a chiefdom that fought against a series of

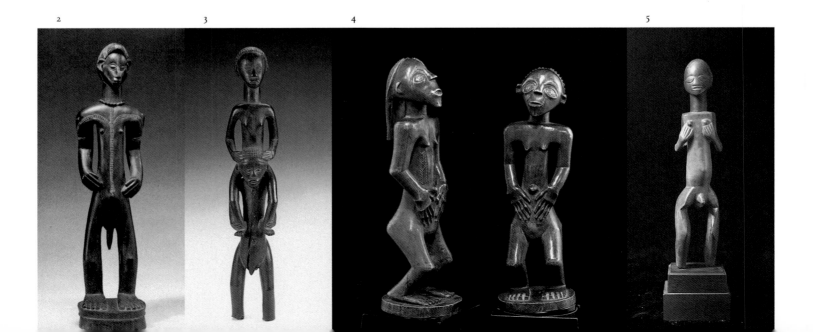

2   3   4   5

6

7

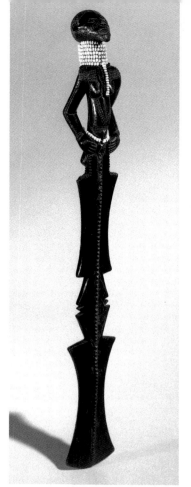

9

8

9 A Tabwa spatula/staff;
wood and beads; height: 51 cm (20 in)

10 A Tabwa zither;
wood; height: 73 cm (28³/₄ in)

10

incursions from the Tabwa, the Luba, the Arabs and the Belgian colonials. Their single chief is assisted by a council of nobles.

Tubwe ancestor figures are often oil soaked and show one man carrying another – a reference to enthronement ceremonies. Tubwe artistic output is strongly influenced by the Tabwa and their figures resemble Tabwa statues except that they lack facial scarifications and have a backward-swept, exaggerated coiffure with a cross-hatched design and an open mouth, often showing their teeth or tongue **[A]**. The Tubwe carved prestige objects such as stools and bow stands influenced by their western neighbours the Luba. Large figures with a cylindrical body and a horn coming out of their head, although found in Tubwe territory, are thought to have been made by Luba artists and then exported to the Tubwe people.

The **Holoholo** people live on the western shore of Lake Tanganyika and should not be confused with the Holo tribe in the west of the Democratic Republic of Congo (formerly Zaire), who are discussed in the Yaka chapter, pp. 184–87. They live in small villages headed by chiefs called *Sultanis*, who are assisted by elders. The Holoholo fish, farm and trade and their statues are influenced by the Tabwa in terms of their general features and by the Luba in terms of their type. Holoholo figures **(5)** are rare and characterized stylistically by a rounded head, elongated split eyes, scarifications on the torso and a ridged coiffure reminiscent of the work of Zela artists.

The 50,000 **Rungu** live in an area which lies between the Democratic Republic of Congo (formerly Zaire), Zambia and Tanzania. They survive from farming and are led by a king called *Mweme Tafuna*, who lives in Isoko (Zambia) and is assisted by elders and district governors. Like other tribes in the area, the Rungu produced prestige objects such as stools,

staffs, spoons and combs – all valued by the Luba – but they show a strong Tabwa aesthetic influence. Their statues are characteristically made of light brown wood with darkened details (a tradition found in East Africa), and often have a vertical face scarification set at the centre of the forehead and incised vertical lines on the cheeks **(6)**.

BIBLIOGRAPHY
A Century of Tabwa Art, Exh. Cat., University of Michigan Museum of Art, Ann Arbor, 1985
DE GRUNNE, B., *La Sculpture Batabwa*, Louvain-la-Neuve, 1980
DELHAISE, C., 'Ethnographie Congolaise: Chez les Warundi et les Wa horohoro', *Bulletin de la société royale belge de géographie*, 32, Brussels, 1908
FELIX, M., *100 Peoples of Zaire and their Sculpture*, Brussels, 1987
SCHMIDT, R., *Les Baholoholo*, Brussels, 1912
VAN GELUWE, H., *Tabwa Metaegomena*, Tervuren, 1986
WILLIS, R., *The Fifa and Related Peoples*, London, 1966

[A] Left: **a Tubwe figure**
wood: 36 cm (14 in); Leloup archives

Only the upper part of this figure remains, but
the backward-swept coiffure and the globular
eyes are characteristic of Tubwe sculpture. As
in illustration C, the oily patina enhances the
mystery of this ancestor figure.

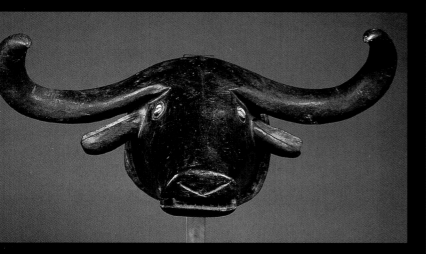

[B] Above: **a Tabwa male mask**
wood; width: 75 cm (29¹/₂ in)

Tabwa male masks, which embody the masculine
spirit, are carved in the shape of a buffalo's
head. The artist who carved the present
example has captured the solidity of this
animal perfectly, particularly through his
treatment of the powerful horns.

[C] Right: **a Tabwa figure**
wood, beads, oil; height: 56 cm (22 in)

Tabwa figures allegedly represent ancestors.
The oily patina covering this figure was caused
by continual libations of palm oil, while the
added jewelry – rarely found in exported African
sculpture – was a token of respect for this
particular ancestor.

Songye

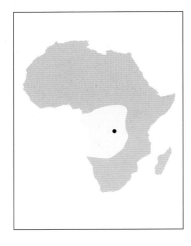

During the 16th century, the Songye migrated from the Shaba area, which is now the southern part of the Democratic Republic of Congo (formerly Zaire), and settled on the left bank of the Lualaba River, on a savannah and forest-covered plateau. Divided into numerous sub-groups, the 150,000 Songye people are governed by a central chief, the *Yakitenge*, whose role demands that he obey special restrictive laws such as not showing grief, not drinking in public and not shaking hands with men. In addition, local rulers, the *Sultani Ya Muti*, distribute plots of land to their villagers and an influential secret society, *Bwadi Bwa Kifwebe*, counterbalances their power. Unlike their neighbours, the Luba, the Songye tribe is a patriarchal society in which agriculture is central to the economy.

The Songye created impressive sculptures and masks used within their secret societies. They are characterized by powerful features, with the figures covered in paraphernalia. Regional variations can be observed owing to the large area occupied by the Songye tribe.

MASKS

The most famous masks created by the Songye are worn in connection with the *Bwadi Bwa Kifwebe* secret society. They are called *Kifwebe*, which means 'mask' in the Songye language. Typically, it has a face covered with linear incisions, a square protruding mouth and a linear nose set between globular pierced eyes. It can be either masculine, if carved with a central crest (10), or feminine if displaying a plain coiffure (9). The size of the crest determines the magical power of the mask. During initiation, circumcision or funeral ceremonies, a dancer will wear the mask and his body will be covered with straw. The dancer who wears the male mask will display aggressive and uncontrolled behaviour with the aim of encouraging social conformity, whereas the dancer who wears the female mask displays more gentle and controlled movements and is assumed to be associated with reproduction ceremonies. *Kifwebe* mask representations also appear on other objects belonging to the *Bwadi Bwa Kifwebe* society – grooved shields (6), for example, are adorned with a central mask.

STATUES

Songye fetish figures **[D]** are numerous and vary in size from 10 to 150 cm. They are usually male and stand on a circular base, have an elongated torso framed by set-apart arms and their hands rest on their abdomen. Their enlarged head has a square or pointed chin, an open mouth and a triangular nose set between enlarged globular eyes. Strips of metal, nails or other paraphernalia are sometimes applied over the face which counteract evil spirits and aggressors and channel lightning against them. Moreover, the top of the head and the abdomen are usually hollowed to allow insertion of fetish material, *Bishimba*, which imbues the figure with power. A 'specialist', called the *Nganga*, then attaches magical objects such as snakeskins, feathers, metal necklaces and bracelets to the figure to enhance its power even more. Occasionally these figures are suspended for apotropaic purposes inside a house by inserting a metal rod under each arm (13). Large fetish figures protect entire villages and are kept in special miniature huts, while smaller ones (3, 7) are used to protect individuals against death and disease. The handling of these fetish figures occurs mostly during new phases of the moon.

Different fetish styles can be distinguished: the Kalebwe style (2) from the north is carved with a square chin; the Kibeshi style is characterized by a pointed chin; the western style, influenced by the

1

1 A bracelet; *ivory; diameter: 12 cm (4⁵/₈ in); private collection*

2 A Kalebwe-style fetish figure; *wood, copper nails and sheets, snakeskin and vegetal-fibre string; height: 62 cm (24³/₈ in)*

3 A small fetish figure; *wood, beads, feathers and vegetal fibres; height: 29.5 cm (11⁵/₈ in)*

4 An adze; *copper; length: 41 cm (16 in)*

5 An axe decorated with faces; *wood and copper; height: 48.3 cm (19 in)*

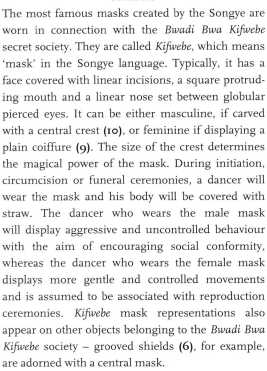

2

3

4

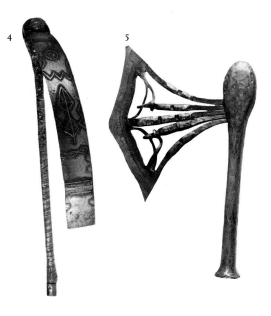

5

6   7   8   9   10

Luba, shows figures with their heads turned to the side [B]; eastern-style figures sometimes wear the Kifwebe mask (7); and finally, the southern-style figures [C] often demonstrate an elongated annulated neck.

A group of around twenty figures and stools with similar characteristics such as flattened feet, prominent breasts and grooved coiffures (8, 11) has been identified as the work of a carver or his workshop, active from the beginning of the century until 1925.

EVERYDAY OBJECTS

The western Songye are famous for their metal axes decorated with faces (5). Influenced by the Luba, they also produced 'prestige objects' such as anthropomorphic stools (8), neckrests, bracelets (1) and copper adzes (4).

RELATED TRIBES

The **Nsapo** are Songye people who, in 1888, following internal wars, moved, with the help of the Belgians, westwards from Songye territory. Like the Songye, they have a patrilineal society wherein the eldest son of the chief is the appointed successor, and traditionally the chief was buried in a dried-up river bed which was subsequently flooded. The Nsapo people did not retain the Songye *Bwadi Bwa Kifwebe* secret society, but replaced it with a *Bushiki* secret society, who were responsible for maintaining social cohesion.

Their art not only reflects their Songye origin, but also shows the influence of the Lula, their western neighbours – in the general composition of their fetish figures [A] and their usage of paraphernalia. The Lula influence is seen in their face scarifications and rounded features. In some cases, Nsapo figures may have been made on demand, to be sold to Europeans. Some of the commercial Nsapo carvers such as the 'Master of Beneki', who carved figures with rounded heads, and the 'Master of the sitting maternity', who produced mother and child groups (12), have been identified.

BIBLIOGRAPHY

FELIX, M., *100 Peoples of Zaire and their Sculpture*, Brussels, 1987
HERSAK, D., *Songye Masks and Figure Sculpture*, London, 1985
MESTACH, J. W., *Etudes Songye: formes et symbolique*, Munich, 1986
TIMMERMANS, P., 'Les Sapo Sapo près de Luluabourg', *Africa-Tervuren 8*, 1962

6   A shield decorated with a *Kifwebe* mask;
    wood; height: 49.5 cm (19 ⁵/₈ in)

7   A small fetish figure wearing a Janus *Kifwebe* mask;
    wood, snakeskin and vegetal fibres; height: 33.7 cm (13 in)

8   An anthropomorphic stool;
    wood and beads; height: 59.5 cm (23 ³/₈ in)

9   A *Kifwebe* female mask;
    wood; height: 34 cm (13 ³/₈ in)

10 A *Kifwebe* male mask;
    wood; height: 60 cm (23 ⁵/₈ in)

11 A figure holding a cup;
    wood and beads; length: 36 cm (14 in)

12 Three 'Master of the sitting maternity' figures;
    wood and beads; height of the tallest: 34 cm (13 ³/₈ in)

13 A fetish figure with rods under the arms;
    wood and metal; height: 23 cm (9 in); private collection

11   12   13

[A] Below: **a Nsapo fetish figure**
wood, horn and metal nails;
height: 58.5 cm (23 in)

Magical substances are contained in the
impressive hollowed horn on top of this
Nsapo figure. The exterior of the horn
symbolizes the male element, and the
interior, the female; both elements give
the figure power.

[C] Below: **a southern-style fetish figure**
wood, vegetal fibres, snakeskin, metal nails;
height: 62 cm (24³/₈ in); provenance:
K. Plasmans, Brussels

This figure, with its annulated neck
characteristic of the southern Songye
territories, exudes an oily patina which
has resulted from numerous libations
offered to it in exchange for protection
against malevolent spirits and curses.

[D] Right: **a Songye fetish figure**
wood, animal skin, snakeskin, beads,
horns, shell and metal; height: 109 cm
(43 in); provenance: Jeff Vanderstraete,
Brussels, 1950

Songye figures take their power from the
fetish material, called *bishimba*, which is
inserted into their heads and abdomen.
External paraphernalia such as hair
and cowrie shells, and leopard, monkey
and snakeskins reinforce its power.
They infuse the fetish with the key
characteristics of the animal they are
derived from.

[B] Above: **a western-style fetish figure**
wood with oily patina; height: 24 cm
(9¹/₂ in); E. Anspach Collection, New York

Principally found in the western and southern
parts of the Songye territory, figures with
turned heads like this one symbolize a
malevolent spirit – the ferryman of the
River of Death. For Songye people, a
side-turned head symbolizes lying or
hidden desires.

Kuba

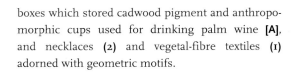

1

During the 16th century, the Kuba people migrated from the north and settled between the Sankuru and Kasai Rivers. Today, they number 250,000 and are subdivided into a number of tribes – the Bushoong, the Ngeende, the Kete, the Lele, the Binji, the Dengese, the Mbuun and the Wongo. Each clan pays tribute to the *Nyim*, the king of the Bushoong ruling clan, but their internal affairs are dealt with autonomously. The Bushoong king and his court lived in a closed palace, known as the *Mushenge*. The king was responsible for the wealth and fecundity of his people.

1   Kuba textiles; *vegetal fibres; length of the longest: 61 cm (24 in)*

2   A Kuba necklace; *beads and claws; diameter: 44 cm (17³/8 in); private collection*

3   A Kete *Ngita* mask; *wood and copper nails; height: 57 cm (22¹/2 in); Van Opstal Collection, Belgium*

4   A Bushoong *Bwoon* mask; *wood; height: 48.2 cm (19 in)*

5   A Ngeende box; *wood and cowrie shells; length: 19.5 cm (7⁵/8 in)*

6   A Kete mask; *wood; height: 42 cm (16¹/2 in)*

2

Each clan within the Kuba kingdom produced artistic objects with specific characteristics, but there are common stylistic features, including a predilection for incised geometric decoration. Cups, zoomorphic divination instruments and boxes were produced throughout the realm.

The Kuba kingdom was founded in the 16th century by the **Bushoong** people. Today, they number about 17,000 and are still ruled by a king – the twenty-first to have held the title.

Bushoong art is characterized by its use of geometric decoration and cowrie shells, and by the application of red cadwood pigment to their carvings. Bushoong carvers are best known for their 'king' figures, called *Ndop*, which have an apotropaic role in childbirth. Each figure portrays a king who can be identified through his totemic animal, which is placed in front of him (11).

Three types of mask have been associated with dances that take place within the royal compound. The first, called *Moshambwooy*, represents Woot, the founder of the Bushoong clan (7). The second, known as *Nady Amwaash*, personifies the 'woman of Woot' (9). The third mask, called *Bwoon*, represents a 'pygmy' (4). Other masks, collectively known as *Isheene Mwalu*, may have been worn in connection with dances and initiations.

Bushoong artists produced everyday objects such as crescent, circular or rectangular-shaped

boxes which stored cadwood pigment and anthropomorphic cups used for drinking palm wine **[A]**, and necklaces (2) and vegetal-fibre textiles (1) adorned with geometric motifs.

The 8,500 **Ngeende** people were integrated into the eastern part of the Kuba kingdom during the 16th century. Their ceremonies incorporate the three main Bushoong types of mask described above, and a *Nyibita* mask **[B]** and a *Mukenge* mask. The latter is influenced by the Bushoong *Moshambwooy* mask, but has a stylized elephant trunk on the top (8). Ngeende artists carved a large array of everyday anthropomorphic objects such as drums, cups, pipes and boxes (5). The figures on these objects have a lozenge-shaped mouth, a slightly flared coiffure and rounded scarifications – called keloids – that are not part of the Bushoong style.

The 25,000 **Kete** people farm along the southern border of the Kuba kingdom and live in independent villages led by family chiefs. They carve figures associated with initiations and helmet masks similar to the Bushoong *Bwoon* mask with large, conical eyes (6). *Ngita* masks have a pair of backward-projecting horns and are worn during funerals (3).

The 20,000 **Lele** people occupy the western region of the Kuba kingdom and live from hunting and agriculture. Lele carvers produced face masks worn

3

4

5

6

7　　　　　　　8　　　　　　　　　　9　　　　　　　　　　10

at the annual founding celebrations which are nearly flat and have slit eyes surrounded by multiple lines **[C]**. The Lele use prestige objects influenced by the Kuba style. The figures on these objects occasionally have a coiffure with two long plaits down the back **(12)**.

Historically, the 35,000 **Binji** people split from the Bushoong clan over a disagreement about initiation processes. Today, they are scattered across a vast area along the eastern border of the Kuba kingdom. Binji artists carved a rougher-looking helmet mask similar in style to the Bushoong *Bwoon* mask and a woven fibre mask used during initiation ceremonies **(10)**.

North of the Kuba kingdom, across the Sankuru River, the 12,000 **Dengese** people claim to be the indigenous population of the area. Their king, known as the *Etoshi*, reigns over local chiefs who are assisted by noble men. Powerful groups such as the black-smith, hunting and witchcraft societies counter-balance the political power of the chiefs. Dengese artists carved legless figures of the king which were believed to embody his power **(15)**. A typical flared coiffure and geometric body scarifications appear on cephalomorphic sceptres and drinking cups.

The 100,000 **Mbuun** people migrated with the Pende from Angola in the 17th century and now live

from trading and cattle rearing. They are led by chiefs, known as *Mfinu*, who are elected by the elders. Artistically, the Mbuun are known for their anthro-pomorphic cups **(13)** and prestige objects that feature a precise geometric decoration.

The 10,000 **Wongo** people migrated from the north and are scattered among villages led by chiefs and structured by secret societies. They farm maize and manioc. Wongo artistic traditions reflect the influence of their neighbours – Bushoong realistic features, Pende-type masks and Lele-style adzes. They carved anthropomorphic cups which are characterized by numerous body scarifications **(14)**.

BIBLIOGRAPHY

BINKLEY, D., *A View from the Forest: The Power of South Kuba Initiation Masks*, Ann Arbor, 1987

CORNET, JOSEPH, 'A Propos des statues N'Dengese', *Arts d'Afrique Noire*, no. 17, 1976

CORNET, JOSEPH, *Royal Art of Kuba*, Milan, 1982

DOUGLAS, M., 'The Lele of the Kasai', *African Worlds*, London, 1954

FELIX, M., *100 Peoples of Zaire and their Sculpture*, Brussels, 1987

LINGUA, FRANK, *Wongo Masking Traditions: A Study in Assimilation*, Mushenge, 1947

NEYT, FRANÇOIS, *Arts traditionels et histoire au Zaire*, Louvain-la-Neuve, 1981

VANSINA, J., *Les Tribus Ba-Kuba et les peuplades apparentées*, Tervuren, 1954

VANSINA, J., *The Children of Woot*, Madison, 1978

7　A Bushoong *Moshambwooy* mask; wood, vegetal fibres, cowrie shells and beads; height: 36 cm (14 in); Van Opstal Collection, Belgium

8　A Ngeende mask; vegetal fibres, cowrie shells, beads and fur; height: 53 cm (21 in)

9　A Bushoong *Nady Amwaash* mask; wood; height: 41 cm (16 in)

10　A Binji mask; vegetal fibres; height: 43 cm (16⁷/₈ in); private collection

11　A Bushoong king figure, 20th century; wood; height: 72 cm (28¹/₈ in)

12　A Lele authority adze; wood (blade missing); height: 40 cm (15³/₄ in)

13　A Mbuun cup; wood; height: 17 cm (7 in); Van Opstal Collection, Belgium

14　A Wongo cup; wood; height: 17.5 cm (6³/₄ in)

15　A Dengese figure; wood; height: 55.2 cm (21³/₄ in); H. Rubinstein Collection, Paris

11　　　　12　　　　　13　　　　　　　14　　　　　　　　　　15

[A] Above: **a Kuba cup**
wood and copper; height: 25 cm (10 in)

Anthropomorphic cups are
commonly found within the
Kuba kingdom, yet examples of
this quality are rare. Its powerful
silhouette and the attention to detail,
including the delicate geometric
abdominal designs, rank it among
the masterpieces of Kuba art.

[B] Right: **a Ngeende** *Nyibita* **mask**
wood; height: 63 cm (24³/₈ in);
private collection

Ngeende masks are extremely rare.
Here its large empty eyes convey a
mysterious presence and its patina
indicates repeated libations.

[C] Far right: **a Lele mask**
wood; height: 35 cm (14 in);
private collection

This flat mask is typical of Lele
artistic production. Its eyes are
surrounded by multiple lines and
the encrusted patina confers great
power and dignity.

Pende

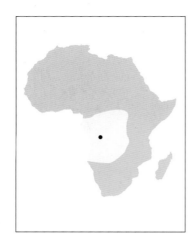

The Pende were pushed northwards by the Lunda people during the 17th century, so they settled in a region near the Loango and Kasai Rivers. Two hundred years later, the Tchokwe people invaded the Pende territory – they were migrating northwards from Angola – but they were pressurized by the Belgian colonial rulers to return the annexed lands to the Pende. The 500,000 Pende people, who are mostly farmers, are not governed by a central authority, but pay allegiance to family chiefs, known as *Djigo*, who are sometimes assisted by various nobles. Young men are organized into age groups and pass through initiation stages, including circumcision at adolescence.

Pende art is divided into two principal aesthetic traditions. The first is derived from the western Pende who live along the Loango River, and the second from the eastern Pende who settled along the Kasai River.

MASKS

Western Pende people use around fifteen different types of mask during their ceremonies. They all have down-cast eyes, a triangular nose and a protruding mouth which sometimes bears teeth.

Three types of mask are found in Western collections. The first has a long beard and is called *Kiwoyo-Muyombo* (6); the second, known as *Mbangu*, has distorted features and is thought to represent the effects of an epileptic seizure [B]; and the third, a chief's mask called *Phumbu*, displays a coiffure divided into three parts (7). Carvers living in villages on the west bank of the Kwilu River carved helmet masks (2). Their purpose is thought to be similar to that of the *Phumbu*.

The helmet masks and face masks associated with the eastern Pende and referred to respectively as *Giphogo* and *Minyangi* were worn by dancers primarily during initiation ceremonies. They have slanted eyes and a pointed chin usually framed by an incised geometric decoration and coloured with red, black and white pigments. The elongated *Panya-Yombe* mask (8) and the tall *Phumbu a Mfunu* (14) mask were used either for dances or for decorating houses.

STATUES

Western Pende figures (10–12) are rare and are thought to represent ancestors, but eastern Pende statues, believed to be used as fetishes, are even rarer. They are carved with elongated features and have added paraphernalia such as a horn inset into their head. Roof figures and decorated lintels frequently appear in the homes of Pende chiefs. These statues usually represent maternity figures and are carved from a light wood. They have found their way onto Western markets and are thought to have been made at the turn of the century to sell to early travellers rather than for ritual purposes.

EVERYDAY OBJECTS

Western Pende amulets (3), called *Ikhoko*, are usually carved from ivory, wood or metal in the shape of human heads or, more rarely, full figures. The authority of the *Djigo*, the family chief, is enhanced by his ownership of prestige objects such as staffs, adzes hung from the shoulder, semi-circular cups adorned with figures, tobacco mortars, anthropomorphic ivory whistles (5) and anthropomorphic or zoomorphic caryatid stools (13). These stools have rarely made their way into Western collections because they were usually buried with their owners. Pende diviners use a device made in the shape of a wooden head which is held at the end of articulated sticks.

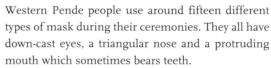

1

3   4

2

5   6   7   8

9   10   11   12   13

RELATED TRIBES

Like the Pende, the 60,000 **Mbala** people migrated from Angola during the 17th century. They are governed by regional and village chiefs who regulate the economy – hunting, fishing and manioc farming. The fame of the Mbala people rests on their production of a red pigment, called *Tukula*, from which their name, 'the red people', emanates. The term *Tukula* is used throughout Central Africa and is applied equally to people, as well as to sculptures during ritual ceremonies.

Mbala figures **[C]** are characterized by a ridged coiffure with a central crest falling below the neck level. Helmet masks are rare and their function is unknown. Among chiefs' possessions were maternity figures and other figures depicting everyday activities, as well as neckrests, cups, knives and sceptres. Fetish figures – used for hunting and divination purposes – are often covered with added paraphernalia which is believed to enhance their powers.

The 5,000 **Hungaan** people left Angola with the Pende and Mbala people and settled north of the Kasai River. They mainly survive from farming. Each village is grouped into associations with two to four others, which are headed by a chief, who is assisted by elders. The eldest man of each family maintains its lineage objects which are kept in a special hut. They include ancestors' skulls and large figures to which power-enhancing paraphernalia are attached. Hungaan people wear apotropaic ivory pendants which represent a stylized human figure **(4)**. Stylistically, Hungaan statues **(11)** can be recognized by their ridged coiffure, similar to the Mbala, which forms a triangle at the back, below the neck level.

Today, the 4,000 **Pindi** are scattered among their neighbours, but they were the first people to migrate from Angola to the Kwango River region. Their social structure is based on the family unit and is headed by the father. Women tend the fields while men hunt and smith. Their artistic tradition is strongly influenced by their neighbours, the Pende and the Suku, but Pindi objects can nevertheless be distinguished as they have a rounder head with a protruding mouth and almond-shaped eyes under a ridged or cross-hatched coiffure. Their figures were carved for apotropaic purposes, but their masks, stylistically influenced by the Pende, were worn by dancers during initiation ceremonies. Pindi carvers also produced prestige objects **(1)** and decorative panels, a tradition found among the Pende.

Unlike the other tribes living in the Kwango River region, the 40,000 **Kwese** people migrated from the west. During the 19th century, they were colonized by the Lunda and the Yaka. A triumvirate of chiefs govern the everyday lives of the Kwese, while territorial and village chiefs organize the farming of millet, corn and manioc. Kwese masks **[A]** have a heart-shaped face and, when not worn by dancers during initiation and circumcision rites, were kept in 'fetish houses' where offerings were made to them. Kwese statues are rare and are artistically influenced by the Pende and Mbala art traditions. Maternity figures **(9)** were probably made to be sold to neighbouring tribes while fetish figures were used and kept on top of small shrines.

Prestige objects such as chairs, slit drums or cylindrical cups for drinking palm wine were carved for the exclusive use of the chiefs.

1   A Pindi staff;
    wood; height: 106 cm (41⁵/₈ in)

2   A Pende helmet mask;
    wood; height: 63.5 cm (25 in)

3   A Pende *Ikhoko* amulet;
    ivory; height: 5.5 cm (2¹/₈ in)

4   A Hungaan amulet; *ivory; height:*
    8 cm (3¹/₈ in); private collection

5   An anthropomorphic whistle;
    ivory; height: 9.5 cm (3⁷/₈ in)

6   A Pende *Kiwoyo-Muyombo* mask;
    wood and hair; height: 43.2 cm
    (17 in)

7   A Pende *Phumbu* mask;
    wood and fibres; height: 40 cm
    (15³/₄ in)

8   An eastern Pende *Panya-Yombe*
    mask; *wood and fibres; height:*
    90 cm (35¹/₂ in); private collection

9   A Kwese maternity figure;
    wood; height: 43 cm (17 in)

10 A western Pende equestrian statue;
    wood; height: 54 cm (21¹/₄ in)

11 A Hungaan figure;
    wood; height: 62 cm (24¹/₄ in)

12 A western Pende figure;
    wood and vegetal fibres; height:
    65 cm (25¹/₂ in)

13 A Pende stool; *wood; height:*
    23 cm (9 in); private collection

14 An eastern Pende *Phumbu a Mfunu*
    mask; *wood; width: 71 cm (28 in)*

BIBLIOGRAPHY

BIEBUYCK, D., *The Arts of Zaire: Southwestern Zaire*, Berkeley, 1985

DE PEIRPONT, J., 'Les Bambala', *Congo*, 1, Brussels, 1932

DE SOUSBERGHE, L., *L'Art Pende*, Brussels, 1960

ENGWALL, R., *An Ethnographic Survey of the Hungana and related Peoples of the Kwilu Province in the Democratic Republic of Congo*, Tervuren

FROBENIUS, L., *Im Schatten des Kongostaates*, Berlin, 1907

LAMAL, F., *BaSuku et Bayaka des districts Kwango et Kwilu au Congo*, Tervuren, 1965

ROULIN, H., *Les Bambala, Bagongo et Bahungana du sud-ouest du territoire du Banningville* (1936–37), Prov. Leo. distr. Kwilu, Terr. Banningville, 1937

VANDEVENNE, *Note sur le Pemba ou Pezo chez les Pende et Kwese*, Prov. Leo. distr Kwilu, Terr. Idiofa, 4, 1, 1934

14

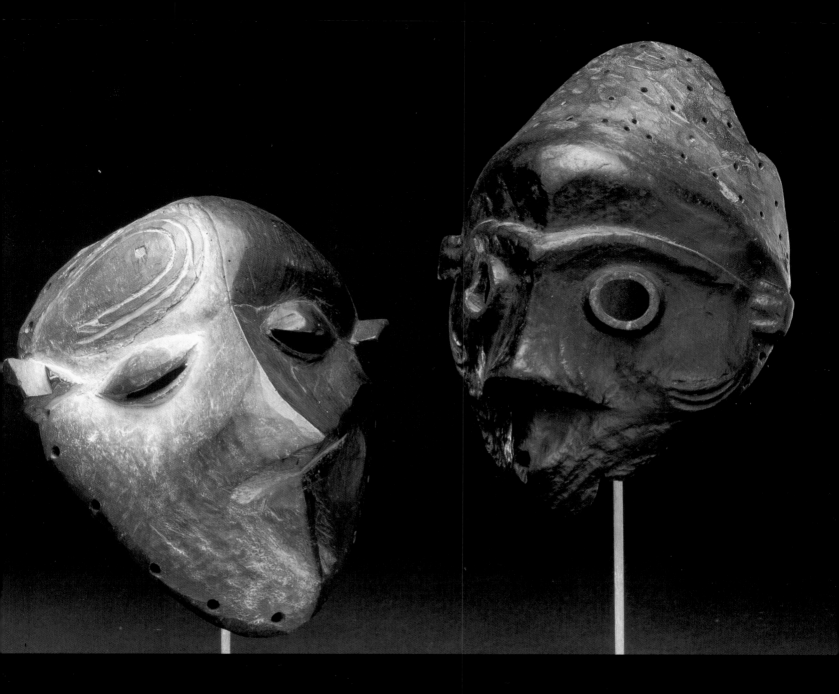

[A] Left: **a Kwese mask**

wood; height: 25 cm (10 in); private collection

This Kwese mask, with its characteristic heart-shaped face, was used during
initiation ceremonies and circumcision rites. This mask shares the Pende
characteristic of applied pigments to underscore the shape of the face.

[B] Above: **two Pende *Mbangu* distorted masks**

wood and pigments; height: 28 cm (11 in); private collection

Distorted faces are rarely depicted in African art. For the Pende, they represent
the effect of an epileptic seizure, which was thought to be a manifestation of
the spirits. The use of black and white pigments emphasizes the overall
distortion of the faces.

[C] Right: **a Mbala figure**

wood; height: 25 cm (9³/₄ in); private collection

With its typical Mbala coiffure, this stern-looking figure is probably the
representation of a spirit whose function was to dispel negative forces.
The rich, smooth patina is the result of much rubbing and handling.

Lulua

The Lulua tribespeople, also known as Bena Lulua, migrated from western Africa during the 18th century and settled in the southern part of the Democratic Republic of Congo (formerly Zaire). They number 300,000 and live in small regional chiefdoms and in times of crisis elect a single common leader. The role of the village chief is to ensure juridical, political and social cohesion. In common with the Luba tribespeople, their social structure is based on a caste system which includes noblemen, warriors, freemen, foreigners and slaves. Their economy is mainly based on agriculture, but they also trade.

During the late 19th century, Lulua culture underwent radical changes. In 1875, the Lulua king, *Kalambam*, introduced new social and religious regulations, including the ending of traditional palm-wine drinking, hemp smoking and the burning of all cult carvings.

1 A Lulua whistle;
  wood; height: 10 cm (4 in)

2 A Lulua pipe;
  wood; height: 25.4 cm (10 in)

3 A Ding mask; *copper; height:*
  28 cm (11 in); private collection

4 A Mbagani mask;
  wood; height: 46 cm (18 in)

5 A Salampasu copper mask;
  wood and copper; height: 24.5 cm
  (9⅝ in)

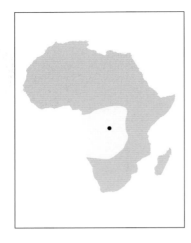

Lulua figures have complex scarifications and a typical pointed coiffure. In 1888, the use of scarifications was banned so any Lulua figures with elaborate scarification patterns must have been produced before this date. During the 1920s, the tradition was reintroduced, but the patterning was simplified.

MASKS
Lulua masks **[C]** are extremely rare and were probably used during circumcision and funeral ceremonies. They display enlarged eyes and complex scarification patterns on their cheeks.

STATUES
Lulua carvers are known mostly for the ancestor figures they produced. The figures carry weapons and shields and represent the ideal warrior, known as the *Mukalenga Wa Nkashaama* **[A]**. They also personify the head of the leopard society who is considered to be an intermediary between the living and the dead – between natural and spiritual forces. The Lulua carved maternity figures which aided pregnant women, who were members of the *Bwanga Bwa Cibola* society, before and after the birth of their child. Another type of female figure, used to protect women and children, was carved holding a cup **(9, 11)**. Rare crouching figures **(10)** are thought to be associated with disease and suffering.

EVERYDAY OBJECTS
Rare prestige objects such as neckrests, whistles **(1)** and pipes **(2)** belonging to village chiefs were adorned with human figures.

RELATED TRIBES
The 60,000 **Salampasu** people live on the frontier between the Democratic Republic of Congo (formerly Zaire) and Angola. They maintain strong commercial and cultural relations with their southern neighbours, the Tchokwe and the Lunda, to whom they pay tribute. The Salampasu are ultimately governed by a few high-ranking chiefs, who are, in turn, assisted by territorial chiefs, who

supervise village chiefs. This hierarchical power structure is counterbalanced by a warriors' society. The Salampasu live mostly from hunting, but the women do some farming.

Salampasu masks **(6)** are famous and are characterized by a bulging forehead, slanted eyes, a triangular nose and a rectangular mouth displaying filed teeth. The age of the masks can be determined by their stylistic variations. The oldest type has keloids and an encrusted red patina; a later style does not have scarifications, while the most recent type characteristically has simplified features and is made of thicker wood. Sometimes the masks were covered with copper plate **(5)** and had vegetal-fibre bells attached at the chin. They were used for initiation ceremonies related to the warriors' society.

Salampasu figures **(8)** are rare and are believed to be representations of their ancestors. Large wooden panels, adorned with human or animal figures, were incorporated into male initiation ceremonies, known as *Mfuku*.

The 50,000 **Mbagani** and **Ding** people belong to an extinct group, the Mpasu. They migrated to their present location from the east during the 16th century. Both tribes were influenced by their southern neighbours, the Lunda, and were almost colonized by the Tchokwe at the end of the 19th century. Economically, they survive by farming and, politically, they are organized into small chiefdoms.

Mbagani carvers are renown for their masks **(4)** which are characterized by a pointed chin, a rectangular protruding mouth, a triangular nose and enlarged coffee-bean eyes set under a domed forehead. Since the Mbagani people do not have major initiation ceremonies, it is thought that these masks are related to healing ceremonies.

The 8,000 Ding people live between Angola and the Democratic Republic of Congo (formerly Zaire). Ding artistic output is limited to copper masks, known as *Ngongo Munene* **(3)**, which are believed to symbolize the Earth spirit. They are physically

3

4

5

6

characterized by a round chin, slanted eyes and a typical rounded scarification in the middle of the forehead.

Another tribe related to the Lulua is the **Lwalwa** who number 20,000 and live on the frontier with Angola. They are of Kete origin and came in close contact with the Lunda people during the 17th century. Nevertheless, they remained independent, although they formed a relationship with the Salampasu and the Mbagani. Each Lwalwa village is headed by either a male or female chief, known as *Dina Dia Bukalenga*, whose power is held in check by a powerful society, the *Bangongo*. In common with their neighbours, Lwalwa men hunt and the women farm.

Lwalwa carvers are famous for their masks which are worn during initiation dances, funerals and to bring good fortune to the tribe. These masks typically display an enlarged nose, a protruding mouth and slanted eyes set under a deeply domed forehead [B].

The 70,000 **Luntu** people originate from Luba territories. They are ruled by regional chiefs, known as *Mfumu*, who are appointed by the Luba king. Like the chief of the Songye tribe, the Luntu king spends most of his time in isolation and is instructed in secret rites. His power is counterbalanced by

the leopard society. The Luntu people are mostly farmers, but the men also hunt.

Their carving style can be distinguished by protruding eyes surrounded by multiple lids, a protruding mouth and elongated features in general. Helmet masks, although rare, are worn during leopard society ceremonies. Small fetish figures **(7)** are used to improve hunting and to protect women during labour.

7

BIBLIOGRAPHY

BASTIN, MARIE-LOUISE, 'Un Masque en cuivre martelé des Kongo du nord et de l'Angola', *Africa Tervuren*, 7, 1961
BOGAERTS, H., 'Bij de Basala Mpasu, de Koppensnellers van Kasai', *Zaire*, 4 (4), Louvain-la-Neuve, 1950, pp. 379–419
BOGAERTS, H., 'Un Aspect de la structure sociale chez les Bakwa Luntu', *Zaire*, 5, Louvain-la-Neuve, 1951
CAMERON, E. L., 'Sala Mpasu Masks', *African Arts*, 22 (1), 1988, pp. 34–43
MAESSEN, A., 'Statuaire et culte de fécondité chez les Luluwa du Kasai', *Quaderni Poro*, Milan, 1954 3, pp. 49–58
PRUITT, W., *An Independent People: A History of the Salampasu of Zaire and their Neighbours*, Ph.D. Dissertation, Northwestern University, 1973
TIMMERMANNS, P., 'Essai de typologie de la sculpture des Bena-Luluwa du Kasai', *Africa Tervuren*, 12, 1966
TIMMERMANNS, P., 'Les Lwalwa', *Africa Tervuren*, 13, 1967
Trésors d'Afrique, Exh. Cat., Musée Royal de l'Afrique Centrale, Tervuren, 1995
VAN COILLIE, G., 'Grepen uit Mbagani-traditie', *Aequetoria*, Coquilhaville, 1947

6 A Salampasu mask;
   wood; height: 25.5 cm (10 in);
   Van Opstal Collection, Belgium

7 A Luntu figure; *wood; height: 27 cm*
   (11 in); Spik Collection; Zurich

8 A Salampasu figure;
   wood; height: 45 cm (17³/4 in)

9 A Lulua figure;
   wood; height: 30.5 cm (12 in)

10 A Lulua crouching figure;
    wood; height: 23 cm (9 in)

11 A Lulua figure;
    wood; height: 50.8 cm (20 in)

8

9

10

11

[A] Left: **a Lulua figure**

wood; height: 31 cm (12 in); private collection

This elegant figure represents an ancestor and was probably used
to reach the spirit world. The elongated neck and the contrast between
the red patina and the black scarifications give the sculpture a refined
sophistication.

[B] Below: **a Lwalwa mask**

wood and pigments; height: 32 cm (12¹/₂ in); private collection

Lwalwa artistic output epitomizes the use of geometric abstraction in
African art. This particular mask, with its contrasting simple geometric
planes, has a strength and power beyond its basic form.

[C] Right: **a Lulua mask**

wood; height: 31 cm (12 in); private collection

Lulua art is characterized by its refinement and serenity. The care taken in
the rendering of the complex face scarifications shows the great artistic skill
of Lulua carvers. The red pigment found on this mask is also seen on small
figures with apotropaic functions.

Yaka

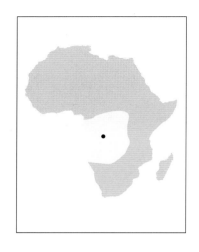

Today, the 300,000 Yaka people live along the Wamba River. They migrated from Angola during the 16th century and settled under the control of the Kongo kingdom. In the 18th century their lands were annexed by the Angola-based Lunda people, but by the 19th century the Yaka had regained their independence. Yaka society is tightly structured and headed by a chief of Lunda origin, the *Kiamfu*, who delegates responsibilities to ministers and lineage chiefs, *Unkwagata*. Young men are expected to pass through various initiation stages, including circumcision. The tribe lives principally from hunting, although subsidiary farming is undertaken by the women.

1   A Yaka neckrest; wood and copper nails; height: 19 cm (7 1/2 in)

2   Two Yaka pipes; terracotta and metal; height: 8 cm (3 in); Van Opstal Collection, Belgium

3   A Suku Janus figure; wood and pigments; height: 56 cm (22 in)

2

Yaka artistic tradition is rich and various, but much of it has been informed by their neighbours – the Suku, the Kongo, the Holo and the Teke. Nevertheless, Yaka statues do have common characteristics – an upturned nose and applied pigments.

MASKS
Yaka masks are worn predominantly during initiation ceremonies related to the *Ngoni* and the *Yiwilla* societies. There are different types which correspond to different functions: the leader's mask, known as *Mbala*, has flared ears and a vegetal-fibre spiked coiffure. The 'ritual expert' male and female masks, called *Kakungu*, have inflated cheeks and enlarged eyes (9), while the initiate's mask, known as *Kholuka*, has a face surrounded by a ridge and surmounted by a vegetal-fibre coiffure which supports figures or animals [B].

STATUES
The majority of Yaka figures were carved in pairs and were associated with *Mbwoolo* shrines. Their abdomen are hollow, enabling the insertion of fetish material and they are also adorned with bundles of paraphernalia (10). Yaka figures are multi-functional and sometimes have contradictory roles, for example, they were used to heal and to cause illness.

EVERYDAY OBJECTS
Prestige objects such as zoomorphic and anthropomorphic neckrests (1), cups, adzes, combs (6) and terracotta pipes (2) were carved specifically for the chiefs and were kept by them. Slit drums ending in a carved human head (7) were used by diviners.

RELATED TRIBES
The 80,000 **Suku** people have lived in the south-western part of the Democratic Republic of Congo

3   4   5   6   7   8

9   10   11

(formerly Zaire) since the 16th century. With the arrival of the Yaka and the Lunda in their territory, they were split into two autonomous groups. Their main economic resource is farming, but occasionally communal hunts are organized. Stylistically, their sculptures are characterized by an enlarged head with an almond-shaped mouth with incised teeth, a triangular nose and coffee-bean eyes, all set under an elaborate coiffure. The Suku carved large figures (3), which were used during fertility ceremonies, and crouching fetish figures [A] to which paraphernalia were attached. These were used either as ancestor figures or as the personification of evil spirits. Large face masks and helmet masks surmounted by animal or human figures [C] were worn by dancers during certain initiation ceremonies. The southern Suku produced hairpins, neckrests and adzes with rounded features, unlike the northern Suku whose everyday objects were more angular in appearance – stylistically influenced by the Yaka.

The 5,000 **Nkanu** people settled along the Lufimi River during the 16th century where they now farm the land. The Nkanu are headed by family chiefs, called *Fumu Nakanda*, who, in turn, report to local chiefs, known as *Mfumu Mpu*, each of whom controls three to five villages. The types of artistic object produced by the Nkanu were influenced by the Yaka, but they achieved a distinctive style through the use of applied polychrome pigments (4). Nkanu statues have a circular line around the eyes while their initiation masks have bulging eyes and inflated cheeks.

Migrating with the Yaka people from Angola during the 16th century, the 15,000 **Lula** settled along the banks of the Nseki River. Today, they live in autonomous villages and their economic survival depends on hunting and fishing. Stylistically, their statues show Teke-like facial scarifications, while the carved coiffure and the general morphology of the figures are influenced by the Yaka.

The Lula carved small apotropaic figures (25 cm high) and prestige objects such as fly-whisks and neckrests. In the 1980s, Lula masks [D] first appeared in the West. They are covered with blue and white pigments and have an oblong shape and typical rounded eyes. They are thought to have been worn by the guardian of the initiation camps.

Led by their queen, Nzigra, in the 16th century, the 10,000 **Holo** people migrated from coastal Angola and settled across the border along the banks of the Kwango River. Today, hunting plays an important part in the lives of Holo men, while the women take

charge of the farming. Stylistically, their artistic output is related to their northern neighbours, the Suku, but their figures have rounded faces, coffee-bean eyes set over vertical scarifications and a smooth coiffure.

Some of their statues are thought to represent their queen, others are carved either standing or in a crouching position (11). Holo helmet masks are like those produced by the Suku and were used during circumcision ceremonies. Prestige objects such as open-worked panels (12), adzes, neckrests, slit drums and combs were made for the ruling class only.

Living near the border with Angola, along the Inkisi River, the 15,000 **Zombo** are historically linked with the Kongo kingdom, but during the 18th century they broke away and enlarged their territories at the expense of the Yaka people. At that time, they gained a reputation as traders in commercial goods and slaves and served as intermediaries between the coastal-dwelling Portuguese and the interior. With the abolition of the slave trade in the 19th century, their economy collapsed and their power vanished.

Today, they are led by several land chiefs who are assisted by village chiefs, usually the oldest person from the oldest family. The Zombo economy is now based on hunting and farming.

Their statues have naturalistic features, probably influenced by Kongo art, but the general morphology of their sculptures relates to Yaka artistic tradition. Small and large fetish figures (5) adorned with paraphernalia and with a realistic face were used for healing, protecting and bringing good fortune to their owner. Slit gongs (8) were used by diviners and helmet masks with large globular eyes and a high coiffure were worn during circumcision ceremonies.

4   A Nkanu panel;
    wood and pigments;
    height: 85 cm (33¹/₂ in)

5   A Zombo double amulet;
    wood and tooth; length:
    22 cm (8¹/₂ in)

6   A Yaka comb;
    wood; height: 12 cm (4⁵/₈ in);
    Van Opstal Collection, Belgium

7   A Yaka slit drum;
    wood; height: 44 cm (17¹/₄ in)

8   A Zombo slit gong;
    wood and copper nails;
    height: 20 cm (7⁷/₈ in)

9   A Yaka *Kakungu* mask;
    wood and vegetal fibres;
    height: 73 cm (28¹/₂ in)

10 A Yaka fetish figure;
    wood, vegetal fibres and feathers;
    height: 28 cm (11 in);
    J. Walscharts, Antwerp

11 A Holo crouching figure;
    wood; height: 35 cm (13³/₄ in);
    Archives Monbrison, Paris

12 A Holo panel;
    wood; height: 28 cm (11 in);
    private collection

BIBLIOGRAPHY
BIEBUYCK, D., *The Arts of Zaire: Southwestern Zaire*, Los Angeles, 1985
BOURGEOIS, A., *Art of the Yaka and the Suku*, Meudon, 1984
DEVISH, R., 'Signification Socio-culturelle des masques chez les Yaka', *Boletin instit. de invest. científico de Angola*, 9, Luanda, 1972
FELGAS, H., *As Populachoes nativas do norte de Angola*, Lisbon, 1965
KOPYTOFF, I., *The Suku of Southwestern Congo, People of Africa*, New York, 1965
NEYT, FRANÇOIS, *The Art of the Holo*, Munich, 1982

12

[A] Left: **a Suku crouching figure**
wood, horn and vegetal fibres;
height: 35 cm (14 in);
private collection

The complexity of this figure
illustrates the skills of African
artists. The curved lines of the
coiffure, the face and the arms
echo each other, and the contrast
between the precisely carved
details and the rough surfaces
breathe life into this carving. The
added paraphernalia on its sides
enhances its power.

[B] Right, above: **a Yaka mask**
wood, vegetal fibres and pigments;
height: 66 cm (26 in)

This initiate's mask has an
upturned nose, a characteristic
of Yaka artistic output. The use
of pigments, vegetal fibres and
the spectacular spikes on top
of the head creates an overall
feeling of mystery.

[C] Left: **a Suku helmet mask**
wood, vegetal fibres and pigment;
height: 44.4 cm (17¹/₂ in)

The open mouth, exposing the teeth,
and the thick eyebrows convey the
aggressive expression of this mask
which was worn during initiation
ceremonies. The bird set on top
of the head was probably a totemic
animal.

[D] Above: **a Lula mask**
wood and pigment;
height: 41.9 cm (16¹/₂ in)

Lula artists used white and blue
pigments to accentuate shapes
and surfaces on their masks.
This one was most likely worn
by the guardian of an initiation
camp. The woven vegetal fibres
attached at the back of the mask
secured it to the wearer's head.

Tchokwe

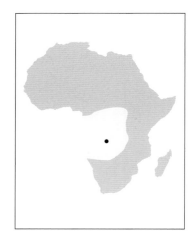

1

During the 15th century, a Lunda queen married a Luba prince called Tshibinda Ilunga. A significant number of the Lunda aristocracy so disapproved of the marriage that they migrated south to present-day Angola. Once settled, they founded several kingdoms, each headed by a god-king. These tribes are now known as the Tchokwe, the Luena, the Songo, the Imbagala and the Ovimbudu. Around 1860, following a major famine, the Tchokwe people migrated back towards the south and settled in Angola, at the source of the Kwango, Kasai and Lungwe rivers. The Tchokwe are governed by a king called *Mwana Ngana*, who distributes hunting grounds and cultivated areas; while the male *Mugonge* and female *Ukule* societies regulate their social life.

1 1 A *Cihongo* mask; *wood and vegetal fibres; height: 20.3 cm (8 in); private collection*

2 A Muzamba-style figure; *wood; height: 57.2 cm (22¹/₂ in)*

3 A Mucomba-style figure; *wood; height: 70 cm (27¹/₂ in); private collection*

4 A Songo figure; *wood; height: 75 cm (29¹/₂ in)*

5 A comb; *wood; height: 17 cm (6⁵/₈ in)*

6 A whistle; *wood and copper nails; height: 7.5 cm (2³/₄ in)*

7 An Ovimbudu box; *wood; height: 33.5 cm (13¹/₄ in)*

8 A Kwilu-Kasai-style chair; *wood; height: 73 cm (28⁵/₈ in); private collection*

9 An Ovimbudu sceptre; *wood and copper nails; height: 41 cm (16 in)*

10 A Pinda figure; *ivory; height: 8.4 cm (31/4 in)*

The vast majority of Tchokwe objects are decorated with figures and geometric motifs. Since the Tchokwe tribespeople were in contact with European tradesmen from the 18th century onwards, some of their figures bear a European influence.

MASKS

The Tchokwe have carved a variety of masks:
• The *Cikungu* is made of vegetal fibres and cloth and is covered with black, white and red pigments. It is used during the *Mukanga* initiation ceremonies and is also worn to exorcise a curse from the village.
• The *Cihongo* mask (1) is a male mask which is made from wood and has a typical horizontal beard and large globular eyes. It symbolizes wealth and power. The wearer of the mask covers himself with a vegetal net and is responsible for collecting the tribute owed to the chief. The mask confers judiciary powers to the wearer.
• The *Pwo* mask [D] symbolizes the ideal mother and woman. It has facial scarifications and is believed to spread fertility wherever it is worn.

• The *Kalelwa* and *Cikunza* are vegetal-fibre masks with highly elaborate coiffures and are used during circumcision ceremonies.

STATUES

Tchokwe carvers have achieved fame on the basis of their statues representing their Luba ancestor, Tshibinda Ilunga [C]. His representations show a man with an enlarged head and an elaborate coiffure, either seated or standing, often engaged in everyday activities. His enlarged, open hands convey a welcoming gesture to his people.

Small female figures, called *Cisola*, are rare. It is thought that each may represent a great queen or, more symbolically, a female ancestor celebrated for her fecundity. They are used during fertility rites and to safeguard pregnant women.

There are several regional styles of figure:
• The Ucokwe style, or 'style from the country of origin' (pre-1860), is characterized by a dynamic attitude and an attention to detail such as the insertion of real hair in the beard area, of metal fragments into

2   3   4   5   6   7

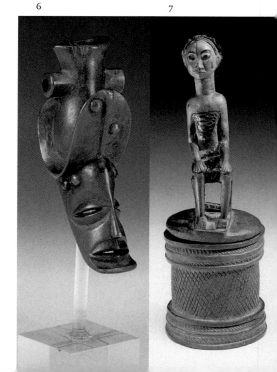

8

9   10

11

the eyes and a large coiffure. There are two sub-styles of the Ucokwe style: the Moxico **[C]** and the Muzamba **(2)** which could be a later style.

After the 1860s, Tchokwe migration appears to have slowed the carving of ancestor figures and given way to the emergence of several simpler styles:
• The Kwilu-Kasai style is mostly represented by monoxylous chairs using carved figures as backrests **(8)**.
• The Shaba-style figures are less detailed and display Luena scarifications on the face. Chairs in this style are made of several pieces of wood and are decorated with figures. They were inspired by European models imported by the Portuguese from the 17th century onwards.
• The Mucomba-style figures are similar to the Shaba with the added Luena feature of a rounded cross-hatched coiffure **(3)**. It has been suggested that these objects were produced for colonials.

EVERYDAY OBJECTS
Figurative 'prestige' and utilitarian objects were produced in large numbers for the Tchokwe court, but after the 1860 migration the production of stools **[B]**, sceptres **(13)** and tobacco boxes made of wood or ivory became more commonplace.
Pipes, whistles **(6)**, combs **(5)**, drums and finger pianos called *Sanzas* were produced for the courtiers' use, as were zoomorphic neckrests.

RELATED TRIBES
Led by a king, the *Mwana Yamvo*, the **Luena** people support themselves from fishing in the wet plains at the source of the Zambeze River, in Angola. Artistically, they appear to have focused their skills on carving female figures which are usually found on

decorative 'prestige' objects such as canes, combs and finger pianos, and on masks **[A]**. These differ from those of the Tchokwe as their statues usually display a spherical cross-hatched coiffure which is often divided by a vertical ridge, and angular linear scarifications on their cheeks.

Another neighbouring tribe of the Tchokwe, the **Songo**, live to the west of the source of the Kwango River, in a trade-route area. Songo craftsmen often took their artistic inspiration from the traders who traversed the route on oxen, transferring this image onto stools **(11)**, small figures and sceptres **(14)**. Sango figures **(4)** are made from a dark red wood, and have a typical coiffure with two horizontal 'wings', the use of which is unknown.

The two million **Ovimbudu** are the largest ethnic group living in Angola. They occupy the high plateau of Benguela where they settled several centuries ago and live mostly from agriculture and cattle rearing.
Ovimbudu carvers are noted for their female figures which generally adorn everyday objects **(9)**. They display an enlarged torso and a typical coiffure with backward-swept plaits joined at the end. The wood is typically light coloured – an influence from East and South Africa – with darkened details. Ovimbudu figures are used either during fertility rites as the Tchokwe *Cisola* figures are, or for female initiation ceremonies. 'Prestige objects' were also produced: canes, boxes **(7)**, combs and pipes.

Several other tribes live in the western and southern part of Angola and have carved rare objects. The **Imbangala** have produced bird-shaped stools **(12)**, neckrests, statuettes displaying a lateral-horned coiffure and pipes with geometric decoration.
The **Cuando** made elongated drums with conical breasts and the **Pinda** carved small ivory figures associated with healing rites **(10)**.

11 A Songo stool;
    *wood; height: 30.8 cm (12 in);
    collected in c. 1885 by Dr Romao
    in Malenge, Angola*

12 An Imbangala stool;
    wood; height: 21 cm (83/8 in)

13 A sceptre with a Janus head;
    *wood; height: 46.3 cm (18 in);
    M. Pinto, Geneva*

14 A Songo sceptre;
    wood; height: 52 cm (20 1/2 in)

BIBLIOGRAPHY
Art et mythologie, figures Tchokwe, Exh. Cat., Musée Dapper, Paris, 1988
BASTIN, M.-L., *Art décoratif Tchokwe*, no. 55, 2 vols, Lisbon, 1961
BASTIN, M.-L., 'L'Art d'un peuple d'Angola, I: Tchokwe, II: Luena, III: Songo, IV: Mbundu', *African Arts*, I–II, 1968–69
BASTIN, M.-L., 'Art Songo', *Arts d'Afrique Noire*, no. 30, summer, pp. 30–43, 1979
BASTIN, M.-L., *La Sculpture Tchokwe*, Meudon, 1982
HAMBLY, W. D., 'The Ovimbudu of Angola', *Field Museum Natural History*, XXI, 2, Chicago, 1934
LOPES CARDOSO, C., 'Mbali Art – A Case of Acculturation', *Memoriam Antonio Jorge Dias*, Lisbon, pp. 69–80, 1974
Sculpture Angolaise: Memorial de Cultures, Exh. Cat., Museu nacional de etnologia, Lisbon, 1994

13   14

[A] Left: **a Luena mask**
wood and vegetal fibres; height: 27 cm (10⁵/8 in)

The characteristic facial scarifications and coiffure of the Luena people can be seen on this mask. A vegetal-fibre net costume which kept the identity of the wearer secret during ritual ceremonies is attached to the mask.

[B] Below left: **a Tchokwe anthropomorphic stool**
wood and copper nails; height: 36 cm (14 in);
private collection

A superb example of the Tchokwe production of prestige objects, this stool is made out of a single piece of wood and pre-dates the chairs that imitate European prototypes.

[C] Left: **a moxico-style Tshibinda Ilunga figure**

wood; height: 37 cm (14¹/₂ in); provenance: collected c. 1895 by Captain Artur de Paiva in Angola

This figure depicts Tshibinda Ilunga, the Luba ancestor of the Tchokwe, with a welcoming gesture. The two smaller figures clasped in his hands symbolize the protection he offers the entire tribe.

[D] Above: **two** *pwo* **masks**

wood, copper nails and vegetal fibres;
height: 27 and 26 cm (10⁵/₈ in and 10¹/₄ in)

Pwo masks, with their typical forehead, cheek and chin scarifications, represent the ideal mother and woman. The vegetal-fibre net secures the mask onto the wearer's head.

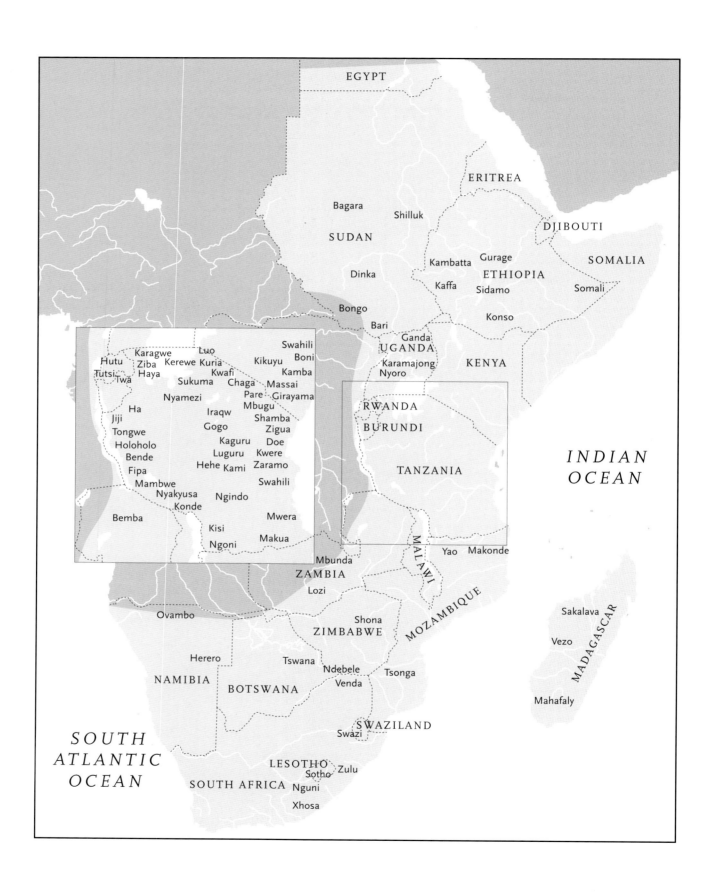

EGYPT

SUDAN

ERITREA

DJIBOUTI

Bagara

Shilluk

Dinka

Kambatta   Gurage

ETHIOPIA

SOMALIA

Kaffa   Sidamo

Somali

Bongo

Konso

Bari

Ganda

UGANDA

KENYA

Karamajong

Nyoro

Hutu   Karagwe   Luo   Swahili   Boni

Ziba   Kikuyu
Kerewe   Kuria
Tutsi   Kamba

Twa   Haya   Kwafi

Sukuma   Chaga   Massai

Nyamezi   Pare   Girayama

RWANDA

Ha   Mbugu

Jiji   Iraqw   Shamba   BURUNDI

Tongwe   Gogo   Zigua

Holoholo   Kaguru   Doe   TANZANIA

Bende   Luguru   Kwere

Fipa   Hehe Kami Zaramo

Mambwe   Swahili

Nyakyusa   Ngindo

Konde

Bemba   Mwera

Kisi

Ngoni   Makua

Mbunda

MALAWI

Yao   Makonde

ZAMBIA

Lozi

INDIAN
OCEAN

Shona

Sakalava

Ovambo

Vezo

ZIMBABWE

MOZAMBIQUE

MADAGASCAR

Herero   Tswana

Ndebele   Tsonga

NAMIBIA   Venda

BOTSWANA

Mahafaly

SWAZILAND

Swazi

SOUTH
ATLANTIC
OCEAN

LESOTHO   Zulu

Sotho

SOUTH AFRICA   Nguni

Xhosa

V

EAST AND
SOUTH AFRICA

SUDAN, UGANDA, RWANDA, BURUNDI
MOZAMBIQUE, MALAWI, ZAMBIA, ZIMBABWE
MADAGASCAR
KENYA, ETHIOPIA, SOMALIA
THE COAST OF TANZANIA
THE NORTH-EASTERN REGIONS OF TANZANIA
THE CENTRAL-WESTERN REGIONS OF TANZANIA
THE WESTERN REGIONS OF TANZANIA
SOUTH AFRICA, NAMIBIA, BOTSWANA

Sudan, Uganda, Rwanda, Burundi

Until recently, Western scholars have not shown a great interest in the culture flourishing in the northern part of East Africa. Nineteenth-century travellers wrote accounts of their meetings with indigenous people, but there was little interest in their artistic output since the majority were nomadic and they tended to carve small, easily portable objects. The impact of the Islamic slave trade at the end of the 19th century and constant inter-tribal wars contributed to the near extinction of some of these peoples. Information about them is scarce and fragmentary.

1

1 A Basoga/Bongo mask;
wood; height: 36 cm (14¹/₄ in);
private collection

2 A Karamajong/Turkana neckrest;
wood; height: 24 cm (9¹/₂ in)

3 A Dinka/Shilluk neckrest;
wood; height: 17 cm (6³/₄ in)

4 A Bari neckrest;
wood; height: 20 cm (7⁷/₈ in)

5 A Bongo *Hegba* neckrest;
wood; height: 15.9 cm (6¹/₄ in)

6 A Ganda vessel;
wood; height: 27 cm (10¹/₂ in);
private collection

7 A Nyoro vessel;
clay; height: 31 cm (12¹/₈ in)

8 A Ganda drum;
wood and hide; height:
80 cm (31¹/₂ in)

2

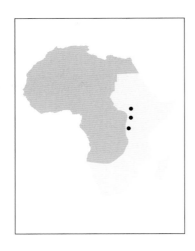

SUDAN

Towards the end of the 19th century, the **Bongo** people were a powerful tribe. They numbered 100,000 and occupied a region of southern Sudan, on a large plain to the west of the White Nile. The Islamic slave trade dramatically reduced their population to 5,000 by the 1920s, although they have slightly grown in number since then. Bongo elders hold political authority and their economy is mainly based on farming sorghum and millet.

The reputation of Bongo artists is based on the posts that they carved for the graves of important men. They are cylindrical in shape and have either a full figure or a head at the top. These posts are believed to represent the deceased and act both as memorials and potent inhibitors of sorcerers' spells. Occasionally, the cylindrical base is notched to represent the number of enemies or large animals killed by the deceased **[B]**.

Bongo masks (1) are extremely rare and characteristically have an elongated flat face with rectangular eyes, a mouth showing teeth and sometimes rows of scars over the nose, eyebrows and on the middle of the forehead. Bongo carvers also produced oval-shaped neckrests with a pair of V-shaped legs (5).

The **Bari** people number 35,000 and occupy swamplands on the eastern side of the White Nile in southern Sudan. Historically, they were cattle farmers, but they migrated due to the pressure of Islamic slave traders and abandoned their nomadic existence and became farmers. Bari society is loosely structured politically – important offices are held by wealthy members of the community.

Bari artists carved elongated figures which were about 50 cm high. They stand on small feet and have a columnar torso set under flattened shoulders. The head is generally oval shaped with a flat face showing incised diminutive features **[A]**. Their purpose is uncertain, although they may have been used as fertility dolls, ancestor figures, or they may have been produced for the tourist trade.

The Bari sleep on wooden neckrests carved with a rectangular concave upper element set over a rectangular open-worked foot covered with vegetal fibres or lizard skin (4).

The **Dinka** and **Shilluk** settled in southern Sudan and their carvers produced wooden headrests which have a three-legged natural shape. They are made from a branch of a tree that has been pruned into the right shape and are often suggestive of animals. A man's status was frequently shown by the quality of his coiffure, so a neckrest was used during the night in order to keep it in place. Dinka elders also use these high neckrests as stools (3) – it is considered undignified for a dignitary to sit on the floor.

The Shilluk created circular mud masks with round pierced eyes and mouths which are thought to represent a leopard's face, although in the West it is not known how they were used. Ivory bracelets (10) are worn by Dinka and Shilluk elders during communal ceremonies.

The **Bagara** and **Ondurman** live in central Sudan. Their carvers made dolls with elongated features and typically a spherical head with eyes inset with white

3

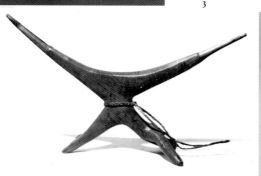

4

5

6   7   8   10   11

glass beads. These dolls (12) are embellished with added cloth, hair, earrings and necklaces.

The people of Darfur, known collectively as the **Nuba**, produce black clay vessels and calabashes decorated with linear motifs either in a giraffe camouflage pattern or in the shape of the net from which objects are often hung.

UGANDA

The **Karamajong** live a nomadic existence, moving with their herds of cattle across Kenya and Uganda. Their artistic output is centred on their production of monoxylous neckrests characterized by a horizontal element supported by a flat foot set on a spherical base (2).

Like the majority of tribes in this area, the **Tutsi** live by rearing cattle. The area they live in spans across the frontiers of Burundi and Rwanda. They are famous for their woven artefacts and their skills in tattooing and hair shaving. Aristocratic women produce extremely fine baskets called *Agaseki*, which are decorated with red and black geometric patterns and capped with a pointed lid (11).

Wristguards, called *Igitembe*, are used by archers to protect their left arm and are usually constructed from vegetal fibres. Dignitaries, however, wear wooden ones which are inlaid with copper wires in the shape of geometric motifs (9).

Tutsi shields are rectangular and convex in shape with a large hemispherical protrusion in the centre that is exposed while the perimeter of the shield is covered in rattan.

The **Nyoro** people from Uganda are associated with the production of black vessels adorned with incised decorations of geometrical motifs that are coloured with white or red pigments (7).

RWANDA/BURUNDI

Scattered across Rwanda and Burundi, the **Hutu** people, unlike the Tutsi, are sedentary. They are known for the quality of their small metal zoomorphic figures.

The **Twa** people are the indigenous 'pygmy' population of Rwanda and Burundi. They are forest dwellers and their livelihood is derived from hunting and trading in terracotta vessels which they exchange with their Tutsi and Hutu neighbours. The vessels are red or black and are often decorated with incised, elongated downward-pointing triangles.

The **Ganda** people of Uganda produce wooden (6), red clay vessels for everyday use and black shiny rounded pots for prestigious functions. Used within the royal court, these vessels are made by a royal potter, known as the *Kujona*, who is given land in exchange for his work. The high lustre on the surface is obtained by applying graphite after firing, followed by rubbing and polishing. Ganda drums (8) are elongated in shape.

BIBLIOGRAPHY

BRAUNHOLTZ, H., 'Pottery figures from Luzua, Uganda', *Man*, 36, no. 92, 1936

BURDOCK, GEORGE P., *Africa, Its People and their Cultural History*, New York

CASTLE, ENRICH, 'Bari Statuary: the Influence Exerted by European Traders on the Traditional Production of Figured Objects', *ROES* (Los Angeles), 14, Autumn 1987

CELIS, G., 'The Decorative Arts in Rwanda and Burundi', *African Arts*, 4 (1), 1970, pp. 40–42

EVANS-PRITCHARD, E. E., 'The Bongo', *Sudan Notes and Records* 12, 1929, pp. 1–61

KRONENBERG, ANDREAS and WALTRUB, 'Die Bongo, Bauern und Jäger in Südsudan', *Studien zur Kulturkunde*, 58, Wiesbaden, 1981

POSNANSKY, P., and J. H. CHAPLIN, 'Terracotta Figures from Entebbe', *Man*, 31, no. 4, 1968

ROSCOE, J., *The Baganda: an Account of their Nature, Customs and Beliefs*, London, 1911

SEITZ, S., 'Die Zentralafrikanischen Wild-beuterkulturen', *Studien zur Kulturkunde* 45, Wiesbaden, 1977

SELIGMAN, CHARLES G., 'A Bongo Funerary Figure', *Man* (London), 18, no. 67, 1917, pp. 97–98

SELIGMAN, CHARLES G. and BRENDA Z., 'The Bari', *Journal of the Royal Anthropological Institute* (London), 58, 1928, pp. 409–79

SELIGMAN, CHARLES G. and BRENDA Z., *Pagan Tribes of the Nilotic Sudan*, London, 1932

TROWEL, MARGARET, and K. P. WACHSWANN, *Tribal Crafts of Uganda*, London, 1953

WESTERN, D., *The Shilluk People and their Language and Folklore*, Philadelphia, 1912

12

9   A Tutsi wristguard;
*wood and copper wire;
diameter: 32 cm (12^1/$_2$ in);
Van Opstal Collection, Belgium*

10   A Dinka/Shilluk bracelet;
*ivory; diameter: 14 cm (5^1/$_2$ in);
private collection*

11   Two Tutsi baskets;
*vegetal fibres; height of the taller:
22 cm (85/8 in)*

12   A Bagara doll;
*wood; textile, vegetal fibres and
glass beads; height: 46 cm (18 in);
private collection*

[A] Right: **a Bari figure**
wood; height: 40 cm (15³/₄ in);
private collection

The strikingly elongated features
of this Bari figure are evocative
of Tanzanian art. Its ritualistic
purpose is unknown, although it
may have been carved as a puppet,
an ancestor figure or possibly for
the tourist trade.

[B] Far right: **a Bongo figure**
wood; height: 42 cm (16¹/₂ in)

This apotropaic figure represents
an important Bongo dignitary and
was placed on top of his grave to
commemorate his life. The notches
on the base symbolize the animals
or enemies that he killed.

Mozambique, Malawi, Zambia, Zimbabwe

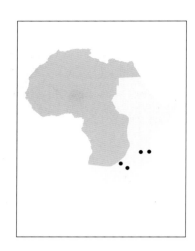

1

MOZAMBIQUE

The **Makonde** belong to the Bantu people who originally lived south of Lake Nyassa and later migrated to their present location on the Mueda plateau in northern Mozambique. They survive economically from farming and, occasionally, cattle rearing.

Makonde carvers are prolific producers of masks, statues and decorative objects.

The most famous Makonde masks are the helmet masks (1) which are used to mark a boy's initiation into adulthood. These masks, called *Lipico*, have realistic features and are often inset with hair and decorated with wax facial scarifications.

Facial and body masks are usually associated with the Makonde people living in Tanzania. The former frequently represents a woman's face with a lip plug (2), while the latter is carved to appear as a body of a pregnant woman (4). These masks are also thought to be worn during boys' initiation ceremonies.

Makonde sculptures measure from 20 to 80 cm in height, are carved as standing men or women, representing ancestors, and have apotropaic functions (6).

Makonde artists like to adorn everyday objects with human faces – empty cartridges were sometimes used as medicine or tobacco boxes and had a lid in the shape of a human head (14). The Makonde also made pipes [A], canes, combs and bark boxes. Contemporary Makonde artists have achieved a reputation for their human-like ebony figures carved with elongated or distorted features.

Tsonga-speaking people live in the centre of Mozambique. In the late 20th century numerous African figures originally thought to have been carved by Zulu artists were reattributed to the Tsonga. Further research may reveal more about the exact provenance of these objects. Tsonga figures, of which there are a significantly large number, demonstrate considerable stylistic variation, although the figures do share common features – a columnar aspect, rounded heads, open mouths and triangular noses. They are thought to have been used in pairs during boys' initiations into adulthood where they served as sexual and social teaching aids [D].

Tsonga neckrests (11) are characterized by appendages hanging under the platform and are usually carved with a flatter base than the neckrests of their southern neighbours, the Shona (12). The feet of the neckrests vary considerably and often have geometric, intricate shapes. However, Tsonga neckrests are very similar to the south-eastern Shona ones and quite often it is impossible to distinguish the exact origin of such pieces.

Tsonga artists carved intricate spoons, wooden chains and staffs with a figure produced from a light-coloured wood with darkened details (13). Such staffs are also found among the northern Nguni people and they cannot be attributed to either tribe with any certainty.

2

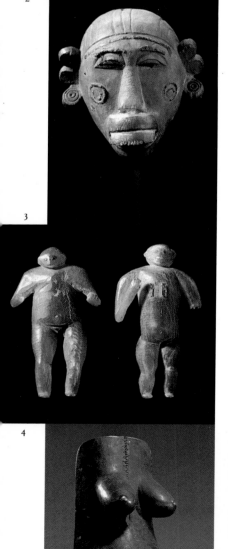

3

4

5

6

7

8

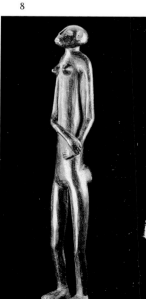

9

10

11

12

13

14

MALAWI
A number of large figures carved with a columnar aspect, enlarged feet and rounded heads (5) have been attributed to artists living in Malawi. There is a remarkable stylistic diversity within this corpus and further research will undoubtedly provide a more accurate provenance for the statues referred to as 'Malawi'.

The artistic output of the **Yao** tribe has not received much attention in the West. The Yao are mostly farmers and their carvers produced large figures which are thought to be used during initiation age-group ceremonies, a common feature of most south-eastern African tribes. Yao figures have a columnar appearance and typical features such as nose plugs and often X-shaped linear scarifications (7).

ZAMBIA
Many Zambian tribes are artistically; among the most prolific are:
The **Lozi** people are ruled by a king and live in western Zambia. They are also called Rotse, which is the name of their kingdom, and includes three sub-groups – the Tsonga, the Mbunda and the Lunda people. Their artistic output appears to be limited to vegetal-fibre baskets, wooden boxes with lids carved with decorative elements, such as human or zoomorphic figures (10), rectangular neckrests (9), small horn figures (3) and terracotta zoomorphic vessels (16).

The **Mbunda** people settled in western Zambia after migrating from Angola. Their masks are character-ized by slanted eyes surrounded by multiple lids and a rectangular mouth which exposes the teeth. Two types of mask have been carved and can be distinguished due to their size. Of the first and larger type, approximately ten examples are known to exist. Called the *Sachango Masaka* **[B]**, it represents the founder of the Mbunda people and is worn by boys at the end of their three to six month initiation period that culminates in the *Mukanda* circumcision ceremony. The second type of mask, called *Malamprevo*, is smaller and symbolizes an imaginary pretty girl. It has a less sacred function and is worn during initiation and circumcision ceremonies, as well as for entertainment festivities.

The **Bisa** people live in northern Zambia and are culturally related to their northern neighbours, the Tabwa. Bisa artists carve elongated figures (8) with rounded heads and thin elongated limbs in common with the Tabwa aesthetic, although these statues also display features related to meridional African art such as a tendency towards abstraction.

ZIMBABWE
Descended from the people who lived in the city of Great Zimbabwe in the 14th century, the **Shona**-speaking people are known for their production of neckrests called *Mutsago*, which have a rectangular upper platform which curves up towards the ends. These neckrests were owned by men and were often buried with them. There are a number of styles – e.g., the eastern style, relating to the Manyika people, with two sets of triangles carved on the platform (12) and the north-central style, related to the Korekore people foot, with triangular and circular motifs separated by horizontal lines **[C]**. Zoomorphic neck-rests have also been carved, although they are rare.

Ivory or wooden knives (15) are rare, but they have also been collected and may have been the prized possessions of highly important men.

Contemporary Shona carvers have developed a significant production of soap-stone figures charac-terized by smooth and abstract features.

BIBLIOGRAPHY
ALPERS, E., 'Trade, State and Society Among the Yao in the Nineteenth Century', *Journal of African History*, 10, 1969
Art and Ambiguity, Perspectives on the Brenthurst Collection of Southern African Art, Exh. Cat., Johannesburg Art Gallery, 1991
Art Makonde, Tradition et Modernité, Exh. Cat., Musée National des Arts d'Afrique et d'Océanie, Paris, 1989
FELIX, MARC, *Makishi*, Munich, 1998
PAPSTEIN, R., ed., *The History and Cultural Life of the Mbunda Speaking People*, Lusaka, 1994
TEW, M., *Peoples of the Lake Nyasa Region*, London, 1950

1 A Makonde *Lipico* helmet mask; *wood; height: 22.5 cm ($8^7/8$ in); private collection*

2 A Makonde face mask; *wood; height: 20 cm (8 in); private collection*

3 A pair of Lozi figures; *horn; height: 6.6 cm ($2^5/8$ in); private collection*

4 A Makonde body mask; *wood and hair; height: 50.8 cm (20 in)*

5 A Malawi monkey figure, possibly from the Lomwe tribe; *wood; height: 48 cm (19 in)*

6 A Makonde figure; *wood; height: 52.7 cm ($20^3/4$ in)*

7 A Yao figure; *wood; height: 19 cm ($7^1/2$ in)*

8 A Bisa figure; *wood; height: 47 cm ($18^1/2$ in); Courtesy Entwistle Gallery, London; private collection*

9 A Lozi neckrest; *wood; length: 32 cm ($12^1/2$ in); private collection*

10 A Lozi box; *wood; diameter: 33 cm (13 in)*

11 A Tsonga neckrest; *wood; height: 17 cm ($6^5/8$ in)*

12 A Shona neckrest; *wood; height: 12 cm ($4^3/4$ in)*

13 A Tsonga staff; *wood; height of the figure: 18 cm (7 in)*

14 A Makonde medicine container; *wood and copper cartridge; height: 10 cm (4 in); private collection*

15 A Shona knife; *wood, copper wire and iron blade; length: 38 cm (15 in); private collection*

16 A Lozi vessel; *terracotta; height: 36 cm ($14^1/4$ in); private collection*

15

16

[A] Left: **a Makonde anthropomorphic pipe**
wood; height: 27 cm (10⁵/₈ in); private collection

In both Eastern and Southern Africa, generally only important people smoke. This extraordinary pipe displays anthropomorphic features, as well as geometric decoration typical of Makonde art.

[B] Below: **a Mbunda mask**
wood; height: 48 cm (19 in); Archives Olivier Klejman, Paris

This Mbunda mask, called *Sachango Masaka*, has typical exaggerated features and was probably used during boys' initiations. Based on field research conducted in Zambia in 1982, it has been attributed to the Mbunda tribe.

[C] Bottom: **a Shona neckrest**
wood; height: 27 cm (10⁵/₈ in); private collection

The decoration on the foot of this Shona chief's neckrest, with circular, triangular and linear motifs, is typical of the North-Central style of Shona art.

[D] Right: **a Tsonga figure**
wood; height: 49 cm (19¹/₄ in); private collection

Very little is known about Tsonga figures, but typically their position is static, they are made of a light-coloured wood worked with a small adze and have a large head.

Madagascar

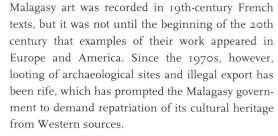

Madagascar is a large island 400 km off the shore of Mozambique. It has a central spine of high dry plateau and is noted for its tropical climate. It was first inhabited during the 7th century by people related to the Polynesians who lived along the Swahili coast of Africa, but they were eventually driven away by Islamic traders. In about 1500, kingdoms began to appear – the Sakalava occupied the west coast of the island; the Betsimisaraka empire, which means 'the many inseparable', was located on the south-east coast, although it was in fact an association of villages isolated within a dense forest; and by 1830 the Merina kingdom, which originally occupied the central highlands and eventually expanded over the entire island, absorbed the Sakalava and Betsimisaraka kingdoms. Towards the end of the 19th century, the island was colonized by the French, but it had gained its independence by 1960.

1

Malagasy art was recorded in 19th-century French texts, but it was not until the beginning of the 20th century that examples of their work appeared in Europe and America. Since the 1970s, however, looting of archaeological sites and illegal export has been rife, which has prompted the Malagasy government to demand repatriation of its cultural heritage from Western sources.

Malagasy artistic output appears to be associated principally with the funerary tradition of the islanders. One funerary tradition, typical of east and central Madagascar – where only a few artefacts have been found – is the practice of 'secondary inhumation'. The practice is that when a person dies their body is either kept in the village to dry, or it is buried in a temporary grave which symbolically 'purifies' the corpse by eliminating all body fluids. After a period of time, the bones are exhumed and re-buried in an ancestral communal tomb. Each time a new corpse is laid to rest in the communal tomb, the bones of the other corpses are taken out, paraded, and wrapped in silk shrouds which are usually decorated with bands of colours, and then returned to the tomb.

The first practice of leaving the corpse to dry is principally related to the **Betsimisaraka** people who live on the east coast of the island. The second practice of burying and then exhuming the body occurs mostly in the middle of the island among the Merina and **Betsileo** people.

On the west and south coasts, where 'primary inhumation' occurs and where graves, graveyards and cenotaphs are more monumental, two main artistic traditions can be distinguished which are related to the Mahafaly and Sakalava people.

The **Mahafaly** occupy an area of desert in the south of the island. They are a nomadic people whose roaming is governed by the migratory patterns of their herds of zebu, a type of buffalo. In spite of their nomadic existence, the Mahafaly construct elaborate tombs for their tribal dignitaries – rectangular, stone monuments surmounted by poles, called *Aloalo*, which are often adorned with figures. Typically, the figures are of naked men/women standing in a frontal position, with short legs, both hands resting on their knees, and with an enlarged rounded head bearing a typical coiffure with a crown of small buns (2, 7). Moreover, the figure is usually set beneath an

2   3

4   5   6   7

open-worked plank which is itself decorated with full and half-moon motifs **(1)**. The very top of the plank is decorated with the form of either a bird or a zebu.

The Mahafaly also created cenotaphs known as *Ajiba*. They were originally surmounted by a single human figure but, during the 20th century, they became more complex and nowadays their iconography sometimes includes elements related to the deceased's life: a car, plane, horse, canoe, etc.

The **Sakalava** occupy a region along the west coast of the island and unlike the Mahafaly, they bury their dead in the forest, far from the village, in wooden rectangular tombs. On each corner and in the middle of the longest sides are large figures of birds **(6)**, men or women – with or without a child **(3, 4)** – or most notably, copulating couples **(5)**. The latter are sometimes called 'Sari Porno' by the natives as tourists take a particular interest in them. These figures can be distinguished from those of the Mahafaly because they lack the plank placed above the head of the figure.

The north-east corner of each grave has a figure representing the deceased **[B]**. The sun rises in the north-east so it is associated with dawn and rebirth. In the opposite corner a figure of the opposite sex is placed which reinforces the idea of sexuality, inherent in Sakalava beliefs. Some scholars have suggested that these figures may in fact have been produced by the Vezo people, a group of fishermen living on the southern coast of Madagascar **[A]**.

EVERYDAY OBJECTS

Figurative Malagasy everyday objects are extremely rare. A miniature figure carved to represent a human couple was found and may have been the upper part of a comb. Wooden spoons are more common and often have an elongated handle on which figures of animals are set, an artistic tradition also found in South Africa. A rare ivory spoon **(8)**, now in a private collection, displays geometric motifs which may have been inspired by Swahili art.

BIBLIOGRAPHY

Art Sakalava, Université de Madagascar, Antananarivo, 1963
ASTUTI, R., 'Invisible Objects: Mortuary Rituals among the Vezo of Western Madagascar', *RES*, 25, 1994, pp. 111–22
BLOCH, M., *Placing the Dead: Tombs, Ancestral Villages and Kinship Organisations in Madagascar*, London, 1971
BOUDRY, R., 'L'Art décoratif Malgache', *Revue de Madagascar*, 1933, pp. 12–71
BOULFROY, N., 'Vers l'art funéraire Mahafaly', *Objets et Mondes*, 16, 3, 1976, pp. 95–116
GUERNIER, N. J., 'Wood Sculpting and Carving among the Betsileo', *Ethnography*, 71, 1976, pp. 5–22
KENT, R., *Early Kingdoms in Madagascar, 1500–1700*, New York, 1970
MACK, J., *Madagascar, Island of Ancestors*, London, 1986
URBAIN-FLAUBEE, M., *L'Art Malgache*, Paris, 1963

1 A Mahafaly figure;
    wood; height: 165 cm (65 in)

2 A pair of Mahafaly figures;
    wood; height of the taller: 78 cm (30¹/₂ in)

3 A pair of Sakalava figures;
    wood; height of the taller: 75 cm (29¹/₂ in)

4 A Sakalava (?)/Mahafaly (?) paternity figure;
    wood; height: 99 cm (39 in)

5 A 'Sari Porno' Sakalava figure;
    wood; height: 80 cm (31¹/₂ in)

6 A Sakalava bird figure;
    wood; height: 73 cm (28³/₄ in)

7 A Mahafaly maternity figure;
    wood; height: 93 cm (36¹/₂ in)

8 A spoon;
    ivory; length: 12 cm (4³/₄ in); private collection

8

[A] Above: **a pair of Vezo figures**
wood; height of the taller: 57 cm (22^1/$_2$ in);
private collection

The Vezo population who carve these figures
live in areas controlled by the Sakalava people.
It is likely that these statues were funerary
objects, but it is unclear whether their dynamic
stance was a deliberate artistic decision or
whether it is due to their exposure to the
extreme weather in this area of Madagascar.

[B] Right: **a Sakalava female figure**
wood; height: 80 cm (31^1/$_2$ in); private collection

Exposure to wind and rain has given this figure
a weathered patina. It was originally set on the
corner of an important dignitary's grave.

Kenya, Ethiopia, Somalia

The art produced by the tribes who live in the eastern corner of Africa is insufficiently documented, yet the corpus of objects found in this region is congruent with the rest of Oriental Africa's artistic output. Nevertheless, the influence of the Islamic world has been particularly strong on the coastal areas of Somalia where Islamic traders have been active since the Middle Ages. The people living in these areas are predominantly nomadic and so produced light and portable objects. Masks are extremely rare and figures were carved for funerary purposes only. In addition, wooden chairs (8), influenced by Tanzanian art traditions, are a feature of nomadic life. The principal tribes of the area are, from north to south: the Gurage, the Sidamo, the Kambatta and the Konso people in Ethiopia, the Boni/Somali people in Somalia, and the Kwafi, the Kikuyu, the Kamba, the Massai and the Girayama people in Kenya.

1 A Girayama post;
wood; height: 89 cm (35 in)

2 A Massai shield; *hide and wood; height: 100 cm (39¹/₄ in)*

3 A Boni/Somali neckrest; *wood; height: 14 cm (5¹/₂ in)*

4 A Sidamo neckrest; *wood; height: 18.5 cm (7¹/₄ in)*

5 A Kambatta neckrest; *wood; height: 17 cm (6³/₄ in)*

6 A Kaffa neckrest; *wood; height: 23 cm (9 in)*

KENYA

The **Kwafi** people live in the south-west corner of Kenya, on the shores of Lake Victoria. Their artistic tradition is related to that of the Luo of Tanzania. They are known for their oval-shaped hide masks which display an applied decoration made from lines of white beads.

Living in the south-western part of Kenya, north of Nairobi, the **Kikuyu** artists are known principally for their wooden shields [C]. They are almond shaped, carved with geometric incisions, and decorated with red and black pigments on both faces. The shields were used as a boy's insignia during his initiation. The design on the face is unique and would be erased if the shield had to be reused.

On the eastern slopes of the Kikuyu highlands in southern Kenya, the **Kamba** people settled in a dry area where they raised cattle. Kamba carvers produced small realistic figures, usually carved from a reddish wood, which have shortened features and a rounded head with eyes inset with metal and enlarged ears [B]. These figures appear to have been created after the First World War when a sculptor called Mutisya Munge began carving for the European colonials after serving an apprenticeship with a number of Zaramo carvers.

Elderly Kamba men sit on small stools with a circular concave seat decorated with metal wires and supported by three flat, open-worked feet (10). These seats symbolize the older generation. Kamba brides and young girls are often associated with the wearing of leather beaded aprons (9).

The **Massai** people made their home in southern Kenya. Traditionally nomads, their artistic output is limited to body ornaments such as beaded necklaces, horn bracelets (7) and leather shields decorated with polychrome decorations (2).

The **Girayama** live in south-east Kenya, on the shores of the Indian Ocean. At the end of the 19th century they were a small tribe living by rearing cattle, but today they number 150,000 and live from farming and the tourist industry. Their artistic reputation rests on their grave posts, called *Kigango*. These have a vertical rectangular base incised with geometric decorations and triangular notches and are surmounted by flat (11) or spherical heads (1). They are thought to provide a new physical body for the deceased and because of this belief the post is kept in the man's house and is offered libations. These posts are only carved for the highest-ranking members of certain secret societies, such as the *Chama Ya Vaja* society, which separated men according to their age group, and the *Chama Ya*

1

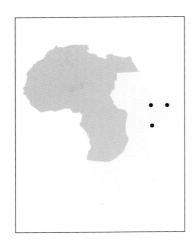

3   4   5   6   7

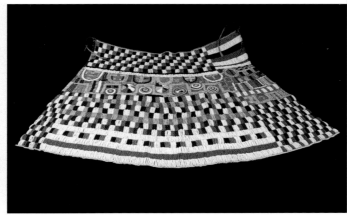

8

9

10

Goghu society, wherein men are initiated as a result of their achievements and financial gifts.

ETHIOPIA

Living in the southern part of Ethiopia, **Gurage** and **Kaffa** men use neckrests in order to protect their coiffure while sleeping. These neckrests have a typical simple or double conical foot supporting a curved platform [D]. Neckrests adorned with small incised triangular decorations are thought to have been made by the Gurage, while the majority with double coned feet are believed to have been carved by the Kaffa people (6).

The **Sidamo** live to the south of the Gurage and the women are believed to use plain rectangular neckrests with a curved upper edge, decorated with incised geometric motifs and a rectangular protrusion on the side (4).

The **Kambatta** people reside west of the Gurage, along the banks of the Upper Omo River, and their men sleep on neckrests with a curved platform supported by rectangular legs over an oblong convex base (5).

Like other Ethiopian tribespeople, the **Konso** are socially structured by the *Gada* male society. The two most important stages in a man's life are his introduction to adulthood and his retirement. The Konso people principally live from farming – hunting is considered to be a prestigious activity. Konso artistic output is restricted to grave markers which adorn the tombs of the highest dignitaries of the *Gada* society [A]. A few months after the death of a dignitary, a set of elongated monoxylous figures representing the deceased, his wives and the animals and enemies he killed are set above the grave and protected by a thatched roof. The dead man's representation is precisely carved with an aggressive expression, an enlarged penis and an abundance of carved jewelry.

SOMALIA

On the frontier between Somalia and Ethiopia, live the **Boni** and **Somali** people who are nomadic cattle herders. Both men and women use two types of neckrest for sleeping and resting. The first type has a curved platform decorated with incised geometric motifs, probably influenced by Islamic designs, and supported by two concave feet joined by a circular base (3). The second type, which might have been used by younger men, has the same decorated platform, but is supported by a single column of intertwined feet on a circular base.

Boni shepherds rest while standing on a single leg, with their head lying on the neckrest set on their shoulder. These neckrests symbolize vigilance because since the base is so small, the resting person could not fall asleep without falling over.

BIBLIOGRAPHY

ADAMSON, J., 'Kaya und Grabfiguren der Kunstenbantu in Kenya', *Paideuma* 4, 1954–58, pp. 251–56

ADAMSON, J., *The People of Kenya*, New York, 1967

BARRETT, W. E. H., 'Notes on the Customs and Beliefs of the Wa-Giriama, East Africa', *Journal of the Royal Anthropological Institute* 41, 1911, pp. 20–28

BROWN, E. J., 'Traditional Sculpture in Kenya', *African Arts* 6, 1, 1972, pp. 16–21, 58, 88

CERULLI, ERNESTA, *The People of South-West Ethiopia and its Borderland*, London, 1956

CHAMPION, A. M., *The Agiryama of Kenya*, J. Middleton, ed., Royal Anthropological Institute of Great Britain, 1967

DEWEY, WILLIAM B., *Sleeping Beauties: The Jerome L. Joss Collection of African Headrests at UCLA*, California, 1993

An Introduction to the Arts of Kenya, Exh. Cat., Smithsonian Institution, Washington, D.C., 1979

KIDANE, G., and R. WILDING, *The Ethiopian Cultural Heritage/ L'héritage Culturel Ethiopien*, Addis Ababa, 1976

LOUGHRAN, K. S., et al., *Somalia in Word and Image*, Washington, D.C., 1986

NOWACK, E., *Land und Volk der Konso*, Bonn, 1954

PUCCIONI, N., *Antropologia e ethnografia della gente della Somalia*, Bologna, 1936

ROUTLEDGE, W. S., *With a Prehistoric People: The Akikuyu of British East Africa*, London, 1910

7   A Massai bracelet;
    horn and copper wires;
    height: 14.8 cm (5³/4 in);
    private collection

8   An Ethiopian chair, Galla (?)/
    Gurage (?);
    wood; height: 95.3 cm (37¹/2 in)

9   A Kamba apron;
    leather and beads; length: 87 cm
    (34¹/4 in); private collection

10 A Kamba stool;
    wood; height: 33 cm (13 in)

11 Three Girayama posts;
    wood; height of the tallest:
    184 cm (72¹/2 in)

11

[A] Left: **a Konso post**
wood; height: 179 cm (69¹/₂ in)

Konso posts were set on top of dignitaries'
graves and were surrounded by wooden
representations of their wives. This dignitary's
exaggerated genitalia, fierce expression and
carved jewelry emphasize his power and status.

[B] Above: **a Kamba figure**
wood; height: 23 cm (9 in); private collection

The use of reddish wood, large round heads
and metal inlaid eyes are typical of Kamba
figures. The stool on which this maternity
figure is seated is associated with the wisdom
of the older generation.

[C] Left, above: **a Kikuyu shield**
wood; height: 64 cm (25^{1}/$_{8}$ in);
Kevin Conru Collection, London

This shield was used as an insignia
during boys' initiations into
adulthood. The abstract geometric
decorations were painstakingly carved
on the surface and erased for each
new ceremony.

[D] Left, below: **a Gurage neckrest**
wood; height: 18 cm (7 in);
private collection

Neckrests such as this one were used
by men to keep their coiffures in
place while sleeping. The present
example is covered in an oily patina,
showing the great care that was taken
to preserve it.

The Coast of Tanzania

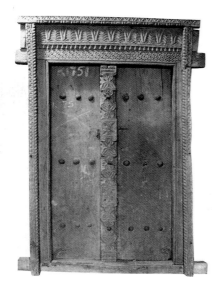

1   A Swahili door;
    wood; height: 204 cm (80¹/₄ in);
    private collection

2   A Zaramo doll;
    wood; height: 9 cm (3¹/₂ in);
    private collection

3   A Luguru figure;
    wood; height: 19 cm (7¹/₂ in);
    private collection

4   A large Zaramo figure;
    wood; height: 85 cm (33³/₈ in);
    Museum für Völkerkunde, Berlin

5   A Doe container and
    anthropomorphic lid;
    calabash and wood; height: 20 cm
    (7⁷/₈ in); private collection

6   A Kwere container and
    anthropomorphic lid;
    calabash and wood; height: 21 cm
    (8¹/₄ in); private collection

7   A Kami doll;
    wood; height: 10.5 cm (4¹/₈ in);
    private collection

The geographical area discussed in this chapter focuses on the southern coast of Tanzania. This region can be divided in two: the first area is centred around the capital Dar-es-Salaam and the second extends to the southerly frontier with Mozambique. Unfortunately, very few Western scholars have studied the Tanzanian people so there is a lack of ethnographic studies which can be drawn upon.

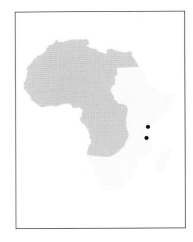

At the beginning of the 19th century, Westerners discovered the art produced in the **first area** before that of the second. Geographically, the first region is a mixture of mangroves and plains where the local population grows corn and wheat and, more recently, fruit. They also rear cattle, goats and sheep. In artistic terms, the tribes who live along a north to south line in this region are the most well documented, from the Swahili along the coast to the Kaguru, the Doe, the Kwere, the Luguru, the Zaramo and the Kami in Zanzibar.

The artistic output of these regions is fairly homogeneous due to the commercial and cultural contacts between the tribes. A feature of their art is the omnipresence of the female form. All over the region, small, stylized, truncated dolls, known as *Mwana Hiti*, are played with by girls and boys during puberty. Later the dolls are preciously preserved and given to the next generation of children. The dolls all have a cylindrical body with pointed breasts and flattened shoulders under a stylized head **(6)**. These *Mwana Hiti* figures also decorate medicine, pigment and oil calabash containers, staffs, zithers and thrones which are used during initiation ceremonies and judgments. Two styles of doll have evolved: a naturalistic style, probably influenced by trade with Malaysia, and an abstract style, probably more indigenous.

The **Swahili** are renowned for their carved doors which display a strong Islamic influence. Usually carved with geometric motifs, these doors **(1)** are a common feature in all the Indian Ocean countries such as Yemen and Oman.

Kaguru thrones are characterized by a plain backrest beneath either a head or a female bust **[D]**. The circular stool to which the back is attached is supported by four concave legs set around a central columnar leg. These, in turn, are linked by an open-worked motif of carved wood.

Doe *Mwana Hiti* dolls are naturalistic in style. They have an elongated, realistic-looking head with inset eyes surmounted by a single or double high crest **(5)**.

Mwana Hiti dolls made by the **Kwere** tribespeople have two separated crests which are sometimes drilled with small holes **(6)**. They have a V-shaped profile, an elongated neck and are slightly more realistic than those of the Zaramo. In the north, they

2   3

4

5   6   7

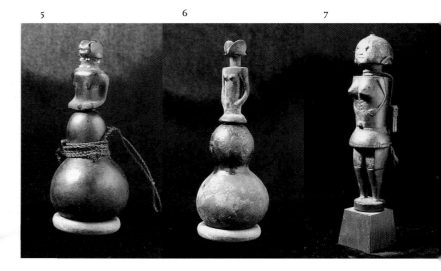

8   9   10

have a smooth, round head. Kwere masks [A, 10] are carved with naturalistic features and have a neck, which is a characteristic of this tribe.

Their throne has a rectangular backrest surmounted by an elongated human head and the circular stool is supported by numerous straight legs with an open-worked carved wooden motif. Kwere stools are carved with three U-shaped feet linked by a horizontal wooden ring.

Figures carved by the **Luguru** (3) have realistic features and usually a long, backward-swept coiffure. Their thrones have a plain backrest [C], often covered with incised geometric motifs, surmounted by a rounded head with a high central crest, and a circular stool usually supported by three outside legs and a central column linked by an L-shaped wooden structure.

Zaramo figures and dolls (2) can be identified by their flattened carved head, often without a face, and their single large sagittal crest. Sometimes this crest is separated slightly by a small groove which is deeper on those made in the southern part of their territory.

Zaramo masks (8) are carved with a high domed forehead, rectangular recessed eyes, a mouth which is sometimes inset with wooden teeth, and flared rectangular ears.

The Zaramo also carved large figures with articulated limbs (4) which were used in funeral ceremonies. During these rites, a nephew of the deceased would speak through the doll and praise the deceased.

Kami dolls (7) are generally carved with a grooved coiffure and usually display abdominal scarifications.

Geographically, **the second area**, which is comprised of the territories in the south-eastern part of Tanzania up to the frontier with Mozambique, is mountainous and covered mostly with forests. Economically, the people in this area live from rearing cattle and from agriculture. The artistic output of the following tribes has been documented: from north to south, the Ngindo, the Mwera and the Makua. The Makonde and the Yao, whose people are scattered between Tanzania and Mozambique, are discussed in the Mozambique chapter, pp. 200–03. Once again, there is a lack of ethnographic, economic and religious studies on these tribes – what is known about them is centred around their artistic output.

The artistic output of this area is similar stylistically to traditions found in Angola (among the Lunda and Tchokwe tribes) – for instance, the use of real hair and body scarifications. The realistic treatment of helmet masks produced by the tribes of this region is obviously influenced by the Makonde of Mozambique.

Ngindo art is rare. Their face masks (9) are rectangular in shape and are characterized by incised geometric decoration on the cheeks or on the forehead.

The artistic tradition of the **Mwera** is related to their southern neighbours the Makonde. The Mwera carved masks with oval faces, linear noses, rectangular eyes, small flared ears and smooth foreheads without scarifications. These masks appear to be a simplified form of a Makonde face mask. Mwera masks carved in the southern part of the territory sometimes have a heart-shaped face and are surmounted by a pair of elongated, hare-like ears. The Mwera people also produced staffs, which often have a top adorned with a bird figure, and human figures which have simplified features and usually incorporate lip plates.

The **Makua** are famous for their half helmet-shaped mask [B], which is stylistically related to the Makonde. They were probably carried at the end of long poles during initiation ceremonies. In addition to these helmet masks, they also made some clay and some wooden face masks (11).

11

8   A Zaramo mask;
      wood; height: 32 cm (12^1/$_2$ in);
      private collection

9   A Ngindo mask;
      wood; height: 24.5 cm (9^1/$_2$ in);
      Leipzig Museum

10 A Kwere mask;
      wood; height: 50.5 cm (20 in);
      Fred Jahn Gallery, Munich

11 A Makua mask;
      wood and hair;
      height: 20 cm (7^7/$_8$ in);
      private collection

BIBLIOGRAPHY

ADIE, J. J., 'Zanzibar Doors', *Guide to Zanzibar*, Zanzibar, 1952, pp. 114–16

BEIDELMAN, T. O., 'The Matrilineal Peoples of Eastern Tanzania (Zaramo, Luguru, Kaguru, Ngulu)', *Ethnographic Survey of Africa, East Central Africa*, XVI, International African Institute, London, 1967

BRAIN, J. L., 'The Kwere of the Eastern Province of Tanganyika', *Tanzanian Notes and Records*, 58/59 (1962), pp. 231–41

FELIX, MARC, *Mwana Hiti, Life and Art of the Matrilineal Bantu of Tanzania*, Munich, 1990

NOOTER, NANCY, 'Zanzibar Doors', *African Art*, XVII, 4, 1984

PRINS, A. H. J., *The Swahili-speaking People of Zanzibar and the East Africa Coast*, London, 1961

SWANTZ, L. W., *The Zaramo of Tanzania*, Dar es Salaam, 1966

Tanzania, Meisterwerke Afrikanischer Skulptur, Exh. Cat., Haus der Kulturen der Welt, Munich, 1994

[A] Above, left: **a Kwere mask**
wood; height: 46 cm (18 in); private collection

Kwere masks are extremely rare and can be identified by their necks and
their weathered patinas. Unlike other Tanzanian mask styles, Kwere masks
have realistic features which reinforce their dramatic expression.

[B] Left: **a Makua mask**
wood; height: 35 cm (13³/₄ in); private collection

Spherical masks are typical of the Makua tribe and were probably attached
to the end of long poles during initiation ceremonies. The additional
elements such as teeth, eyelashes and beards are part of a common
artistic tradition also found among the Makonde people.

[C] Above: **a Luguru throne**
wood; height: 100 cm (39¹/₄ in); Marceau Rivière Collection, Paris

Thrones from this part of Tanzania can be distinguished from one another
by their legs and feet. Luguru thrones characteristically have three delicately
incised legs set around a central column linked by L-shaped stretchers,
although they are partly broken in this example.

[D] Right: **a Kaguru throne**
wood; height: 94 cm (37 in)

This is a typical Kaguru throne with concave legs linked by an open-worked
motif to a central column. The anthropomorphic backrest represents the
notion of ancestry and thus asserts the status of the chief.

The North-Eastern Regions of Tanzania

The area discussed in this chapter includes two principal regions – north-east Tanzania and central-eastern Tanzania. As with most of Oriental Africa, little research has been done and most of the artistic output of this area has only recently been accurately attributed to specific tribes.

North-east Tanzania is on the frontier with Kenya, on the shores of the Indian Ocean and has a strong cultural identity. It is a region of mountains and high plains, covered by forest and savannah. The principal tribes living there are, from north to south, the Chaga, the Pare, the Shamba, the Mbugu and the Zigua.

The artistic traditions of this region are fairly homogeneous and show a strong stylistic relationship with the Malagasy and Batak aesthetic emanating from Indonesia. As yet, academic research has not confirmed their connection, but it is likely that traders travelling by boat along the coasts of India and the Arabian Peninsula made contact with the tribespeople – containers, magical horns and calabashes with anthropomorphic lids have been found on both continents. Characteristically, clay and wooden figures from north-east Tanzania are covered with a piece of cloth or leather impregnated with a liquid substance which gives them a 'mummified' look. Most of these figures are also hollowed so that they can hold magical substances. The figures often appear in pairs and are usually used during initiation ceremonies into secret societies or by healers during curing rites. Very few masks from this region have been discovered and Westerners still do not know what their function is.

I

Chaga artists carved small wooden or clay figures covered with cloth, which stand on shortened legs and have an enlarged round head (7). The faces often have eyes inlaid with white glass beads, large rounded ears and a small mouth.

Pare figures are similar to Chaga ones, but have longer legs (9). They are either full figures or are set on top of animal horns believed to hold magical substances (5). The Pare also made seated clay figures, but their function is unknown (6).

Shamba artists created small wooden and clay figures, which are usually covered in a thick sacrificial patina [B]. They often have an enlarged head with a broad smile and circular ears.

Mbugu figures are predominantly made from a dark shiny wood and are carved with more realistic features than those made by their neighbours. They

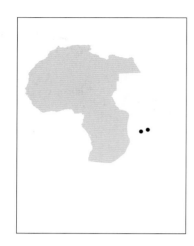

1   An Iraqw mask;
    leather, beads and feathers; height: 21 cm (8³/₈ in); Linden Museum, Stuttgart

2   A Mbugu figure;
    wood, beads and cloth; height: 22.5 cm (9 in); private collection

3   A large Zigua figure;
    wood; height: 70.5 cm (28 in); Museum für Völkerkunde, Berlin

4   A Hehe(?)/Pare(?) figure;
    wood; height: 46.5 cm (18¹/₄ in); private collection

2   3   4   5   6

7   8   9

are often covered with fetish materials, a stylistic tradition of north-eastern Tanzania (2).

The **Zigua** people's artistic tradition is more realistic than that of the other tribes living in this part of Tanzania. Zigua artists carve large wooden figures similar to the Sukuma who live in central-western Tanzania. They have splayed legs and their surface is covered by a weathered patina (3). The Zigua have also produced anthropomorphic clay figures (10) and containers with a dynamic attitude, exaggerated features and almost comical expressions (8). These figures were used during initiations as visual teaching aids and sometimes represent ancestors or spirits.

The second area is **central-eastern Tanzania** which has plains in the north and volcanoes in the south. The main tribes living in this area are, from north to south, the Massai, the Iraqw, the Gogo and the Hehe.

  The art produced by people living in this area is scarce and many figures have been re-attributed to neighbouring tribes. Field research has recently documented the existence of clay figures which are principally zoomorphic in character. The omni-presence of the animal representations is related to the main activities of the tribe: cattle breeding and agriculture.

The **Massai** people live a nomadic existence between Kenya in the north and Tanzania in the south. Since most of them live in Kenya, their artistic output is discussed in that chapter, pp. 208–11.

The **Iraqw** people number 300,000 and produce leather aprons and masks decorated with rows of beads which are often adorned on the top with feathers [A, 1]. It is likely that they were worn during girls' initiation ceremonies.

Gogo artists produced a large number of clay figures in the shape of bulls and buffaloes with exaggerated horns (11). Their function is unknown.

Hehe artefacts are rare. Only a few figures [C, 4] and seats have been discovered, so little is known about this tribe.

BIBLIOGRAPHY

CLAUS, HEINRICH, 'Die Wagogo: Ethnographische Skizze eines Ost-Afrikanischen Bantustammes', *Baessler-Archiv, Supplement 2,* 1911

Tanzania, Meisterwerke Afrikanischer Skulptur, Exh. Cat., Haus der Kulturen der Welt, Munich, 1994

10

5   A Pare magical horn;
    horn, fur and clay; height: 54 cm (21¹/₄ in); private collection

6   A Pare zoomorphic maternity figure;
    terracotta, beads and cloth; height: 11.1 cm (4³/₈ in); private collection

7   A Chaga (?)/Chamba (?) figure;
    clay, cloth and glass beads; height: 27 cm (10¹/₂ in); private collection

8   A Zigua container;
    terracotta; height: 13.5 cm (5¹/₄ in); private collection

9   A pair of Pare figures;
    wood, magical substances and beads; height: 18 cm (7 in); private collection

10   A pair of Zigua figures;
    clay, cloth and glass beads; height of the taller: 30 cm (11³/₄ in); private collection

11   A Gogo buffalo figure;
    terracotta; length: 14.5 cm (5⁵/₈ in); private collection

11

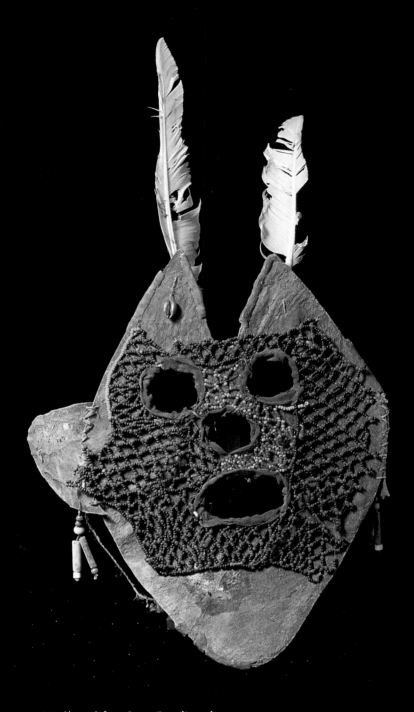

[A] Above, left: **an Iraqw/Luo (?) mask**
leather, beads, shells and feathers; height: 38 cm
(15 in); private collection

Leather masks are frequently produced by
north-eastern Tanzanian tribes. They were
worn during initiation ceremonies and are
often decorated with beads, enhancing their
aesthetic appeal.

[B] Above, right: **a Shamba figure**
wood and cloth; height: 20 cm (7⁷/8 in);
private collection

This figure is covered in a thick encrusted
patina which has resulted from numerous
libations of blood and other liquids. The statue
is wrapped in a cloth, typical of the art from
this part of Tanzania.

[C] Right: **a Hehe figure**
wood; height: 35 cm (13³/4 in); private collection

Examples of Hehe art are rare. Few figures
appear to have been made by this tribe, but the
ones that do exist all have diminutive limbs and
an enlarged head with realistic features.

The Central-Western Regions of Tanzania

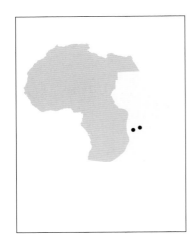

This area includes the entire central part of Tanzania, from Lake Victoria in the north to Lake Rugwa in the south and can be divided into two regions – the shores of Lake Victoria and the inland area. The latter is called Nyamezi after some of its inhabitants. The shores of Lake Victoria have a range of mountains, between 1000 and 2000 metres high, which are covered in bushes and savannah. The main town is Mwanzya. Traditionally, the inhabitants of this area have bred cattle and fish. Archaeological excavations have unearthed early ceramics and ironwork which suggests that this area may have been the East African birthplace of such techniques. The region is inhabited by a number of tribes – the Luo, the Kuria, the Kerewe, the Haya/Ziba and the Karagwe. As with all of East Africa, very little ethnographic, religious or economic information is available and therefore discussions about these tribes will focus on their artistic endeavours.

1 A Kerewe figure;
wood; height: 92 cm (36^1/$_8$ in);
private collection

2 A Nyamezi figure; wood; height:
61 cm (24 in); private collection

3 A Nyamezi container;
calabash, wood, horn and magical
substances; height: 26 cm (10^1/$_4$ in);
private collection

4 A pair of Sukuma figures;
wood and glass beads; height:
92.1 cm (36^1/$_4$ in)

5 A Nyamezi figure;
wood; height: 61 cm (24 in);
private collection

6 A Sukuma necklace;
ivory and glass beads; length:
30 cm (11^3/$_4$ in); private collection

7 A central (?) Tanzanian mask;
leather, horn, vegetal fibres and cowrie
shells; height: 25 cm (9^7/$_8$ in)

Objects from this area are rare and a Luo artistic style seems to dominate the output of the whole area. Masks carved from heavy wood are rectangular in shape, and in the northern part of this territory they have large pierced eyes and a rectangular mouth. In addition, they made leather masks (7), elongated figures and funerary poles.

The **Luo** tribe is scattered across Tanzania and Kenya and they are known predominantly for their polychrome leather masks which are worn as part of an outfit which includes a costume and shield. Wooden stools supported by four high tubular legs were also made.

The **Kuria** tribe is scattered across Tanzania and Kenya and they also use leather masks in their dances and rituals. They are either oval or pear shaped and are often decorated with linear motifs on a darkened surface. Moreover, their mouth is sometimes inset with human teeth.

On the homonymous island, the **Kerewe** tribespeople live principally from fishing and from cultivating banana and millet. They are members of a highly structured society headed by a central chief. Kerewe carvers are famous for their rare, rough-looking figures (1) which display elongated features, splayed legs, flattened hands showing their palms and a round head which is slightly bent forward. Traditionally, they carved elongated wooden shields with surfaces entirely covered with incised black, white and red triangles.

The **Haya** and the **Ziba** tribespeople live on the western shore of Lake Victoria. Their carvers have produced wooden masks **[C]** with oblique eyebrows, round eyes and an enlarged square mouth inset with human teeth. These masks have no ears and sometimes have hide eyebrows and a beard. They may be painted white to imitate the dancer's face. Although rare, some leather masks have been made.

Several tribes live within the **Karagwe** territory, on the eastern shore of Lake Victoria. They are associated with cast iron and copper zoomorphic figures, as well as highly elaborate metal tree-branch holders (9).

1

2

3

4

5

The **inland region** is called Nyamezi, which is also the name of the main tribe living in this area. Geographically, the northern part of this region is a high plateau covered with grass and baobab trees and is favoured by elephants. The southern part is lower and is covered with savannah. The tribes living in this area are, from north to south, the Sukuma, the Nyamezi, the Kimbu and the Sangu. The majority of artistic objects produced in this region are made by the Sukuma and the Nyamezi. Both tribes are famous for their large figures, which usually have static postures. On the whole, the masks of this region have a rough appearance and are often inset with teeth.

The **Sukuma** people are a comparatively large tribe and number approximately one million. They live in small villages in the northern part of Tanzania, each of which is headed by a chief who is also a sorcerer and whose power is counterbalanced by secret societies.

Sukuma carvers are associated with large, rough-looking, standing figures, which have a weathered patina. In some instances these statues were made either with articulated limbs or were carved without any arms and legs at all (4). Their bold, rounded heads usually have eyes inset with beads. The later figures may have been used as scarecrows and the figures carved with articulated limbs, known as *Amaleba*, are used by musicians and dancers during ceremonies in the dry season, following the harvest. Another type of tall, carved figure, to which fetish material is attached, is thought to represent an ancestor.

Sukuma masks (8) have a fearful expression, exaggerated features, including applied eyebrows, and a beard and moustache, and, like their statues, have a weathered patina. In common with the *Amabela*, Sukuma masks were also employed during dance ceremonies in the dry season. Steatopygous terra-cotta figures with a small head and hands resting on their hips and long ivory necklaces (6) were also made by Sukuma craftsmen.

The 500,000 **Nyamezi** people, whose name means either 'Men of the West' or 'Men of the Moon', are the largest ethnic group living in central Tanzania. Socially, they are organized into villages which correspond to small chiefdoms and each chief is responsible for the material wealth of the village, while the spiritual welfare is governed by the village sorcerer. The cult of ancestors, which protects each family, plays an important role in the religious life of Nyamezi people.

6

Nyamezi carvers are known for their thrones **[A]** which are designed with a circular seat supported by three convex legs, sometimes alternating with three pegs. In some cases, the high plain backrest is decorated with a female figure, a head or with incised geometric motifs.

Nyamezi carvers are also famous for their figures (2, 5) which are usually carved out from a dark, heavy wood with a shiny surface. They tend to have elongated features with the statue's face divided into two planes and the eyes inset with circular white beads. Such elongated figures with distorted limbs **[B]** were used in water divination ceremonies.

The same dark wood from which they carve their statues is used by the Nyamezi to produce masks (10) with elongated features and domed foreheads.

Small objects for everyday and magical use – combs, horns or calabashes (3) – also feature in the work of Nyamezi carvers.

BIBLIOGRAPHY

ABRAHAMS, RALPH G., 'The Peoples of Greater Unyamwezi, Tanzania (Nyamwezi, Sukuma, Sumbwa, Kimbu, Konongo)', *Ethnographic Survey of Africa, East Central Africa*, XVII, London, 1967

BLOHM, W., *Die Nyamwezi, Gesellschaft und Weltbild*, 3 vols, 1933, Hamburg

KROLL, H., 'Plastische Menschendarstellungen von der Insel Ukerewe im Victoria-See', *Ethnologischer Anzeiger* 3, 1933, pp. 142–44

ROBERTS, ANDREW, 'The Nyamezi', in *Tanzania Before 1900*, Nairobi, 1973, pp. 117–50

STUHLMAN, F., *Handwerk und Industrie in Ostafrika*, Hamburg, 1910, pp. 77–78, ill. 41–45

Tanzania, Meisterwerke Afrikanischer Skulptur, Exh. Cat., Haus der Kulturen der Welt, Munich, 1994

8

9   10

8 A Sukuma mask;
   wood and teeth; height: 36 cm (14 in);
   Fred Jahn Gallery, Munich

9 A Karagwe tree-branch holder;
   iron; height: 72 cm (28 3/8 in);
   private collection

10 A Nyamezi mask;
   wood, hair and vegetal fibres;
   height: 22.5 cm (9 in); collected
   before 1914 by Captain Weiss;
   private collection

[A] Far left: **a Nyamezi throne**
wood; height: 94 cm (37 in); private collection

This anthropomorphic throne was probably only put on display to show prestige since there is no space on which to sit. As found on other stools from Tanzania, the female figure epitomizes the idea of fertility and the passing of the generations.

[B] Left: **a Nyamezi figure**
wood; height: 149 cm (58³/4 in); private collection

Among the corpus of Nyamezi figures, a small group have elongated features, reminiscent of the Western artist Alberto Giacometti. Field research has shown that these figures were used by water diviners.

[C] Above: **a Haya mask**
wood; height: 24 cm (9¹/2 in); private collection

Like most Tanzanian masks, this Haya mask has rough features, which have been further enhanced by the addition of hair and human teeth. The use of these masks is unknown, although it is likely that they were worn during initiation ceremonies.

The Western Regions of Tanzania

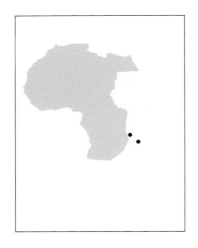

The area surveyed in this chapter covers the territories along the eastern shore of Lakes Tanganyika and Nyasa. An area of savannah, it ultimately reaches 2500 metres above sea level at its southernmost point. The tribespeople of this region survive economically from rearing cattle and farming maize and rice. The area can be divided into two regions – the first lies along the shores of Lake Tanganyika and is, from north to south, inhabited by the following tribes – the Ha, the Jiji, the Tongwe, the Holoholo, who also live on the western side of the lake, which is in the Democratic Republic of Congo (formerly Zaire), and the Bende, the Fipa and the Mambwe.

The second region is along the shore of Lake Nyasa, on the frontier with Malawi and Mozambique. This volcanic area, rich in minerals and exceptionally fertile, supports a rich agriculture of maize, rice and banana groves. From north to south, the most famous tribes living in this region are – the Nyakusa/Konde, the Kinga, the Bena, the Pangwa, the Kisi, the Manda, the Mpoto and the Ngoni. In spite of the numerous tribes that live in these two regions, scholars have not studied them as extensively as their Zairean neighbours.

1   A Ha figure;
    wood; height: 37 cm (14 1/2 in);
    private collection

2   A pair of Jiji figures;
    wood and beads; height of
    the taller: 45 cm (17 5/8 in)

3   A Tongwe figure;
    wood; height: 23.5 cm (9 1/4 in);
    Bareiss Family Collection

4   A pair of Mambwe figures;
    wood; height of the taller: 25 cm
    (10 in); Vincke Collection

The artistic tradition of the tribes living in the **first region** along the eastern shore of Lake Tanganyika is strongly influenced by the aesthetic of Zairean tribes living across the lake – in particular, the Tabwa, the Luba and the Bembe. Therefore figures are often found in pairs, standing on a round base or seated on a throne. The position of one figure on the shoulders of another and the treatment of the eyes demonstrate the influence of the Tabwa.

Located south of Burundi, the **Ha** people are famous for their standing figures **(1)** which are set on round bases and display strong features, enlarged feet and hands, almond-shaped eyes and a lopped-off coiffure. They are thought by Western scholars to represent ancestor figures, which is often the case in Zairean art.

Tabwa influence is strongly apparent in the art of the **Jiji**. Their figures **(2)** are carved standing on a round base, with their hands resting on their abdomen, and they have almond-shaped eyes and mouths. Unlike

the Tabwa, the head of a Jiji statue is slightly tilted upwards and its chin is often pointed. The majority of these figures were produced for the tourist trade, but there is an earlier style of statue that can be distinguished by its incised teeth. No Jiji masks have come to light so far.

The **Tongwe** and **Bende** artistic styles are related to those of the Tabwa and Bembe. Their masks **(7)** characteristically have almond-shaped eyes and mouths, and protruding ears, while their figures **[A, 3]** have shortened legs, an elongated torso framed by set-apart arms, stylized incised hands and a columnar neck supporting a rounded head which is often carved with large hollowed eyes reminiscent of the Bembe artistic tradition.

The **Holoholo** also carve figures influenced by the Tabwa aesthetic. They are discussed in more detail in the Tabwa chapter, pp. 164–67. Nevertheless, their statues have realistic features and a typical rounded head with split eyes. They carved fetish figures into

1

2

3

4

5

6

7

whose hollowed heads magical substances are inserted (see illustration 5 on p. 164).

The bust figures carved by the **Fipa** are used during initiation rituals. Their maternity and female statues **[B, D]** characteristically have elongated features and asymmetrical poses. They are carved from a light-coloured wood which is highlighted with darkened details, a tradition commonly found in southern Africa. The Fipa also made masks **(6)**, but it is not known what their function was.

The Tabwa influenced the **Mambwe** as well. Mambwe figures **(4)** stand on slightly bent legs, and have an elongated torso framed by set-apart arms, with their hands resting on their abdomen. Their heads look upwards and they have a pointed chin and a typical cross-hatched incised coiffure unlike the Jiji figures.

The artistic traditions of the tribes who live in the **second area** are comparatively less well known. Nevertheless, there is evidence that carvers were active in this area and that they were influenced by their southern neighbours such as in the use of light wood highlighted with darkened details.

The **Konde**, who live on the northern shore of Lake Nyasa, are known for their terracotta zoomorphic figures with exaggerated humps and horns which represent water buffaloes **(9)**. It is thought that these may have played a part in initiation ceremonies. They carved elongated masks **[C]** from a light-coloured wood and the eyes and mouth are represented by rectangular holes. The mouths were sometimes inset with wooden teeth.

The **Kisi** carved stylized anthropomorphic terracotta figures **(5)** with columnar bodies supported by enlarged feet and an exaggerated navel and breasts. The heads have drilled eyes.

In terms of artistic production, the **Ngoni** people are reputed for their neckrests **(8)** which are decorated with stylized animals carved with elongated bodies and often black triangles. Zulu influence can be seen in the design of the legs. The Ngoni produced calabashes over which coloured beads were applied in the shape of a face.

BIBLIOGRAPHY

AVON, R. P., 'Vie Sociale des Wabende au Tanganyika', *Anthropos*, 10, 1915, pp. 98–113
KAKAYA, MAKOTO, 'Subsistence Ecology of the Tongwe, Tanzania', *Kyoto University African Studies*, 10, 1976, pp. 143–212
SCHERER, J., 'The Ha of Tanganyika', *Anthropos*, 54, 1959, pp. 841–904

5   A Kisi figure;
    terracotta; height: 20.3 cm (8 in);
    Museum für Völkerkunde, Berlin

6   A Fipa mask;
    wood; height: 24 cm (9¹/₂ in);
    private collection

7   A Tongwe mask;
    wood; height: 23.5 cm (9¹/₄ in);
    private collection

8   A Ngoni neckrest;
    wood; length: 27 cm (10⁵/₈ in);
    Linden Museum, Stuttgart

9   A Nyakusa/Konde buffalo figure;
    terracotta; height: 8 cm (3 in)

8

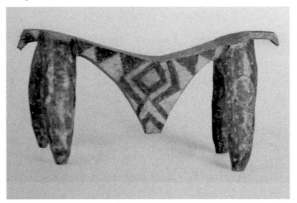

9

[A] Far left: **a Tongwe/Bende figure**

wood; height: 28 cm (11 in); private collection

Tongwe and Bende figures are rare and often have an emphasized round head, as in the present example. The representation of an entwined pair of figures may refer to the primordial couple in Tongwe mythology.

[B] Left: **a Fipa staff figure**

wood and glass beads; height: 24 cm (9¹/₂ in); private collection

The Fipa artistic tradition of this figure, set on top of an authority staff, is different to that of the figure in illustration D. Made of heavy wood, the contrast between the rounded head inset with white beads and the elongated legs fusing into the staff suggests dynamism in an otherwise static figure.

[C] Below: **a Nyakusa/Konde mask**

wood; height: 45 cm (17³/₄ in); private collection

Like most of the masks found in this area, this Nyakusa or Konde mask has a weathered patina. In addition to terracotta figures, such masks probably appeared during initiation ceremonies.

[D] Right: **a Fipa figure**

wood; height: 28 cm (11 in); private collection

Fipa sculpture is often characterized by the use of a light-coloured wood – a southern African artistic influence. The asymmetrical pose is also typical of Fipa statuary.

South Africa, Namibia, Botswana

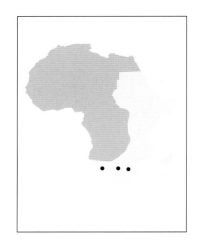

The artistic production of meridional Africa – South Africa, Namibia and Botswana – is not properly understood. Until the 1960s, most of the objects collected in these areas were attributed to the Zulu tribe – the most important political force in the region. Today, the corpus of South African objects has grown dramatically, but unfortunately scholars and collectors are quite often unable to give a precise attribution. It is frequently not known exactly where they were found and the traditionally carved objects have now been replaced by mass-produced pieces. Moreover, extensive travel and the exchange of objects between tribes occurred before the arrival of colonials, making their provenance even more difficult.

Nevertheless, some common artistic characteristics do exist among the art produced in this part of Africa. Figures are scarce and were carved only by the northern Nguni and Venda people in the north-eastern corner of South Africa, and masks are even more rarely documented in this part of the world.

The majority of the people living in these areas are nomadic – they follow their herds of cattle – and so their artistic output is mainly limited to utilitarian objects such as clubs, vessels, neckrests, pipes and snuff boxes.

There are a number of tribes living in meridional Africa – from the north to the south, they are the Venda, the Ndebele, the Sotho and the North and South Nguni in South Africa, the Herero and the Ovumbo in Namibia and the Tswana in Botswana.

1 A number of Zulu beadworks; *glass beads; height of the longest: 19 cm (7¹/₂ in)*

2 A number of Ovumbo beads; *ivory; width of the largest: 6 cm (2³/₈ in)*

3 A Sotho doll; *clay and glass beads; height: 10 cm (4 in); private collection*

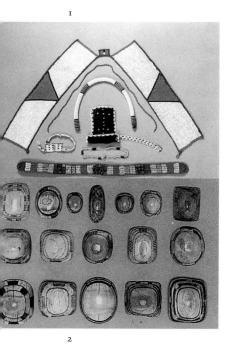

SOUTH AFRICA

The **Venda** people live in northern Transvaal and south-eastern Zimbabwe and are ruled by a king. Their carvings are reserved for the Royal Court and for women's initiation ceremonies.

Venda court art consists mostly of stone monoliths adorned with concentric designs, and carved doors and drums used in rain-making ceremonies. Their initiation objects are usually wooden or clay figures, called *Matano*, which are brought out during ceremonies to illustrate a story. These figures are thought to represent either an ideal girl, a man [D], a renegade man or even an animal.

The **Ndebele** people settled in northern South Africa and carved objects which they decorated with polychrome geometric motifs on white backgrounds. These motifs are also found on the walls of their houses and are incorporated into their beadwork from which aprons (6), dolls (4) and wands in the shape of telegraphic poles are made.

The centre of South Africa is occupied by several tribes who speak the **Sotho** language. They have been divided into three major groups – the Northern, Southern and Western Sotho (who are also called

Tswana and live in Botswana). They live in villages of cylindrical huts and their economy is based on cattle herding and hunting. Socially, the Northern Sotho people are organized into small chiefdoms.

The artistic production of the Sotho people consists predominantly of geometrically shaped wooden headrests, meat plates, leather aprons, which are decorated with rosette and rectangular motifs on a white background and are usually worn by married women, and beadwork where the colour red dominates.

Sotho artists are also famous for their dolls (3) produced either from a core of reed, or clay, or even a bottle, which are entirely covered with multi-coloured bands of beads (except for the head). Both boys and girls played with these dolls prior to their initiation ceremonies. They also made objects related to their smoking habits – anthropomorphic pipes (5) and snuff containers carved from horn with either abstract (8) or human figures in relief on the surface.

At the beginning of the 19th century, several tribes joined together and took the name of one – the **Zulu**. Their king reigned over local chiefs, called *Iduma*, who, in turn, ruled over the people. Zulu men were organized in warrior age classes and were allowed to

7   8   9

10

11

12

13

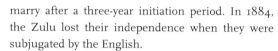

marry after a three-year initiation period. In 1884, the Zulu lost their independence when they were subjugated by the English.

It is extremely difficult to distinguish Zulu art from that of their immediate neighbours – the Tsonga in the north and the Natal chiefdoms in the south. Zulu objects are usually called North Nguni and this term includes the artistic output of the Natal chiefdoms.

North Nguni artists carved clubs with anthropomorphic features **(7)**. Their smoking habits also generated an array of objects such as snuff containers carved from horn in the shape of a human head with two long plaits **[A]**, small ivory spoons decorated with black motifs, gourds inlaid with copper wires and club-shaped snuff containers. Large wooden vessels with grooved surfaces were made and may have been used as milk containers **(9)**. Neckrests supported by oval-shaped feet were used by important North Nguni dignitaries **(10, 11)**. Finally, a large number of beaded body ornaments decorated with geometric polychrome motifs were produced **(1)**.

The Swazi people, who live north of the Zulu, carved neckrests with vertically grooved rectangular legs **(12)**.

The **South Nguni** people are represented among seven tribes, including the Xhosa and the Thembu, and were originally nomadic people who followed their herds of cattle, but today they live in small villages. Xhosa boys are initiated into the *Khwetha* society.

Xhosa artistic output is limited to rare ivory knives which are decorated with geometric and zoomorphic motifs **[C]**. More generally, South Nguni artists produced abstract or anthropomorphic wooden pipes inlaid with metal **(14)** and zoomorphic containers made of intestine.

NAMIBIA

The majority of people living in South West Africa are members of the **Herero** tribe who settled in the area at the beginning of the 18th century. Herero carvers are known for their abstract-shaped neckrests **(13)**.

The **Ovumbo** people live on the frontier between Namibia and Angola and their artistic production appears to be limited to large square ivory beads decorated with a linear black motif **(2)**. Worn by Ovumbo women during important ceremonies, they are attached to a leather belt and were originally a wedding gift from a groom to his bride.

BOTSWANA

Little is known about the **Tswana** people and very few objects have been attributed to them except for zoomorphic spoons **[B]** and dolls carved with articulated arms.

BIBLIOGRAPHY

Art and Ambiguity, Perspectives on the Brenthurst Collection of Southern African Art, Exh. Cat., Johannesburg Art Gallery, 1991
ELLIOT, A., *The Magic World of the Xhosa*, Charles Scribner, ed., New York, 1970
KENNEDY, CAROLEE, *The Art and Material Culture of the Zulu-Speaking Peoples*, Exh. Cat., UCLA Museum of Cultural History Vol. I, 3, 1978
TYRELL, B., *Tribal Peoples of Southern Africa*, Cape Town, 1968

4 Ndebele dolls; *wooden core and glass beads; height: 12 cm (4³/4 in)*

5 A Sotho pipe; *wood and glass beads; height: 34.3 cm (13¹/2 in)*

6 A Ndebele apron; *leather and glass beads; height: 47 cm (18¹/2 in)*

7 A North Nguni club; *wood; length: 60 cm (23¹/2 in); K. Conru Collection*

8 A Sotho snuff container; *horn; height: 12 cm (4³/4 in); K. Conru Collection*

9 A Nguni milk (?) vessel; *wood; height: 51 cm (20 in)*

10 A Nguni neckrest; *wood; height: 12 cm (4³/4 in)*

11 A Nguni neckrest; *wood; height: 13 cm (5¹/8 in)*

12 A Swazi neckrest; *wood; length: 30 cm (11³/4 in)*

13 A Herero neckrest; *wood; height: 13 cm (5¹/4 in); private collection*

14 A South Nguni pipe; *wood and metal inlay; length: 8 cm (3¹/8 in)*

14

[A] Far left: **a Zulu anthropomorphic snuff container**
horn; length: 20.5 cm (8¹/₈ in); private collection

This striking object displays the ability of African carvers to use natural shapes and textures. The animal horn has been carved in the shape of two legs, while the head is hollow to hold snuff.

[B] Left: **a Tswana zoomorphic spoon**
wood; length: 16 cm (6 ¹/₄ in); Kevin Conru Collection, London

The ceremonial function of elaborately carved Tswana spoons is unclear. Nevertheless, the attention given to the carving of the handle suggests it was reserved for important ceremonies.

[C] Above: **a Xhosa knife**
ivory and iron; length: 20 cm (7⁷/₈ in); private collection

Ivory was used in South Africa for carved objects such as spoons and knives. This knife was painstakingly decorated with an elephant and a tortoise and was the property of an important dignitary.

[D] Right: **a Venda figure**
wood and ivory; height: 45.1 cm (17³/₄ in); private collection

Little is known about Venda figures, but they are thought to have been used in pairs during initiation ceremonies. The emphasis on the head and the angular treatment of the body features is characteristic of meridional African art.

Bibliography

General

Bassani, E., *Le Grand héritage*, Exhibition Catalogue, Musée Dapper, Paris, 1992

Bastin, Marie-Louise, *Introduction aux arts d'Afrique noire*, Arnouville, 1984

De Grunne, B., and R. Farris-Thompson, *Chefs-d'oeuvre inédits de l'Afrique noire*, Exhibition Catalogue, Musée Dapper, Paris, 1988

Kerchache, J., J. L. Paudrat and L. Stephan, *Art of Africa*, Paris, 1988

Leiris, M., and J. Delange, *Afrique noire: La création plastique*, Paris, 1967

Meauze, Pierre, *L'Art nègre: Sculpture*, Paris, 1979

General Exhibition Catalogues

Africa, Royal Academy of Art, London, 1996

Die Kunst von Schwartz Afrika, Kunsthaus, Zurich, 1970

Ouvertures sur l'art Africain, Musée des Arts Décoratifs, Paris, 1986

Rubin, William, ed., *Primitivism in 20th Century Art: Affinity of the Tribal and the Modern*, 2 vols, The Museum of Modern Art, New York, 1984

Statuary in Wood by African Salvages: The Root of Modern Art, Gallery 291, New York, 1914

Sweeney, James J., ed., *African Negro Art*, The Museum of Modern Art, New York, 1935

Ghana

Cole, Herbert, and Doran Ross, *The Arts of Ghana*, University of California, Los Angeles, 1977

Ivory Coast

Barbier, Jean-Paul, ed., *Art of the Côte d'Ivoire*, Musée Barbier-Mueller, Geneva, 1993

Nigeria

Art du Nigeria, Collections du Musée des Arts d'Afrique et d'Océanie, Exhibition Catalogue, Paris, 1997

Eyo, Ekpo, *Two Thousand Years of Nigerian Art*, Lagos, 1977

Eyo, Ekpo, *Treasures of Ancient Nigeria*, London, 1982

Neaher, Nancy, *Bronzes of Southern Nigeria and Igbo Metalsmithing Traditions*, Stanford University, 1976

Cameroon

Harter, Pierre, 'Arts anciens du Cameroun', *Arts d'Afrique Noire*, Arnouville, 1986

Gabon

Perrois, Louis, 'Arts du Gabon, les arts plastiques du Bassin de l'Ogooue', *Arts d'Afrique Noire*, Arnouville, 1979

Zaire

Félix, Marc, *100 Peoples of Zaire and their Sculpture*, Brussels, 1987

Trésors d'Afrique, Exhibition Catalogue, Musée Royale de l'Afrique Centrale, Tervuren, 1995

Angola

Bastin, Marie-Louise, *Sculpture Angolaise: Memorial de cultures*, Exhibition Catalogue, Museu Nacional de Etnologia, Lisbon, 1994

Zambia

Brelsford, W. V., *The Tribes of Zambia*, Lusaka, 1965

Félix, M., *Makishi*, Munich, 1998

Tanzania

Holy, Ladislas, *Masks and Figures from Eastern and Southern Africa*, London, 1967

Krieger, Kurt, *Ostafrikanische Plastik*, Museum für Völkerkunde, 1978, 2nd edn 1990

Leurquin, Anne, and Georges Meurant, 'Tanzanie Méconnue, I-IV', *Arts d'Afrique Noire*, vols 73, 75, 81, 84

Tanzania, Meisterwerke Afrikanischer Skulptur, Catalogue Exhibition, Haus der Kulturen der Welt, Munich, 1994

Whartwig, Gerald, 'Sculpture in East Africa', *African Arts*, vol. 2, no. 4, July 1978, pp. 62–65, 96

South Africa

Art and Ambiguity, Perspectives on the Brenthurst Collection of Southern African Art, Exhibition Catalogue, Johannesburg Art Gallery, 1991

Special interest

Barley, Nigel, *Smashing Pots: Feasts of Clay from Africa*, London, 1994

Beauté Fatale: Armes d'Afrique centrale, Exhibition Catalogue, Galerie du Crédit Communal, Brussels, 1993

Brincard, Marie-Thérèse, *The Art of Metal in Africa*, Exhibition Catalogue, The African-American Institute, New York, 1982

Brincard, Marie-Thérèse, *Afrique: formes sonores*, Exhibition Catalogue, Musée National des Arts d'Afrique et d'Océanie, Paris, 1990

Dewey, William B., *Sleeping Beauties: The Jerome L. Joss Collection of African Headrests at UCLA*, California, 1993

Falgayrettes, C., *Supports de rêves*, Exhibition Catalogue, Musée Dapper, Paris, 1989

Falgayrettes-Leveau, C., *Masques*, Exhibition Catalogue, Musée Dapper, Paris, 1995

Fisher, Angela, *Africa Adorned*, London, 1984

Garrard, Timothy, *Akan Weights and the Gold Trade*, Harlow, 1980

Sieber, Roy, *African Textiles and Decorative Arts*, Exhibition Catalogue, Museum of Modern Art, New York, 1972

Major museums

AUSTRIA

Vienna
Museum für Völkerkunde
Neue Hofburg
Heldenplatz
1014 Vienna
Tel: 43 1 521 770 Fax: 43 1 535 53 20

BELGIUM

Antwerp
Etnografisch Museum
Suikerrui 19
2000 Antwerp
Tel: 32 3 232 08 82 Fax: 32 3 220 86 57

Tervuren
Musée Royal de l'Afrique Centrale
Steenweg op Leuven 13
3080 Tervuren
Tel: 32 2 769 52 11 Fax: 32 2 767 02 42

BRITAIN

Cambridge
University Museum of Archaeology and
Anthropology
Downing Street
Cambridge CB2 3DZ
Tel: 44 1223 337733

Edinburgh
Royal Museum of Scotland
Chambers Street
Edinburgh EH1 1JF
Tel: 44 131 225 7534 Fax: 44 131 220 4819

London
British Museum (which now holds the Museum
of Mankind collection)
Great Russell Street
London WC1B 3DG
Tel: 44 171 636 1555

Horniman Museum
100 London Road
Forest Hill
London SE23 3PQ
Tel: 44 181 699 2339 Fax: 44 181 291 5506

Oxford
Pitt Rivers Museum
University of Oxford
South Parks Road
Oxford OX1 3PP
Tel: 44 1865 270927

CANADA

Toronto
Royal Ontario Museum
100 Queen's Park
Toronto
Ontario M5S 2C6
Tel: 1 416 586 8000 Fax: 1 416 586 5863

DENMARK

Copenhagen
National Museum of Denmark
Frederiksholms Kanal 12
1220 Copenhagen
Tel: 45 33 13 44 11 Fax: 45 33 14 84 11

FRANCE

Marseille
Musée des Arts Africains, Océaniens
et Amérindiens
Centre de la Vieille Charité
Rue de Charité
13002 Marseille
Tel: 33 91 56 28 38 Fax: 33 91 90 63 07

Paris
Musée Dapper
50 Avenue Victor Hugo
75016 Paris
Tel: 33 1 45 00 01 50 Fax: 33 1 45 00 27 16

Musée de l'Homme
17 Place du Trocadéro
75116 Paris
Tel: 33 1 45 53 70 60 Fax: 33 1 44 05 72 72

Musée National des Arts d'Afrique et d'Océanie
293 Avenue Daumesnil
75012 Paris
Tel: 33 1 44 74 84 80 Fax: 33 1 43 43 27 53

GERMANY

Berlin
Museum für Völkerkunde
Staatliche Museen zu Berlin
Preussischer Kulturbesitz
Stauffenbergstrasse 41
10785 Berlin
Tel: 49 30 266 2610 Fax: 49 30 266 2612

Dresden
Museum für Völkerkunde
Karl Marx Platz
Japanisches Palais
01097 Dresden
Tel: 49 351 52 591 Fax: 49 351 53 298

Frankfurt am Main
Museum für Völkerkunde
Schaumainkai 29
60594 Frankfurt am Main
Tel: 49 69 212 353 91 Fax: 49 69 212 307 04

Hamburg
Hamburgisches Museum für Völkerkunde
Rothenbaumchaussee 64
20148 Hamburg
Tel: 49 40 44 19 55 05 Fax: 49 40 44 19 52 42

Leipzig
Museum für Völkerkunde zu Leipzig
Postfach 969
04009 Leipzig
Tel: 49 341 214 20 Fax: 49 341 214 22 62

Munich
Staatliches Museum für Völkerkunde
Maximilianstrasse 42
80538 Munich
Tel: 49 89 22 85 506 Fax: 49 89 22 45 82

Stuttgart
Staatliches Museum für Völkerkunde
Hegelplatz 1
70174 Stuttgart 1
Tel: 49 711 123 12 42

HUNGARY

Budapest
Néprajzi Muzeum (Ethnographic Museum)
Kossuth Lajos tér 12
1055 Budapest
Tel: 36 1 332 63 40

ITALY

Rome
Museo Nazionale Preistorico Etnografico Luigi
Pigorini
Viale Lincoln 3
00144 Rome
Tel: 39 6 592 30 57/59 Fax: 39 6 591 91 32

NETHERLANDS

Amsterdam
Koninklijk Instituut voor den Tropen Museum
Linnaeusstraat, 2
Amsterdam
Tel: 31 20 568 82 15

Leiden
Rijksmuseum voor Volkenkunde
Steenstraat 1
Postbus 212
2300 AE Leiden
Tel: 31 71 168 800 Fax: 31 71 128 437

Rotterdam
Museum voor Volkenkunde
Willemskade 25
3016 Rotterdam
Tel: 31 10 411 10 55 Fax: 31 10 411 83 31

PORTUGAL

Lisbon
Museu Etnográfico
Rua Portas de Santo Antao, 100
1100 Lisbon
Tel: 351 1 325 401

SOUTH AFRICA

Cape Town
South African National Gallery
Government Avenue
PO Box 2420
Cape Town 8000
Tel: 27 21 45 16 78 Fax: 27 21 461 00 45

Johannesburg
Johannesburg Art Gallery
PO Box 23561
Joubert Park 2044
Johannesburg
Tel: 27 11 725 31 30 Fax: 27 11 720 60 00

SWITZERLAND

Basel
Museum für Völkerkunde
PO Box 1048
Augustinergasse 2
4001 Basel
Tel: 41 61 266 55 00 Fax: 41 61 266 56 05

Geneva
Musée Barbier-Mueller
10 Rue Jean-Calvin
1204 Geneva
Tel: 41 22 312 02 70 Fax: 41 22 312 01 90

Musée d'Ethnographie
65–67 Boulevard Carl-Vogt
1205 Geneva
Tel: 41 22 328 12 18

Neuchâtel
Musée d'Ethnographie
4 Rue Saint-Nicolas
2006 Neuchâtel
Tel: 41 38 24 41 20 Fax: 41 38 21 30 95

Zurich
Rietberg Museum
Gablestrasse 15
8002 Zurich
Tel: 41 1 202 45 28 Fax: 41 1 202 52 01

USA

Brooklyn
The Brooklyn Museum
200 Eastern Pkwy
New York
NY 11238
Tel: 1 718 638 5000 Fax: 1 718 638 3731

Cambridge
Peabody Museum of Archaeology and Ethnology
Harvard University
Cambridge
MA 02138
Tel: 1 617 495 22 48 Fax: 1 617 495 75 35

Chicago
The Art Institute of Chicago
Michigan Avenue at Adams Street
Chicago
IL 60603
Tel: 1 312 443 3600 Fax: 1 312 443 0849

Cincinnati
Cincinnati Art Museum
Eden Park, Cincinnati
OH 45202-1596
Tel: 1 513 721 5204 Fax: 1 513 721 0129

Cleveland
Cleveland Museum of Art
11150 East Boulevard
Cleveland
OH 44106
Tel: 1 216 421 7340 Fax: 1 216 421 0411

Dallas
Dallas Museum of Art
1717 North Harwood
Dallas
TX 75201
Tel: 1 214 922 1200 Fax: 1 214 954 0174

Denver
The Denver Art Museum
100 W. 14th Avenue Pkwy
Denver
CO 80204
Tel: 1 303 640 2295 Fax: 1 303 640 5627

Detroit
The Detroit Institute of Arts
5200 Woodward Avenue
Detroit
MI 48202
Tel: 1 313 833 7900 Fax: 1 313 833 2357

Indianapolis
Indianapolis Museum of Art
1200 West 38th Street
Indianapolis
IN 46208
Tel: 1 317 923 1331 Fax: 1 317 926 8931

Kansas City
The Nelson-Atkins Museum of Art
4525 Oak Street
Kansas City
MO 64111
Tel: 1 816 561 4000 Fax: 1 816 561 7154

Los Angeles
Fowler Museum of Cultural History
University of California
405 Hilgard Avenue
Los Angeles
CA 90024
Tel: 1 310 825 4361 Fax: 1 310 206 7007

Minneapolis
The Minneapolis Institute of Arts
2400 Third Avenue S.
Minneapolis
MN 55404
Tel: 1 612 870 3000 Fax: 1 612 870 3004

New York
The Metropolitan Museum of Art
1000 Fifth Avenue
New York
NY 10028
Tel: 1 212 879 5500 Fax: 1 212 570 3879

Center for African Art
54 East 68th Street
New York
NY 10021
Tel: 1 212 861 1200

Philadelphia
University of Pennsylvania Museum of
Archaeology and Anthropology
33rd and Spruce Streets
Philadelphia
PA 19104
Tel: 1 215 898 4000 Fax: 1 215 898 0657

Richmond
Virginia Museum of Fine Arts
2800 Grove Avenue
Richmond
VA 23221–2466
Tel: 1 804 367 0878 Fax: 1 804 367 9393

Saint Louis
The Saint Louis Art Museum
71 Fine Arts Drive
Forest Park
Saint Louis
MO 63110
Tel: 1 314 721 0072 Fax: 1 314 721 6172

Santa Barbara
University Art Museum
Arts Building
University of California
Santa Barbara
CA 93106
Tel: 1 805 893 2951 Fax: 1 805 893 7206

Washington
Smithsonian Institution
National Museum of African Art
950 Independence Avenue SW
Washington, DC
DC 20560
Tel: 1 202 357 4600

Major dealers

BELGIUM

Antwerp
Lucien Van de Velde
90 Desguinlei 5a, 2018 Antwerp, Tel: 32 3 248 46 60

Brussels
P. Ancart
1559 Chaussée de Waterloo, 1180 Brussels,
Tel: 32 2 375 91 39

Gallery Joseph Christians
Eikstraat 23, 1000 Brussels, Tel: 32 2 512 24 89

Marc Félix
20 Avenue Marie-Clothilde, 1170 Brussels,
Tel: 32 2 672 70 54

P. Guimiot
16 Avenue Lloyd George, 1000 Brussels,
Tel: 32 2 640 69 48

L'Impasse Saint-Jacques Gallery, P. Dartevelle,
D. Henrion,
7–8 Impasse Saint-Jacques, 1000 Brussels,
Tel: 32 2 513 01 75

BRITAIN

London
Kevin Conru
53 Oberstrand Mansions, Prince of Wales Drive,
London SW11 4EY, Tel: 44 171 720 8614

Entwistle Gallery
6 Cork Street, London W1X 2EE, Tel: 44 171 734 6440

Wayne Heathcote
100 Eaton Square, London SW1 9AQ,
Tel: 44 171 235 7034

AUCTION HOUSES

Bonhams
Montpellier Street, London SW7 1HH,
Tel: 44 171 393 3900

Phillips
101 New Bond Street, London W1Y 0AS,
Tel: 44 171 629 6602

FRANCE

Avranches
Galerie P. and L. Dodier
1 Rue Bremesnil, 50300 Avranches,
Tel: 33 2 33 58 05 81

Paris
Galerie A. de Monbrison
2 Rue des Beaux-Arts, 75006 Paris,
Tel: 33 1 46 34 05 20

Galerie P. and H. Leloup
9 Quai Malaquais, 75006 Paris, Tel: 33 1 42 60 75 91

Galerie Ratton-Hourdé
10 Rue des Beaux-Arts, 75006 Paris,
Tel: 33 1 46 33 32 02

GERMANY

Düsseldorf
Galerie Simonis
Poststrasse 3, 40213 Düsseldorf, Tel: 49 211 32 48 73

Munich
Fred Jahn
Maximilianstrasse 10, 80539 Munich,
Tel: 49 89 22 07 14/22 01 17

HOLLAND

Amsterdam
Kunsthandel van Bussel
De Lairessestraat 165/4, 1075 HK Amsterdam,
Tel: 31 20 671 34 33

SPAIN

Barcelona
Anna Ricard
Alfonso XII, 107, 08006 Barcelona,
Tel: 34 3 200 46 32

SWITZERLAND

Magliaso
Paolo Morigi
Casa Calmo, via Fiume, Magliaso 6983,
Tel: 41 91 71 19 62

USA

Dallas
Steven Alpert
Pacific American Corp., PO Box 140939, Dallas,
TX 75214, Tel: 1 214 692 8311

New Orleans
Davis Gallery
3964 Magazine Street, New Orleans, LA 70115,
Tel: 1 504 897 0780

New York
Alan Brandt
363 Greenwich Street, 2B, New York, NY 10013,
Tel: 1 212 431 1503

Wayne Heathcote
1438 3rd Avenue, #29d, New York, NY 10021,
Tel: 1 212 472 4647

Pace Primitive
32 East 57th Street, New York, NY 10022,
Tel: 1 212 421 3237

Merton D. Simpson Gallery
1063 Madison Avenue, at 80th Street, New York,
NY 10028, Tel: 1 212 988 6290

Tambaran Gallery
5 East 82nd Street, New York, NY 10028,
Tel: 1 212 570 0655

AUCTION HOUSES

Christie's
502 Park Avenue, New York, NY 10022,
Tel: 1 212 546 5807

Sotheby's
1334 York Avenue, New York, NY 10021,
Tel: 1 212 606 7325

San Francisco
James Willis
1637 Taylor Street, San Francisco, CA 94133,
Tel: 1 415 885 6736

Glossary

age-classing society: an organization that separates people into groups according to their age

anthropomorphic: describes an object in the shape of a human form

apotropaic: describes an object whose main function is to cast away harmful forces such as diseases or curses

aquamanile: a receptacle used to pour liquid over the hands of a dignitary, usually zoomorphic in shape

autodafe: a communal ceremony where religious objects are burnt

'cache-sexe': a garment that hides the sex of the wearer

calabash: a gourd whose shell is used as a receptacle

caryatid figure: a sculpture used as a pillar

caryatid stool: a stool with a foot in the shape of a human figure

caste system: the division of a society into different classes. Classification is usually determined by birth

cephalomorphic: describes an object made in the shape of a head

chiefdom: an area controlled by a chief

clan: a group of people who claim a common ancestor

court art: art produced for the use of a royal court

cult of ancestors: a belief system whereby ancestors are honoured, usually through sculptures made in their image, and are held responsible for the welfare and protection of an individual or a tribe

'detective' mask: a mask whose function is to detect anyone guilty of a crime

family: a small group of people, usually from three generations

fetish: an object with magical powers which is worshipped

grave marker: a sculpture set on the top of a grave to indicate its emplacement

initiation: a period of time or a special rite which allows a person to enter a society or to pass one of its grades

Janus figure: a figure with two faces, one opposite the other

keloid: rounded scarification set on the temple

libation: a liquid offering made to a figure or a mask, resulting in an oily or encrusted patina

lip plug: an ivory or wooden rounded implement inset in the upper or lower lip

'lost-wax' technique: a method of creating a metal sculpture. A model is made in wax, which is surrounded by a terracotta mould and then melted. In the void space the liquefied metal is poured, taking the shape of the original wax model

mask: a wooden sculpture hiding the wearer's face (face mask), head (helmet mask), bust (shoulder mask) or torso (body mask). Often a vegetal-fibre or material dress is attached to the edges of the mask and this hides the wearer's body

maternity figure: a sculpture which represents a mother and child

monoxylous: describes an object made of a single piece of wood

nose plug: an implement inset in the nostril for decorative purposes

Oriental Africa: the area of Africa to the east of the Democratic Republic of Kongo

paraphernalia: objects added on the surface of an object to enhance its power

'passport' mask: a small mask (no more than 10 cm high) worn on the arm or on the back. It is used either for apotropaic purposes or for identification

paternity figure: a sculpture which represents a father and child

patina: the surface of an object due to much handling, libations or exposure to the elements

prestige object: an object whose main function is to testify to the wealth and power of its owner

primary inhumation: the burial of a corpse in a grave set in the earth

reliquary box: a box containing ancestors' bones

reliquary figure: a sculpture which contains ancestors' bones, generally in a space set in its back; or a sculpture set on top of a reliquary box or basket

Sanza: a small musical instrument made of a wooden case on which metal blades are set; also called a finger piano

'Sari Porno': a sculpture from Madagascar which represents copulating couples

satellite culture: a civilization strongly influenced by a neighbouring civilization

scarification: a mark in relief on the skin which is made by a needle injecting a foreign substance

secondary inhumation: the burial of bones which have been inhumed previously

secondary mask: a mask which acts as attendant to a major mask or head mask

secret society: an organization whose members have to be initiated, which includes secret rites and the teaching of secret knowledge. Members of the same society usually show solidarity and within a tribe can be an important political or military force

slit drum: an elongated drum which is usually hollowed through a large slit along its length

totemic: said of an animal or an object which is used as an emblem for a tribe or a society

tribe: a large group of people governed by the same rules and religion. A tribe can include several clans and families

tumulus: a grave built in relief, usually circular in form

warrior society: a hierarchical organization which regroups warriors

zoomorphic: describes an object in the shape of an animal

Photographic credits

Jean-Baptiste Bacquart 21 (9); 29 (10); 32 (3, 6); 37 (13); 45 (11, 12); 47 (C); 48 (1); 56 (2, 3, 7); 61 (14); 68 (3, 4, 7, 9); 72 (4); 73 (11, 12); 80 (1, 3, 4, 5); 81 (11); 88 (1); 89 (9); 93 (14); 100 (1); 103 (C); 105 (10, 11); 109 (10); 117 (9, 13); 124 (1); 125 (10); 128 (2, 3); 136 (2); 137 (7, 8, 10); 141 (9); 144 (1, 3); 145 (6, 7); 148 (4); 149 (10–13); 152 (2); 153 (7, 9); 157 (14); 161 (6, 7, 11); 164 (5); 165 (6–8); 168 (1, 4); 169 (13); 172 (2, 3); 173 (7–9, 13); 176 (3, 4); 177 (13); 181 (3, 6); 184 (2, 6); 185 (12); 188 (1); 189 (10); 196 (1, 2); 197 (6, 9–12); 200 (2, 3); 201 (9, 14–16); 205 (8); 208 (6, 7); 209 (9); 211 (D); 212 (1–3, 5–7); 213 (11); 214 (A, B); 216 (2, 4, 5); 217 (7–10); 218 (A, B); 220 (3, 5); 221 (6, 7, 10); 223 (C); 224 (1); 226 (A, B); 227 (C, D); 228 (3); 229 (10, 13); 231 (C)

Staatliche Museen zu Berlin - Preussischer Kulturbesitz. Museum für Völkerkunde 212 (4); 216 (3); 224 (5)

Christie's 21 (12); 86 (B); 104 (2, 5); 109 (12); 125 (11); 135 (C); 137 (12); 138 (B); 141 (11); 143 (D, E); 149 (7); 156 (1); 169 (9, 10, 12); 170 (A); 173 (14); 190 (C); 191 (D); 197 (8)

L'Impasse Saint-Jacques Gallery archives, Brussels 111 (D); 129 (12); 157 (12)

Fred Jahn Gallery archives, Munich 10; 213 (8, 10); 220 (1); 221 (8); 224 (3, 4); 225 (6, 7)

Andrea Jungman 73 (9); 156 (3); 181 (7)

O. Klejman Gallery archives, Paris 203 (B)

R. Lehuard archives, Paris 135 (B)

Leipzig Museum 213 (9)

Galerie Leloup archives, Paris 60 (7); 61 (11, 13, 15); 62 (A); 151 (C); 166 (A)

Linden Museum, Stuttgart 225 (8)

Richard Pearson 11; 13 (1); 18; 30 (A, B); 31 (C); 34 (A); 38 (A); 39 (C); 42 (B); 43 (C, D); 47 (B, C); 48 (2); 50 (B); 55; 58 (A); 59 (B, C); 66 (A); 67 (C); 70 (A); 78; 82 (A); 90 (A); 94 (A, B); 95 (D); 98 (A); 99 (B, C, E); 106 (A); 110 (A, C); 114; 115 (1); 117 (7, 11); 118 (A, B); 119 (C, D); 122 (B); 123 (C, D); 126 (A); 127 (B, D); 130 (B); 138 (A); 142 (C); 146 (B); 147 (D); 149 (6, 8); 151 (E); 159 (B); 161 (5, 10); 163 (B, C, D); 175 (C); 178 (A); 182 (A, B); 186 (A); 190 (B); 194 (2); 195; 198 (A); 219 (C); 222 (A); 223 (B)

Galerie Ratton-Hourdé archives, Paris 74 (B); 109 (13); 116 (2)

Galerie Sao archives, Paris 104 (1)

Sotheby's 1; 2; 6; 8; 9; 12; 13 (2); 14; 19 (1); 20 (1–6); 21 (7, 8, 10, 11, 13); 22 (A); 24 (1–3, 5); 25 (6–8, 10); 26 (A, B); 28 (1–4); 29 (5–9, 11); 32 (1, 2, 4, 5, 7); 33 (8–13); 35 (B, C); 36 (1–3, 5–7); 37 (8–11); 38 (B); 40 (1–5); 41 (6–10); 42 (A); 44 (1, 2, 5–7); 45 (8–10); 46 (A); 48 (3–5); 49 (6–11); 50 (A); 54; 56 (1, 4, 5); 57 (8–11); 60 (1, 5); 61 (8–10, 12); 62 (B); 63 (C); 64 (1–5); 65 (7–13); 67 (B); 68 (1, 2, 5, 6, 8); 69 (16); 71 (B, C); 72 (1–3, 5); 73 (6, 8, 10, 14); 74 (A); 75 (C, D); 79 (2); 84 (1–8); 85 (9–16); 86 (A); 87 (C); 88 (2–5); 89 (6–8, 10–13); 92 (1–7); 93 (8–13); 94 (C); 96 (1–8); 97 (9–12); 100 (2–5); 101 (6–12); 102 (A); 103 (B, C); 105 (6–9, 12); 107 (B, C); 108 (2, 3); 109 (5–9, 11); 110 (B); 116 (1–4, 6); 117 (10, 14); 120 (5, 6); 121 (7–11); 124 (2, 3, 5–7); 125 (8, 9, 12); 128 (1, 4–8); 129 (9–11, 13–15); 131 (C); 132 (1, 2); 133 (3–8, 10); 136 (3–5); 137 (6, 9, 11); 139 (C); 140 (1, 7); 141 (8, 10, 12, 13); 142 (B); 143 (F); 145 (4, 5, 8–10); 148 (1–3, 5); 150 (A, B); 151 (D); 152 (1, 3–6); 153 (8, 10); 155 (C); 156 (2, 4–6); 157 (7–11, 13, 15–19); 158 (A); 159 (C); 160 (2–4); 161 (8); 162 (A); 164 (2, 3); 166 (A); 167 (B, C); 168 (2, 3, 5); 169 (6–8, 10, 11); 170 (B); 171 (D); 172 (1, 4–6); 173 (11, 12, 15); 176 (1, 2, 5–8); 177 (9–12); 180 (1, 2); 181 (4, 5, 8–11); 184 (1, 3–5, 7, 8); 185 (9–11); 187 (B–D); 188 (2–7); 189 (8, 9, 11–14); 190 (A); 194 (1); 196 (3–5); 197 (7); 199 (B); 200 (4–7); 201 (10–13); 203 (D); 204 (1–3); 205 (4–7); 208 (1–3); 209 (8, 10, 11); 210 (A); 220 (2, 4); 224 (2); 228 (1, 2, 4–6); 229 (9, 11, 12, 14); 230 (A); 231 (D)

J. Van Overstrate Gallery archives, Brussels 136 (1); 173 (10); 177 (14); 179 (C)

Mr Veignant, Paris 59 (D); 142 (A); 154 (B)

Index

Figures in **bold** refer to pages on which colour illustrations appear